PALLIATIVE CARE
FOR OLDER PEOPLE
IN CARE HOMES

FACING DEATH

Series editor: David Clark, Professor of Medical Sociology,
University of Sheffield

The subject of death in late modern culture has become a rich field of theoretical, clinical and policy interest. Widely regarded as a taboo until recent times, death now engages a growing interest among social scientists, practitioners and those responsible for the organization and delivery of human services. Indeed, how we die has become a powerful commentary on how we live and the specialized care of dying people holds an important place within modern health and social care.

This series captures such developments. Among the contributors are leading experts in death studies, from sociology, anthropology, social psychology, ethics, nursing, medicine and pastoral care. A particular feature of the series is its attention to the developing field of palliative care, viewed from the perspectives of practitioners, planners and policy analysts; here several authors adopt a multidisciplinary approach, drawing on recent research, policy and organizational commentary, and reviews of evidence-based practice. Written in a clear, accessible style, the entire series will be essential reading for students of death, dying and bereavement and for anyone with an involvement in palliative care research, service delivery or policy-making.

Current and forthcoming titles:

PALLIATIVE CARE
FOR OLDER PEOPLE
IN CARE HOMES

Edited by
JO HOCKLEY
DAVID CLARK

OPEN UNIVERSITY PRESS
Buckingham · Philadelphia

Open University Press
Celtic Court
22 Ballmoor
Buckingham
MK18 1XW

email: enquiries@openup.co.uk
world wide web: www.openup.co.uk

and
325 Chestnut Street
Philadelphia, PA 19106, USA

First Published 2002

A catalogue record of this book is available from the British Library

ISBN 0 335 21060 0 (pb)   0 335 21061 9 (hb)

Library of Congress Cataloging-in-Publication Data
Pallitive care for older people in care homes / edited by Jo Hockley and David Clark.
        p. cm. — (Facing death)
    Includes bibliographical references and index.
    ISBN 0-335-21060-0 (pbk.) — ISBN 0-335-21061-9 (hb)
    1. Terminal care. 2. Palliative treatment, 3. Aged—Care. I. Hockley, J. M. II. Clark, David, 1953– III. Series.
    R726.8 .P3429 2002
    616'.029—dc21
                                                                    2002022777

    Typeset by Graphicraft Limited, Hong Kong
    Printed in Great Britain by St Edmundsbury Press, Bury St Edmunds, Suffolk

Contents

List of tables, figures and boxes

List of contributors

Frans Baar has been a nursing home doctor since 1980, mainly working with the Antonius IJsselmonde facility, in Rotterdam, The Netherlands. He is a past chairman of the Palliative Care Network for Terminal Patients in The Netherlands and is chair of the organizing committee of the 2003 Congress of the European Association of Palliative Care.

Kenneth Boyd is Senior Lecturer in Medical Ethics in the Medical Faculty of Edinburgh University, Research Director of the Institute of Medical Ethics and Deputy Editor of the *Journal of Medical Ethics*. He has written on many aspects of medical ethics and has been actively involved in the education of health care professionals since 1975, often in collaboration with colleagues in palliative care. His current interests include the history of medical ethics, the role of medical humanities, development of the undergraduate medical curriculum and the use of animals in science.

Chris Burridge is a senior lecturer in the School of Nursing Studies at the University of Northumbria. With a background in general nursing she teaches aspects of continuing care, and has a particular interest in loss and grief developed during her MA in counselling, and local voluntary loss and grief counselling. She has a clinical liaison role in care of the older person in hospitals and nursing homes and has been involved in research in care homes.

David Clark is Professor of Medical Sociology within the Academic Palliative Medicine Unit of the University of Sheffield. He has written widely on the sociology of religion, family life and end-of-life care and he has been involved in research and teaching in palliative care since 1989. His current interests include: the history of hospice, palliative care and related fields;

policy development and international issues in the growth of palliative care; and palliative care ethics.

Ailsa Cook is a PhD student in the Department of Applied Social Science at the University of Stirling. Her thesis explores the ways in which people with dementia manage their communication in a residential care setting. Prior to commencing her PhD, Ailsa worked in the Centre for Social Research on Dementia, also at the University of Stirling, where she was involved in a number of projects exploring social aspects of dementia, including the ability of people with dementia to self-report pain.

Glenda Cook qualified as a registered nurse in 1982 and now works as a senior lecturer in nursing research within the Centre for Care of Older People at the University of Northumbria. Her teaching activities are related to risk, law and ethics in professional health care practice and her current research interests relate to all aspects of living and working in care homes.

Sylvia Cox is a qualified social worker with many years' experience as a practitioner and senior manager in a range of community services, including care homes. Since 1995 she has been Planning Consultant at the Dementia Services Development Centre, at the University of Stirling, where she is involved in consultancy, policy and practice development and research. Her current interests include end-of-life care and user involvement.

Sue Davies is a lecturer in nursing in the Department of Community, Ageing, Rehabilitation, Education and Research at the University of Sheffield. Before moving into higher education she worked as a health visitor and as a senior nurse within a unit providing services for older people in London. Current research interests focus upon the needs of older people in care homes and the development of conceptual and theoretical frameworks to inform practice with older people in a range of care settings and to guide education for service providers.

Katherine Froggatt is Head of the Macmillan Practice Development Unit at the Centre for Cancer and Palliative Care Studies, Institute of Cancer Research, London. After studying for a geography degree she trained as a nurse and subsequently worked in radiotherapy and care of the elderly settings before moving into research, working in both universities and hospital trusts. Her current interests include generic palliative care, care provision for older people and practice development.

Jo Hockley is currently research fellow/clinical nurse specialist at St Columba's Hospice, Edinburgh. She has worked within the hospice movement since 1979 but has spent most of her energies disseminating palliative care into the acute hospital sector. She has set up two hospital-based palliative care teams in the UK and has published widely on this subject and other practice issues in palliative care. She is currently working on a collaborative action research project with independent nursing homes in Edinburgh, developing palliative care at the end of life.

Carol Komaromy is a lecturer in health studies in the School of Health and Social Welfare at The Open University, where she has worked since 1994. She is a medical sociologist with a background in health care and her main research interests lie in the area of death and dying.

Alison McLeod is a palliative care clinical nurse consultant in South Australia and has conducted workshops and presented at conferences in the Asia Pacific region. She has a particular interest in the provision of palliative care for elderly people dying from chronic degenerative disease. She conducted the 'Link Nurse' project in South Australia, educating and consulting in residential care facilities, and co-edited a book focusing on symptom management in the elderly. Presently Alison shares her time between practising as a palliative care clinician in the community and conducting education and training in residential care facilities for the aged.

Helen Orchard is Honorary Research Fellow at the Lincoln Theological Institute, University of Sheffield, and an Anglican ordinand and research student at Cambridge University. She worked for the NHS between 1990 and 2001 in managerial positions at hospital, health authority and regional levels. She has researched and written in the area of spirituality and health care, specifically hospital chaplaincy, as well as on the Gospel of John.

Deborah Parker is a PhD candidate in the Department of Palliative Care, Flinders University of South Australia. She has worked as a registered nurse in a variety of aged care settings for 15 years. For the past ten years she has researched in the areas of aged and palliative care.

Ian Philp is the National Director for Older People's Services within the Department of Health. He has a brief to stamp out ageism in the NHS and to win over hearts and minds in implementing the National Service Framework for Older People. Prior to publication, he was co-chair of the External Reference Group of the National Services Framework (NSF).

Jan Reed is Professor of Health Care for Older People and Director of the Centre for Care of Older People, a research and practice development centre at the University of Northumbria. She trained as a nurse and worked with older people before taking up a lecturing post at the then Newcastle Polytechnic. She held a Department of Health post-doctoral nursing fellowship from 1993 to 1995, when she carried out a study of older people moving into care homes. Her current research interests continue to include care homes for older people, and also the role of the voluntary sector in providing support for older people, and partnership working with older people.

Jane Seymour is a nurse and sociologist. She is a research fellow in the Sheffield Palliative Care Studies Group, which comprises the University of

Sheffield Academic Palliative Medicine Unit and Trent Palliative Care Centre. Jane has worked in palliative care research and education since 1994, prior to which she pursued a career in clinical nursing. Her research interests include end-of-life decision-making in intensive care, older people and end-of-life care, and palliative care policy.

Jo Vallis is Research and Training Officer at the Lister Institute, Edinburgh, where she is responsible for research on junior doctors' training needs. Jo is from a long-standing nursing/nurse education background. She obtained her PhD in 1998, from Queen Margaret University College, Edinburgh, and has subsequently worked on two health service research projects at the University of Edinburgh before taking up her current position. Both projects focused on aspects of care of elderly people. The first, based in the Department of Nursing Studies, concerned hip fracture care, whereas the second, based in Geriatric Medicine, was about ethics and end-of-life decision-making. Her current research interests include junior doctors' communication skills, particularly in relation to death, dying and breaking bad news.

Herman van der Kloot Meijburg is a theologian and a bioethicist at Antonius IJsselmonde, Rotterdam, The Netherlands, where he is currently helping to set up an Education Centre for palliative terminal care. He studied at the Universities of Leiden and Edinburgh and worked for many years as the general secretary of the Standing Committee on Religious and Ethical Affairs of the Hospital Association of The Netherlands. He has lectured in and outside the country and published on a wide range of subjects dealing with ethical quandaries in health care institutions. He is a member of the International Work Group on Death, Dying and Bereavement.

Series editor's preface

Many nations of the world are facing a significant challenge in responding to the question of end of life care for older people. It is a serious indictment of policy makers, researchers and service providers that there should be a sense of political, historical and organizational 'surprise' about this. Indeed the founders of modern palliative care and of modern geriatrics had much to say about the issue as long ago as the early 1950s. The challenge of providing good care to older people who are approaching death should not be seen as an aspect of demographics or population ageing, rather it reflects institutionalized ageism, negative stereotypes, and a failure to spread good practice where it occurs. For too long hospices and specialist palliative care services have been islands of excellence, providing their services primarily to older people with cancer. Those older people with other diseases, chillingly referred to as 'the disadvantaged dying', have all too often failed to benefit from such help, in a context where it is the diagnostic label, rather than the level of suffering, which determines access to the best standards of care. At the same time those providing mainstream care for dying older people have been starved of resources and have enjoyed little in the way of public sympathy and support.

Care homes of various types are becoming a steadily more common place for older people to live for some part of their lives, and for many this is where they will eventually die. The clinical and financial status of care homes varies across societies. There are differing criteria for entry, varying levels of provision and staff expertise, numerous arrangements for reimbursement. In whatever guise, such organizations and settings occupy a pivotal place between the domestic home and the hospital. They are places of long-term care and they are communities where residents experience and contribute to a particular kind of culture. Until recently, they were not places associated with a high level of commitment to palliative care goals and ideals. Nevertheless, in several countries we can see examples where pilot initiatives, demonstration projects and research studies are focusing on such issues and where there are encouraging signs of improvement.

This book is one such contribution. It acknowledges that, gradually, older people are becoming more central to the aims of health and social care policy, and that the organization of care homes is a part of this. It also demonstrates that the character of the care homes population is changing, with greater levels of dependency at admission. Moving into a care home is likely to be experienced as a process of loss, which is continued as other residents die and as levels of dependency increase further. This places great demands on staff seeking to provide person-centred care and grappling with complex and sensitive situations, often in the absence of a well-developed ethical framework. It this context it becomes important to fully assess the changing palliative care needs of resident, including their spiritual as well as their physical, social and psychological aspects. Good care does not just rely upon the resources within the care home, it is also dependent on effective external partnerships: with relatives, with primary care and social services, with specialist palliative care providers and with hospitals.

The contributors to *Palliative Care for Older People in Care Homes* address all of these issues and explore their implications from a variety of perspectives. There are contributions from social scientists, nurses, doctors, service managers, ethicists, and from those engaged in educational and development programmes in this field. Such a multi-disciplinary orientation is vital to the formation of a rounded and balanced view of the important issues and should in turn stimulate policy making and service development which reflects the same approach. Moreover, the book combines perspectives from the increasingly diverse health and social care system of varying parts of the United Kingdom, as well as from the Netherlands and from Australia. This approach lies at the heart of the Facing Death series, which since it began in 1997 has worked hard to foster creative thinking and evidence-based approaches to questions of end of life care in the international context. *New Themes in Palliative Care*, with its sections on policy ethics and evidence, on service developments, and on clinical issues is one such example (Clark, Hockley and Ahmedzai 1997). The analysis of palliative care developments in seven Western European countries in *The Ethics of Palliative Care: European Perspectives* also tackled these questions in a comparative manner (ten Have and Clark 2002). Another book to do so is *Transitions in End of Life Care: Hospice and Related Developments in Eastern European and Central Asia*, which provides a massive sweep over the palliative care situation in 28 countries among the poorest in the European region (Clark and Wright 2002).

Palliative Care for Older People in Care Homes tackles a topic which few concerned about health and social welfare can afford to ignore. It gets to the heart of an issue which has for too long been relegated to the back-burner of policy making. Now that is changing. Older people are becoming more vocal, they recognize the authority they have as consumers of services with a right to fair hearing. They are concerned about inequities in provision. It appears that their voices are being heard by planners and providers of services. In the coming years, many more citizens will end their lives in some type of care home. This book stands every chance of influencing the quality of care they receive there.

David Clark

References

Clark, D., Hockley, J. and Ahmedzai, S. (eds) (1997) *New Themes in Palliative Care*. Buckingham: Open University Press.

Clark, D. and Wright, M. (2002) *Transitions in End of Life Care: Hospice and Related Developments in Eastern Europe and Central Asia*. Buckingham: Open University Press.

ten Have, H. and Clark, D. (eds) (2002) *The Ethics of Palliative Care: European Perspectives*. Buckingham: Open University Press.

Acknowledgements

We had the idea for this book while having lunch in Edinburgh one day in the autumn of 2000. One of us (J. H.) had already embarked on a major action research project concerning end-of-life care in nursing homes. The other (D. C.) had recently been involved in the nursing home world as the family member of a resident. Then, as now, we were enthusiastic about bringing together a volume which would explore the issues and challenges of end-of-life care in such homes. We have now done so, and for that we thank the following: St Columba's Hospice, Edinburgh, for supporting Jo Hockley in her action research project alongside the stimulation from colleagues and co-researchers involved in the project; David Clark's colleagues in the Sheffield Palliative Care Studies Group, for their continuing encouragement and inspiration; all of our authors, for their enthusiasm and commitment; and finally – but by no means least – Margaret Jane for her usual exemplary job in preparing the manuscript.

Jo Hockley and David Clark

Introduction

IAN PHILP

Although in recent years there has been a focus on developing and providing palliative care services for people dying of cancer, such services are equally relevant for people dying with other diseases. Indeed, in old age, where multiple pathology is common, it is necessary to respond to the complex interaction of physical, mental and social status, and the resulting impact on functioning and well-being of the older person, rather than to just the consequences of a single disease. In these circumstances, increased skill is required to recognize when a person is dying, but the palliative care approach is entirely appropriate in responding to the complexity of death in old age. This book explores many of the issues which arise when we begin to think in these terms.

In the United Kingdom it is now acknowledged that older people should receive care based on their individual needs, priorities and circumstances, rather than their age (Department of Health 2001a). This includes access to palliative care services. It is unfortunate that needs for palliative care are often overlooked in old age, particularly as death and dying are part of the 'ageing process' and therefore predictable. Indeed, failure to provide palliative care for older people who are dying is one of the most serious consequences of age discrimination in terms of impact on quality of life.

Care should be provided irrespective of setting. One in five people die in residential or nursing homes (Addington-Hall 2000). Most older people recognize a move to a care home as the last refuge before death, so it is vital that palliative care services are available to people in these settings, and palliative care must be a central feature of care provision in residential and nursing home care.

In England, national standards have been set which define the baseline for acceptable practice. The three key documents in this area are the *NHS*

Cancer Plan (DoH 2000a), The Report of the National Care Standards Commission (DoH 2001b) and *The National Service Framework for Older People* (DoH 2001a). A variety of inspection and performance management systems are in place to hold organizations to account against these national standards.

Older people's care is one of the UK government's four top priorities in health care (the others are cancer, mental health and coronary heart disease). There is an overlap for palliative care policy between older people and cancer. It is necessary to have both perspectives to develop effective end-of-life care policy for older people. Policies developed only from the cancer perspective would overlook important issues relating to non-cancer death and death outside hospices and hospitals. Furthermore, practitioners and managers often fail to extrapolate palliative care principles into practice for non-cancer patients, so policies for non-cancer patients must be explicit.

Workforce development is required, particularly where there are skill gaps. These are most notable among care assistants (Henwood 2001), but other practitioner groups are important. The need to ensure high-quality medical care from general practitioners and specialists in geriatric medicine and palliative care in the residential and nursing home sector is a pressing issue, as is the need to develop the competencies of registered general nurses in old age and palliative care.

A new partnership approach between the statutory and independent sectors is being developed (DoH 2000b) to encourage strategic commissioning and sharing of expertise to deliver person-centred care in the care home setting.

In England, joint commissioning by health and social care agencies will have a strong local focus through increasing partnership between primary care trusts and local government councils. There will be increased involvement of service users in planning services, building local partnerships which have been less of a tradition in English health and social care than, for example, in Scandinavian countries.

Strong central direction, a quality workforce and partnership between the independent sector, the local NHS, local government and older people representatives will be a necessary, but not sufficient, requirement for ensuring that older people receive palliative care services according to need. The involvement of stakeholders in building on these foundations is also required. 'Bottom-up' development of good practice is being supported through collaborative networks. Collaborative networks were pioneered in cancer services (DoH 2000a) and are now being extended to support implementation of the older people's modernization programme.

Reforming the National Health Service to ensure person-centred care through a whole systems approach as described above is one of the greatest challenges facing government. Meeting that challenge for older people, dying people and people in the residential sector – groups which are traditionally at the margins of the health and social care system – will be the true measure of success of the programme of reform. This book, with its contributions from a variety of disciplines and perspectives, sets out some of the key elements of knowledge, understanding and practice, which must exist within that programme.

References

Addington-Hall, J. (2000) *Briefing Paper: Care of the Dying and the NHS*. London: The Nuffield Trust.

Department of Health (2000a) *The NHS Cancer Plan*. London: Department of Health.

Department of Health (2000b) *For the Benefit of Patients: A Concordat with the Private and Voluntary Health Care Provider Sector/Department of Health*. London: Department of Health.

Department of Health (2001a) *National Service Framework for Older People*. London: Department of Health.

Department of Health (2001b) *The National Care Standards Commission (Registration): Regulations 2001*. London: Department of Health.

Henwood, M. (2001) *Future Imperfect? Report of the King's Fund Care and Support Enquiry*. London: King's Fund.

NHS Executive (1995) *Purchasing Specialist Palliative Care Services EL(95)22 (Annex A)*. London: HMSO.

1 Historical and policy contexts

SUE DAVIES AND JANE SEYMOUR

Although largely hidden from the view of the rest of society, the provision of institutional care for older people has become a major industry. What does this phenomenon mean for the experience of dying older persons and their families? What does palliative care have to offer and what problems are associated with meeting the needs of residents with palliative care needs?

This chapter addresses these questions, setting the scene for the chapters that follow. We chart briefly the evolution of the care 'industry' from the middle years of the twentieth century, locating this development in relation to the more recent policy context of the United Kingdom. We then sketch out the demography of dying in institutional care and discuss the relevance of palliative care, in terms of its meaning and core goals, to meeting the needs of people with life-limiting conditions who live in care homes. We conclude by looking closely at what is known about the experiences of older people in care homes and their families, and identify some critical issues that currently constrain the successful application of the palliative care model in care home settings.

Institutional care: past and present directions

The roots of current provision of long-term care can be traced back to the early eighteenth century with the establishment of institutions for the provision of Poor Law relief (Webster 1991). In the early part of the twentieth century there was no separate provision for the aged poor and older residents were subject to the strict discipline of the workhouse regime. It was not until immediately after the Second World War that legislation was introduced for the development of community-based services for older people. The National Assistance Act of 1948 provided a major change in emphasis, suggesting that continuing care provision should be developed on a 'hotel' model. A distinction was made between those requiring continuous nursing care, who were cared for either in long-stay geriatric wards within the NHS or in private nursing homes if they had sufficient resources, and those requiring care and supervision. The latter group became eligible for placement in local authority residential homes, or could seek care in a private residential home. During the second half of the twentieth century a body of influential literature raised doubts about the appropriateness of institutional care for a range of client groups (Goffman 1961; Townsend 1962; Robb 1967). Townsend, for example, noted in the conclusion to his seminal study *The Last Refuge* that homes for the elderly 'do not adequately meet the physical, psychological and social needs of the elderly people living in them and that alternative services should quickly take their place' (Townsend 1962: 222). Subsequently, there was growing recognition that NHS hospital wards in particular did not provide an appropriate care environment for older people with continuing care needs (Bond and Bond 1987). Although the potential solution of enabling older people to remain within their own homes with adequate support services was slow to be realized, the drive towards providing appropriate community-based alternatives was gaining pace. In addition, anxieties about escalating costs of institutional care also provided an incentive (Symonds 1998).

Explicit intentions in community care policy have included widening the choices available to older people and their families by offering a range of continuing care options, and ensuring that older people receive the right amount of care and support to maintain maximum independence (Reed and Payton 1998). Where older people decide to move into some form of residential care, the emphasis has been on creating a homely environment that maximizes opportunities for both social engagement and privacy (Davies 2001). However, the extent to which successive governments have been successful in achieving these goals has been influenced by financial constraints and fragmentation of services (Cotter *et al.* 1998). It is therefore important to review some of the important features of UK health and social care policy as they relate to these concerns, focusing on the later twentieth and early twenty-first centuries. Key elements of these policy initiatives are summarized in Table 1.1.

Community care policy in the post-Second World War United Kingdom

During the early post-war period, the provision of health and social care services for older people and others in need of care was marked by a heavy reliance on residential services. This was despite a dominant rhetoric of 'community care' in which home care was lauded as the ideal. In old age

Table 1.1 Key UK policy developments in the field of community and continuing care since 1980

1981	White Paper *Growing Older*	Emphasizes that care 'in' the community must increasingly mean care 'by' the community.
1983	Health and Social Services and Social Security Adjudications Act	Payment of fees for voluntary and private care homes by social services becomes statutory for anyone in receipt of supplementary benefit. An assessment of need is not required. Prompts a massive expansion of the private care home sector.
1982	National Health Service Act	District health authorities replace area health authorities – less representation from local authorities.
1984	Registered Homes Act	Establishes a regulatory body for the private homes sector.
1985	Select Committee Report *Community Care*	Calls for government action to move care away from local authority provision and hospitals to be linked more closely to the community.
1986	Audit Commission Report *Making a Reality of Community Care*	Highlights lack of progress in shifting care from institutional to community based services.
1988	Griffiths Report *Community Care – An Agenda for Action*	Recommends a leading role for local authorities in the arrangement and funding of community care.
1989	White Paper *Caring for People*	Expresses an explicit commitment to the policy of community care and defined responsibilities of health and social services.
1990	NHS and Community Care Act	Local authorities to have responsibility to manage care but not to provide it – a purchasing role. Formal mixed economy of care of statutory, voluntary, private and informal care. No extra funds available. Older people in receipt of income support have all costs of care (after assessment and up to a national limit) met by local authority. Those with assets of £3,000 make a contribution. Those with over £8,000 must fund themselves.

Table 1.1   *(cont'd)*

1994	Audit Commission Report *Taking Stock – Progress with Community Care*	Identifies over-stretched resources, with some local authorities running out of funds.
1995	Carers Recognition and Services Act	Entitles those providing care in excess of 20 hours a week to an assessment of need.
1999	Carers' National Strategy	Charges those responsible for health and social care to give a commitment to identify and address carers' needs.
1999	*With Respect to Old Age.* Report of the Royal Commission on Long Term care	Recommends that nursing care and personal care should be free of charge to those needing long-term care. Recommends establishment of a national care commission to set and monitor standards.
2000	NHS Plan – Annexe	Nursing care to be centrally funded for all in need of continuing care. Upper limit for contributions to personal care and accommodation costs raised to £30,000.
2000	Care Standards Act	All private health care to be regulated by a single national body – the National Care Standards Commission. Distinction between nursing and residential homes to be abolished.
2001	National Service Framework for Older People	Identifies standards of care for older people in a range of care environments.

Source: adapted from Symonds (1998)

care this latter discourse was strengthened by the emergent discipline of geriatric medicine and the gradual development of organizations devoted to the health and social well-being of older people. The following is a typical sentiment from the period: 'certain postulates are basic to any clear thinking on the care of the elderly . . . other things being equal, home is the right place for everybody, well or ill, without distinction of age' (National Council of Social Service 1950: 6).

Perversely, initiatives that would have made home care a real option for the majority of older people and their families were never pursued with the necessary coordination of effort or state financial investment. It has been well documented that, 'in practice, care in the community equals care by family and in practice, care by family equals care by women' (Finch and Groves 1980: 494). Furthermore, a significant proportion of older people, especially older women, are without family support yet despite this do not receive the services they need to remain in their own homes (Audit Commission 1997). It has been observed across the decades that older women aged 85 years and over are most likely to be living on their own but, compared to people in the 65–85 age group, are less likely to receive visits from GPs and district nurses even though they are also less likely to be admitted to a hospital or hospice (Cartwright *et al.* 1973; Seale and Cartwright 1994). Indeed, it has been shown that some older people living at home may have an unacceptably low quality of life (Lawton *et al.* 1995). In these circumstances 'home' as a physical location becomes less important than the reconstruction of intimacy and familiarity in a safe care environment (see Chapter 3).

Community care policy in the latter part of the twentieth century

The ambivalence surrounding 'community care' for older people, combined with the funding of residential and nursing home care through the Department of Social Security during the 1980s, meant that the fundamental reliance on institutional options rather than care at home for frail older people was, if anything, strengthened in the latter years of the twentieth century. Changes in funding arrangements meant that individuals were able to refer themselves to a care home, with costs covered centrally by flat-rate social security payments following a basic means test, but without a test of care need. This sparked a rapid expansion of private sector care home accommodation throughout the UK, with many older people entering residential and nursing homes who might have remained in their own homes if alternative support services had been available (Audit Commission 1986).

The Griffiths Report of 1988 lamented the lack of progress in making community care a reality and proposed that, in order to encourage local authorities to put more resources into supporting people to remain in their own homes, local authorities should have a care needs assessment role with funds transferred from social security. The government's response to the Griffiths Report took the form of the White Paper *Caring for People* (Department of Health 1989). Here the aims and intentions of community care were laid out explicitly:

- to promote the development of domiciliary, day and respite services in order to enable people to live in their own homes wherever feasible and sensible;
- to ensure that service providers make practical support for carers a high priority;

- to make a proper assessment of need and good care management the cornerstone of high-quality care;
- to promote the development of a flourishing independent sector alongside good quality public services;
- to clarify the responsibilities of agencies and so make it easier to hold them to account for their performance;
- to secure better value for taxpayers' money by introducing a new funding structure for social care.

In an attempt to make this vision of community care a reality, the NHS and Community Care Act of 1990 introduced a contract culture to arrangements for funding continuing care. This involved a system of assessment and case management, with social services departments purchasing packages of care from a range of service providers across the private and voluntary sectors as well as statutory services. Older people and their carers were referred to as 'service users' and a stated intention of the Act was to increase flexibility and 'consumer' or 'user' choice. Paradoxically, however, the accompanying proposals to speed the relocation of older people from NHS beds to 'the community' resulted in huge numbers entering nursing homes in the private sector. Between 1978 and 1999, independent nursing home places rose from 26,100 to 213,300, while between 1988 and 1999, NHS long-stay beds for older people fell from 80,700 to 36,900 (Laing 1998). This had significant consequences for older people needing continuing care, summarized succinctly by Walker (1999: 166):

> It was the imposition of market principles, coupled with the hurried removal of long-term care functions from the NHS and the forceful application of the crudest form of least-cost efficiency that had such a deep impact on older people and their family carers. A tighter and tighter rationing of community care budgets has been imposed, with the result that, in many places, support is available only for those in greatest need.

In 1997, in view of mounting concerns over the costs of long-term care and the quality of care in some homes, the Labour government set up a Royal Commission on Long Term Care under the chairmanship of Sir Stewart Sutherland. The aim of the commission was to examine the short- and long-term options for a sustainable system of funding of long-term care for older people, both in their own homes and in other settings. The Commission's recommendations relate principally to funding arrangements, with a key proposal that nursing and personal care should be centrally funded for anyone needing long-term care, with means testing remaining for accommodation and food costs (Royal Commission on Long Term Care 1999). Recommendations also relate to the quality of care in nursing homes, with a National Care Commission proposed to oversee implementation of the new system, provide information and monitor standards. Other recommendations are that nurses should be more involved in assessments for entry to care homes and that services for ethnic minority users should be improved. The Commission's report was generally well received by service user groups and practitioners, but the key message that care should be centrally funded was considerably weakened by the production of a minority report written by two of the commissioners who disagreed with this important proposal. Their argument was that central funding for personal care would do very little to raise the quality of care within the majority of care homes and that resources would be better directed towards intermediate care (Lipsey 2001).

The government's response to the report is included as an Annexe to the NHS Plan (Department of Health 2000b). Significantly, the government chose not to implement the recommendations of the Commission in full. While the proposal that nursing care should be free at the point of delivery was accepted, charges for personal care would continue to be means-tested, along with accommodation costs. In financial terms these changes are likely to have the greatest impact for those residents who pay the full cost of their nursing home care. However, the picture in Scotland is at variance with that in England and Wales, with the Scottish Executive making an announcement in January 2001, following a prolonged political debate, that personal care will be provided free of charge to people living in care homes in Scotland. This has raised concerns that the Scottish executive's decision will create a 'two-tier system' of elderly care in the UK (Butler 2001).

In March 2001, the government launched the National Service Framework (NSF) for Older People, with the aim of improving and standardizing the quality of care for older people in a range of care environments (Department of Health 2001). The NSF for older people embraces the principles of dignity, autonomy and independence within its recommendations and is likely to make an important impact on care at the interface between acute, intermediate and continuing care. The likely effects of implementation of the framework on care practices within care homes in the private and voluntary sectors are more difficult to estimate. The Care Standards Act 2000 introduces a range of minimum standards that proprietors and managers of care homes must achieve from April 2002. These include minimum standards for building specifications, room occupancy, staff training and management. However, there are concerns that many homes within the independent and voluntary sectors will be forced out of business as a result of these requirements, resulting in compulsory relocation for some residents.

All of these changes and initiatives are likely to impact upon the experiences of older people and family caregivers around and beyond the time of admission to nursing home care. The introduction of minimum standards, together with a national body with responsibility for overseeing their implementation should, in the longer term, improve experiences of admission to, and life within, a care home. However, in the absence of adequate levels of government funding, some homes will inevitably close, resulting in disruption and trauma for the residents, their relatives and the staff involved. In reality, inequalities and inconsistencies in standards of care are likely to persist, at least for the foreseeable future.

The demography of dying in institutional care

This section looks at the numbers and types of community care institutions in the UK and the place and causes of death of older people who die in England and Wales. Laing and Buisson (2001) report on the basis of their survey of care homes that the total value of the care home market for elderly and physically disabled people at April 2001 was estimated at £9.1 billion, of which private sector operators accounted for £7.2 billion. They estimate that there are 525,900 places in residential settings (including independent nursing and residential homes, local authority residential homes and NHS long-stay facilities) for long-stay care of elderly and physically disabled people across all sectors (private, public and voluntary) in the UK.

The number of residential care homes remained steady after 1999, having been on an upward trajectory until 1998. In England, between 1999 and 2000, the total number of nursing homes and private hospitals and clinics fell by 3 per cent, returning to the same level as in 1996. Four-fifths of the residents who have their care costs partly or fully met by the local authority are aged over 65 years, and just over half (52 per cent) of all residents supported financially are living in independent homes (Department of Health 2000a). In the UK as a whole, during 1998, 78 per cent of *all* nursing and long-stay hospital care for elderly, chronically and physically disabled people was provided by the private sector, with the NHS providing 15 per cent and the voluntary sector 7 per cent. Similarly, 60 per cent of residential care for elderly and physically disabled people was provided by the private sector in 1998, with the NHS providing 22 per cent and the voluntary sector 18 per cent (Laing and Buisson 2001).

The huge size of the care industry obscures considerable regional variation. For example, in England, there are 243 beds per 10,000 population over 65 in the North West, while in North Thames the rate is 124. Similarly, a picture of diversity in the types, size, management and organization of homes predominates. Laing and Buisson (2001) identify six main types of home across the UK: private and voluntary residential homes; small residential homes; private and voluntary nursing homes; private and voluntary dual registered homes; local authority owned homes; and NHS Trust owned homes. Such variation, underpinned by the huge growth of the independent care sector, has been highlighted as giving rise to particular problems in planning and delivering care to residents. For example, the Clinical Standards

Advisory Group reported the following on the basis of its inquiry into community health care for older people:

> The rapid and largely unplanned development of private and residential nursing homes has had several adverse consequences. Concentration of homes in particular areas was distorting the workload for GPs and district nurses. Concern was expressed that people who were discharged from hospital directly to residential or nursing home care did not receive adequate rehabilitation and that people in need of nursing home care were sometimes admitted to residential care because this was cheaper.
>
> (Clinical Standards Advisory Group 1998: 3)

What do these figures tell us about death and dying in institutional care? Most glaringly it is clear that residential and nursing homes are increasingly places where older people die (Froggatt 2001), with the percentage of deaths occurring in such institutions increasing year on year. In 1998 in England and Wales, 19 per cent of all deaths and almost a quarter of deaths in over 65-year-olds (23 per cent) took place in nursing or residential care.[1] In all cases, it is *women* aged over 85 who make up the majority of those who die in such settings. Similar figures apply to the USA (Zerzan *et al.* 2000).

Table 1.2 shows that the place of death for all ages and for those aged over 65 in England and Wales in 1998. Figures are also available from the Office of National Statistics (2000) for causes of death at different ages and in different places in England and Wales during 1998. Table 1.3 summarizes the available figures for deaths in care homes.

As we can see, neoplasms and circulatory and respiratory disease are major causes of death among residents in institutional care, with considerable numbers also dying from unknown causes or from dementia or diseases of the nervous system. These are all conditions characterized typically by a dying trajectory punctuated with periods of troublesome and distressing symptoms and complex psychosocial needs. While people suffering from cancer may experience a number of intensely distressing symptoms which have a rapid onset over a shorter period of time, those with circulatory and respiratory conditions may have experienced similar symptoms for at least a year, and are more likely to have been restricted in activities of daily living for a longer time period and to have experienced additional symptoms such as mental confusion, incontinence, difficulties with hearing and vision and dizziness (Addington-Hall *et al.* 1998). Even in the absence of any active disease, it is known that those older people who move into care homes tend to have overall greater physical and mental frailty than those who live at home and a poorer quality of life, and to be more socially isolated (Seale and Cartwright 1994; Seymour and Hanson 2001). Many do not have families or friends to support or care for them – again a feature that is especially true for very old women. We can see, then, that older people dying in institutional care are among the most needy, and that their

Table 1.2   Place of death in England and Wales, 1998

Place of death	Number of deaths (% of all deaths) at all ages (over 28 days)		Number of deaths (% of all deaths in people aged 65 and over) for those aged 65 and over	
NHS hospitals and other communal establishments for the care of the sick	300,536	(54)	249,903	(56)
Non-NHS hospitals and other communal establishments for the care of the sick	58,491	(11)	56,494	(13)
Other communal establishments	45,147	(8)	44,538	(10)
Hospices	23,274	(4)	16,342	(4)
Psychiatric hospitals (NHS and non-NHS)	4,062	(0.7)	1,944	(0.4)
At home	109,035	(20)	82,620	(19)
In other private houses and other places	14,469	(3)	8,022	(2)
Total deaths	555,015	(100)	444,286	(100)

Source: compiled using data from Office of National Statistics, Mortality Statistics: general 1998

Table 1.3   Cause of death among residents of care homes aged 65 and over, England and Wales

Cause of death	Number of deaths in care homes among those aged 65 and over	Percentage of all deaths among people aged 65 and over	Percentage of all deaths in care homes among people aged 65 and over
Neoplasms	13,284	3	13
Mental disorders	5,883	1.3	6
Diseases of the nervous system	3,713	0.8	3.7
Circulatory disease	37,880	8.5	37
Respiratory disease	25,646	5.8	25
Symptoms and signs in ill-defined conditions	8,520	2	8.4
Other causes	6,106	1.4	6

Source: compiled using data from Office of National Statistics, Mortality Statistics: general 1998 needs span the physical, social and psychological domains. It is this complex fusion of problems and needs that the contemporary model of palliative care seeks to address.

Our attention now turns first to a brief analysis of the palliative care model and the evolution of palliative care policy, and second to an exploration of whether the stated aims of health care policy relating to palliative care fit with older people's experiences of institutional care. We conclude with an overview of the problems attendant on the application of palliative care in the institutional setting. All these areas are subsequently covered in more detail in later chapters of this book.

What is palliative care?

Historically 'palliative care' has been associated with the delivery of care by hospices to cancer patients. However, from its early beginnings, promoters of the palliative care model have been at pains to emphasize that palliative care is a *philosophy* of care with no necessary association with a particular setting, disease or type of caregiver (Clark and Seymour 1999; Seymour and Hanson 2001). Indeed, increasingly, palliative care is being recognized as an essential component in the care and treatment of all those who suffer from a life threatening or life limiting illness. Clark and Seymour (1999: 80), drawing on Morris (1997), examine how the term palliative care is associated with the metaphor of the 'shield' as well as the 'cloak': the relief and palliation of the symptoms of disease is associated with the protection and support of the person in need. The most widely accepted definition of palliative care is that provided in 1990 by the World Health Organization (WHO). At that time, the definition was framed to apply to cancer patients but it is now recognized that its key elements are also applicable to people suffering from non-cancer conditions:

> Palliative care is the active total care of patients whose disease is not responsive to curative treatment. Control of pain, of other symptoms, and of psychological, social and spiritual problems is paramount. The goal of palliative care is achievement of the best quality of life for patients and their families. Many aspects of palliative care are also applicable earlier in the course of the illness, in conjunction with anticancer treatment. Palliative care:
>
> * Affirms life and regards dying as a normal process
> * Neither hastens nor postpones death
> * Provides relief from pain and other symptoms
> * Integrates the psychological and spiritual aspects of patient care
> * Offers a support system to help patients live as actively as possible until death

- Offers a support system to help the family cope during the patient's illness and in their own bereavement

(WHO 1990)

Throughout the last quarter of the twentieth century, a developing concern can be traced within health and social care policy of successive UK governments to widen access to palliative care. Clark and Seymour (1999) observe how, from an early position in which the government gave tacit support to the charitable hospices with their somewhat patchy and locally contingent development, the notion expanded that government should take a much more strategic approach and provide a tight 'steer' to health authorities with regard to the assessment of palliative care needs and the planning of palliative care services, whether provided by the NHS or the voluntary sector (see Table 1.4 for key policy landmarks after 1980).

In order to refine and elucidate policy relating to palliative care, it has been necessary to define and clarify the boundaries and relationship between different types and modes of delivery of palliative care. Clark and Seymour (1999) discuss the tangled relationship between 'terminal care', 'the palliative care approach' and 'specialist palliative care', although their discussion has in part been superseded by the publication of a briefing document (National Council for Hospice and Specialist Palliative Care Services 2001), which outlines the 'principal definitions of the principal elements of care provided to meet the full spectrum of palliative care need' (p. 1) and in so doing affords the provision of palliative care in nursing homes a crucial role in the mobilization of the much heralded supportive care strategy for England and Wales (Box 1.1).

Box 1.1   Definitions of palliative care

General palliative care: palliative care provided by the patient's and family's usual professional carers as a vital and integral part of their routine clinical practice. It is informed by a knowledge and practice of palliative care principles. A practitioner within a general palliative care service should be able to: assess patients' palliative care needs; meet those needs within the limits of their knowledge, skills and competence; know when to seek advice from or refer to specialist palliative care services.

Specialist palliative care: palliative care provided by health and social care professionals who specialize in palliative care and work within multiprofessional specialist palliative care teams. A specialist palliative care service should be available in all care settings for patients with a moderate to high complexity of palliative care need.

Source: adapted from NCHSPCS (2001).

Table 1.4   Key UK policy landmarks in palliative care

Year	Landmark
1980	Report of the Working Group on Terminal Care (1980) produced by the Standing Subcommittee on Cancer of the Standing Medical Advisory Committee (The Wilkes Report), encouraging the dissemination of the principles of terminal care throughout all sectors of the health service
1987	The publication of the government's first official circular on terminal care, requiring health authorities to take the lead in co-ordinating integrated services for terminally ill people. Palliative Medicine recognized as a speciality
1991	National Council for Hospice and Specialist Palliative Care established as a pressure group and begin to publish a series of influential reports and commentaries that help to shape national policy
1992	Standing Medical Advisory Committee and Standing Nursing and Midwifery Committee publish their report (SMAC and SNMAC 1992) on the principles and provision of palliative care, recommending that greater effort be directed at meeting the needs of people with palliative care needs arising from non-cancer disease and in non-specialized settings
1995	The Expert Advisory Group on Cancer (1995), established in 1994, reports its findings, in what is known as the Calman-Hine report. It recommends sweeping changes in the organization of cancer and palliative care services
1997–2001	New Labour government is elected and re-elected. The NHS is reorganized, with an emphasis on national standards and strategies of care
2000	The NHS Cancer Plan is published, incorporating a supportive care strategy that embraces palliative care and has a key goal providing palliative care to all those in need. The National Council for Hospice and Specialist Palliative Care Services send out for consultation proposals for a National Plan and Strategic Framework for Palliative Care 2000–2005
2001	The National Service Framework for Older People is published and makes explicit reference to the value of palliative care for older people

We can see that by 2000, for the first time in England, palliative care became a key aspect of a wider supportive care strategy. The National Council for Hospice and Specialist Palliative Care Services (NCHSPCS 2000) identified the provision of palliative care as underpinned by the following 'landmarks':

• Designation of palliative care as a national priority and inclusion for the first time in health authorities' service and financial frameworks.
• Allocation of an additional £50 million per year by the NHS to enhance equity of access to services – this represents a 20 per cent increase on current NHS/voluntary sector expenditure.
• NHS investment of £2 million a year on training and support in palliative care for district nurses and other community staff.
• NHS commitment to agree a more realistic NHS funding contribution to voluntary hospices that provide agreed core services.
• Steps to achieve a major increase in the supply of palliative care physicians.
• Department of Health commitment to agree definitions of core services and to review out-of-hours services.
• Establishment of palliative care networks as forerunners of supportive and palliative networks alongside Cancer Networks.
• Recognition in National Service Frameworks of the palliative care needs of elderly people and those with coronary heart disease (NCHSPCS 2000).

Within the rhetoric of policy there is a powerful emphasis on partnerships between health and social services and between the public, private and voluntary sectors (Department of Health 1998). But how do the stated aims of health care policy as they relate to palliative care fit with older people's experiences of institutional care? We examine now the range of experience from the point of entry to a care home to death, drawing on the developing range of research in this field. Our central thesis is that older people who live and die in care homes, and (where they have them) their family carers, have been systematically disadvantaged in relation to the provision of palliative care.

The experiences of older people in institutional care: from entry to care to death

This section draws upon a review of the literature on experiences of life in a care home prepared by one of us in the context of a research study to explore the educational needs of staff working in care homes (Davies 2001). We consider experiences of admission to care from the perspectives of older people and their family carers. It has been recognized for some time that admission to care is rarely anticipated in advance, with little evidence of a proactive and planned approach (Nolan and Caldock 1996). This is largely a consequence of pervasive and deeply rooted negative perceptions of institutional care (Jack 1998). A majority of older people and family carers reject the idea of admission to care (Victor 1997) and rarely discuss the possibility openly with the person they care for (McAuley *et al.* 1997; Lewyeka 1998). As a consequence, older people and their families have often gathered little information on which to base a judgement about the pros and cons of institutional care, and make care decisions all too frequently from a position of crisis (Aneshensel *et al.* 1995; McAuley *et al.* 1997). Assessments during this period are often fragmented and confusing (Cotter *et al.* 1998), with a lack of coordination and adequate documentation (Audit Commission 1997). It is apparent that older people themselves frequently do not figure prominently in the decision-making process and may not have the opportunity to visit the home before moving in (Audit Commission 1997; Cotter *et al.* 1998; Reed and Morgan 1998; Wright 1998). Yet the selection of a home is crucial if residents are to achieve an optimal quality of life and maintain links with family and friends (Reed *et al.* 1998). While the role of nursing and residential homes in providing respite care and rehabilitation is expanding (Baltes *et al.* 1994; Blair 1995; Salgado *et al.* 1995) and, increasingly, admission to a care home may not necessarily be a permanent decision, for most new admissions the care home will indeed provide a final resting place.

Living in a care home

A number of studies and first hand accounts have explored the experience of living in a care home from the older person's perspective (Laird 1982; Nystrom and Andersson-Segesten 1990; Nystrom and Segesten 1994; Casey and Holmes 1995; Liukkonen 1995). While experiences are varied these accounts suggest that, for many residents, life in a care home is characterized by a sense of powerlessness, vulnerability and loss of personal identity. Links with family and friends often prove difficult to maintain and residents experience social exclusion from the wider community. These experiences are compounded by low levels of interaction between staff and residents and minimal involvement in decision-making and social activities (Gilloran *et al.* 1994; Ballard *et al.* 2001). There is evidence that care home staff prioritize residents' needs for physical care over their needs for social and emotional support (Liukkonen 1995; Wilde *et al.* 1995). Furthermore, there appears to be a gap in understanding between the older residents of care homes, their families and the staff caring for them in terms of perceptions of need. Accordingly, a recurrent theme within the literature is that professional caregivers have different priorities for frail older people in their care to those which older people have for themselves (Bartlett 1993; Bliesmer and Earle 1993; Bowsher 1994; Oleson *et al.* 1994; Davies and Nolan 2000).

Vulnerability and powerlessness

The vulnerability that older people feel as a result of their dependence on nursing home staff has been vividly described in many first hand-accounts (Laird 1982; Nystrom and Segesten 1994; Reed and Payton 1996). Numerous studies have described how care staff, sometimes inadvertently, adopt a gatekeeping role *vis-à-vis* essential care (Herzberg 1993), medical care (Gillick and Mendes 1996), pain control (Ferrell 1995) and opportunities for social interaction (Gilloran *et al.* 1994; Nolan *et al.* 1995). The regular exclusion of older people and their families from discussions about their care and progress (Norburn *et al.* 1995; Davies and Nolan 2000) is a further example of the ways in which older people living in nursing homes can be disempowered. This is disturbing in the light of evidence to suggest that involvement in decision-making has positive benefits for the residents of nursing homes, with studies demonstrating a relationship between the maintenance of personal control and important outcomes such as psychological well-being and satisfaction with care (Chen and Snyder 1996; Warner 1997).

Loss of personal identity and self-esteem

The challenge to personal identity and self-esteem presented by the move to a care home has significant implications for quality of life in old age (Nystrom and Andersson-Segesten 1990), and the value of basing care for older people within the framework of their personal biography and life history has been demonstrated (Reynolds 1992; Ford and McCormack 1999). Knowledge of individual characteristics such as family relationships, occupation, cultural background, spiritual beliefs and sexuality is essential to the development of an appropriate plan of care. However, biographical detail within assessment documentation is often limited (Brocklehurst and Dickinson 1996) and there is evidence that family caregivers are frequently not involved in the care planning process (Norburn *et al.* 1995; McDerment *et al.* 1997; Davies and Nolan 2000). This has important implications for the extent to which care can be person and relationship centred (Nolan *et al.* 2001).

The importance of relationships

The importance of maintaining family relationships following the move to a nursing home, both for older people and for their family members, has been clearly demonstrated (Bogo 1987; DePaola and Ebersole 1995; Lawton *et al.* 1995; Ross *et al.* 1997). However, few studies have considered the effects on a relationship of a spouse or partner moving into a care home. In particular, the need for intimacy and a continuing sexual relationship has received little attention (Kaplan 1996). For the partner who remains at home adjusting to living alone, dealing with loneliness and a lack of companionship is a major challenge (Ade-Ridder and Kaplan 1993). For some, the grieving process is 'elongated' because they are not free to resume an independent life (Sommers and Shields 1987; Beyleveld 1997).

Residents also benefit from opportunities to build relationships with other residents and their families (Powers 1992; Patterson 1995; Reed and Payton 1996). Yet frequently staff in care homes fail to recognize the significance of the relationships residents have with each other (Reed *et al.* 1998). In particular, there are implications for support needs when an older person dies (Costello and Kendrick 2000).

In summary, the literature describing experiences of living in a nursing home confirms the potential for older people to feel isolated within an alien environment if they are not encouraged and enabled to maintain important relationships and create new ones. Similarly, the frailty of many older people at the time of admission renders them vulnerable to the loss of personal autonomy and identity. The potential benefits of creating a sense of community within care homes, nurturing relationships and creating links with the outside world seem clear. However, contemporary evidence does little to expel the negative images of long-stay care settings evoked so strongly by early observational research (Townsend 1962; Robb 1967; Miller and Gwynne 1972).

The experience of dying and death in institutional care

Hockey, writing in 1988, observed how the care of the sick and dying in the nursing home she studied was 'an intrinsic aspect of its role... deterioration and death were always waiting in the wings' (Hockley 1988: 201). Despite the presence of dying and death, these phases of life are frequently concealed in institutional care:

> On entering residential care there is a covert understanding that elderly people will end their days there, and yet it is often not considered 'decent' to broach the subject of how they wish to be cared for when dying, and what services the home offers... Hinton (1972) observed further that there was a veil of silence in some residential homes. A game was thus devised, with its own unspoken rules and rituals.
>
> (Shemmings 1996: 32)

More recently, Komaromy has reported on a major study of death and dying in nursing homes that incorporated some in-depth ethnographic study of selected homes (Komaromy 2001; see also Chapter 8, this volume). She observes how, within the homes studied, 'ageing bodies, when they have become immobile, lend themselves to an object like status' (Komaromy 2001: 306). One root of this type of objectification, argues Komaromy, is the tendency for staff to 'represent residents as institutionalized into a homogenous group who all share the same life experiences, responses and expectations' (p. 310).

The wider study from which these observations are drawn suggests that such phenomena are related in no small measure to a lack of formal preparation and training of care staff to look after dying residents, and a lack of awareness among care home managers of the elements of good practice in relation to death and dying, despite their aspirations to provide a 'good death' and an individualized care approach for residents. This was especially the case for pain relief and symptom control (Katz *et al.* 1999). Moreover, this study shows that even where knowledge and preparation were of a reasonable standard, homes were constrained by many factors, including resource constraints, and the variable levels of support and differing perspectives and practices of GPs, specialist and community nurses. Medical input into homes is of particular note here: GPs assume the responsibility for the medical care of residents yet are burdened heavily with competing duties and responsibilities (Black and Bowman 1997).

Analysis of the quality of care given to people with dementia highlights concerns that the day-to-day care of people with palliative care needs is lacking in fundamental ways. Ballard *et al.* (2001) mapped the care of 218 people with dementia in seven NHS and ten private care homes by observing their activities over six hours. Only 14 per cent of that time was spent communicating with staff or other residents, and less than 3 per cent was spent in everyday constructive activities other than watching television. The facilities chosen were not selected because of perceived poor standard of care and were considered to be representative. They conclude by stating that: 'quality of care was rated as needing radical improvement or much improvement in all homes, and no home showed even a fair standard of care' (Ballard *et al.* 2001: 426).

Not surprisingly, this picture is found elsewhere. Zerzan *et al.* (2000), reporting on the access of nursing home residents to hospice and palliative care in the USA, note that although most nursing home residents in the USA have incurable chronic diseases and more than half have been diagnosed with a progressive dementia, only 1 per cent are enrolled in a hospice care programme. Zerzan *et al.* (2000) note that the area they live in or organizational features influence the access of nursing home residents to hospice care. It has little to do with residents' preferences. Other research in the USA observes that dissatisfaction with terminal care management is most frequently expressed by surviving family members of nursing home residents (Hanson *et al.* 1997). There is a growing body of evidence that suggests similar trends in the UK. We know that, once in institutional care, older people in the UK tend not to be referred to specialist palliative care inpatient units proportionally to their needs for such care (Grande *et al.* 1998; Eve and Higginson 2000). This is most problematic among older people with non-cancer palliative care needs, but is even the case among older cancer patients – a group which at all ages has preferential access to specialist palliative care (Eve and Higginson 2000). Why is this? Clearly there are a number of complex and interrelating factors, all of which are addressed in some depth in forthcoming chapters. Our task here is to give the reader an overview of some key issues, in order to 'set the scene' for what follows.

The problems in applying palliative care in the institutional setting: a summary of key issues

This section considers the barriers and challenges facing those with the responsibility to ensure that people living in care homes and their families receive appropriate and effective care at the end of life.

Regulation and standard setting in a mixed economy of care

To date, the focus of legislation and health authority guidance in relation to the provision of continuing care for older people has been largely on adequacy and quality assurance rather than quality of life (Bartlett and Burnip 1998). Within the UK, the role of the nursing home inspectorate in maintaining standards has been criticized, with varying standards applied in different parts of the country (Royal College of Nursing 1994). Few health authorities inspect registered homes more than twice a year. There have also been calls for standards to be identified in terms of resident outcomes rather than structural features and processes of care (Bartlett and Burnip 1998). Within the context of continuing care services, the potential for the voice of the consumer to raise care standards has yet to be fully realized. This is significant, since the few attempts that there have been to involve residents and relatives in quality specification have suggested that older people and their families prioritize different aspects of care when compared to staff members (Raynes 1998).

Given the fragmentation of continuing care services, an effective regulatory mechanism is essential. With the market increasingly dominated by profit-making corporate providers, there is an imperative for government intervention in areas that affect profit margins, such as staffing, skill mix, staff training and the range and quality of services provided (Harrington 2001). The Care Standards Act 2000 introduced a range of minimum standards that proprietors and managers of care homes must achieve. Historically care services for older people throughout the UK have been beset with inequity, so that older people with similar needs have received very different levels and forms of care. This situation has been attributed to chronic underfunding of statutory services, which has resulted in a forced mixed economy of care, including private (for profit), voluntary (not for profit) and informal arrangements. It has been suggested that the absence of effective collaboration between the statutory sector and these non-state providers has resulted in inefficiency and a lack of fairness (Laing 1998; Wright 1998).

Furthermore, it is generally acknowledged that the continuing separation between health and social services militates against effective teamwork (Walker 1995).

Viability of care homes and consumer choice

Many private nursing homes have been forced out of business in the wake of the reforms of the early 1990s and the tightening up of funding requirements (Bartlett and Burnip 1998). As a consequence, the proportion of homes managed by large corporations has increased. While this has the advantage of enabling staff to have improved access to support services and programmes of professional development, the fluidity of the market continues to create uncertainties for residents, their families and employees. The requirements of the Care Standards Act are likely to result in further closures as home owners struggle to meet new building standards and training stipulations. A report carried out by an independent firm of financial consultants in 1998 found wide discrepancies between the level of state funding for continuing care and the economic cost of providing such care (Laing 1998). This situation also results in inequities: shortfalls between the level of funding which local authority social services departments allow for residential and nursing home placements and the fees charged by many care homes have resulted in a two-tier system, with those able to 'top up' social services payments from their own resources able to choose from a wider range of homes (Wright 1998).

Workforce issues

Historically, little attention has been paid to the characteristics of the continuing care workforce (Maslin-Prothero and Masterson 1998). However, a report published by the Kings Fund in 2001 concluded that: 'immediate action is needed to avoid a catastrophe. A coherent and integrated strategy that includes government, the NHS, local authorities, training and regulatory bodies and private providers, is essential to improve the quality of care services and avert a crisis' (Henwood 2001: 2). The care home sector suffers from a history of employing predominantly unskilled labour and this, together with expenditure constraints, leaves workers with little time to spend with individual residents. This is a major factor limiting the quality of care that can be delivered. Despite a heavy reliance on an untrained workforce, it is worth noting that between 1995 and 1999 there was an 8 per cent increase in the number of qualified whole-time equivalent nursing staff employed in nursing homes, leading to fears that the care home sector will need to recruit a growing proportion of the nursing workforce from a health service already experiencing nursing shortages. Mainly anecdotal evidence suggests that the care home workforce, both qualified and unqualified, is usually female, older and employed on a part-time basis (Maslin-Prothero and Masterson 1998). In urban areas, a significant proportion of staff are black (Gerrish *et al.* 1996). Many home-owners, particularly those operating independently, are forced to minimize labour costs in order to offer fees at competitive rates. Consequently, staff turnover is high; one study suggests an annual staff turnover in excess of 20 per cent (Laing and Buisson 2001). Thus it appears that the care workforce shares the marginalized status of those to whom it delivers care. In these circumstances, it is difficult to create a culture of career development. Care homes currently offer comparatively poor preparation for specialist roles in gerontological care, widely acknowledged to be a key element in driving up standards of care (Ford and McCormack 1999).

As the foregoing suggests, within the nursing profession caring for older people is frequently perceived as an unattractive career option. As a result many care homes experience difficulties in recruiting and retaining qualified nursing staff. Furthermore, the very definition of 'nursing' in continuing care settings is contested and under threat. In the wake of the report of the *Commission on Long Term Care* and the government's response, the government debated with stakeholder groups an appropriate definition of nursing in the context of continuing care with stakeholder groups in order to inform decisions about funding (Cayton 2001). The Royal College of Nursing rejects the notion that 'nursing care' should refer only to care provided by registered nurses, thus excluding care provided by health care assistants under the supervision or delegation of a registered nurse, currently defined as 'personal care' (Hancock 2001). Despite the decision taken by the Scottish Executive to reject the distinction between personal and nursing care, confusion and disagreement in relation to the distinction between nursing and personal care are likely to persist, clouding developments aimed at improving and enhancing standards.

Valuing the role of family caregivers

The temporal nature of family caregiving (Nolan *et al.* 1996) implies that the needs of family caregivers will change at key points over time and that supportive interventions need to be tailored to the particular stage reached. However, the literature suggests that family caregivers' needs are poorly addressed at all stages of the move to a care home and beyond, particularly with respect to information upon which to base an informed choice and preparation for the emotional consequences of the placement process. Family members experience loss, guilt and grief, and report that these emotions continue throughout the time that their relative is in the nursing home (Nolan *et al.* 1996; McAuley *et al.* 1997; Lewyeka 1998). There are, however, few published reports of practice interventions to help relatives to prepare for the move (Nolan and Dellasega 1999).

It is clear that most family caregivers wish to maintain active involvement in the life and care of their relatives (Bogo 1987; Naleppa 1996); however, staff rarely negotiate the nature and extent of this involvement. Admission assessment normally focuses entirely upon the needs of the new resident to the extent that the difficulties relatives experience are often ignored. Furthermore, care staff may be largely unaware of their potential role in supporting family caregivers in adjusting to the transition and in enabling them to develop a modified caregiving role (McDerment *et al.* 1997; Pillemer *et al.* 1997), and this despite the unique potential for relatives to provide 'a lifeline of special care' (Fleming 1998: 140).

Care at the end of life provides an important indication of the extent to which care home staff perceive that they have a role in supporting family members. Regular confrontation with the processes of death and dying is a feature of nursing home life and this is likely to be stressful for staff, residents and relatives (Savishinsky 1991; Aday and Shahan 1995). Yet there are few studies which have considered the support needed by relatives and staff following the death of a resident. One North American study (Murphy *et al.* 1997) looked at bereavement services available for families of older people with Alzheimer's disease living in long-term care facilities. This survey of 121 nursing homes revealed that 98 per cent of homes did not visit, make phone calls or provide written information to family members in the period following a resident's death. This is clearly an area for research and practice development.

Conclusion

The emergence of the care home as a pivotal site of life and death for older people, yet the evolution of a policy context that constrains the translation of the stated aims of palliative care into high-quality, individualized care for the residents in care homes results from a complex, tangled history. In this chapter we have tried to elucidate this history, before outlining the current profile and population of care homes in the UK. Experiences of living and dying in a care home, from the perspectives of both residents and their family caregivers, have been gleaned from a developing body of literature. Here we have seen that residents and their families can experience isolation and a lack of opportunity to continue with existing, or to establish new, relationships. This is despite the potential for these relationships to contribute positive experiences of care and caregiving, even as death approaches. We have discussed broadly some of the important issues and factors influencing and constraining the development and provision of palliative care to older people in need within care homes, pointing to the complex relationship among financial and workforce resources, clinical education and training, and the wider organization of health and social care.

We hope that this chapter will act as a point of reference for readers as they go on to explore and reflect upon, through the subsequent contributions to this volume, the pressing problem of providing high-quality care to some of the most needy, frail and marginalized people in our society.

Implications for practice

- Older people who move into care homes tend to have greater overall physical and mental frailty than those who live at home. This renders them vulnerable to the loss of personal autonomy and identity and to social isolation, resulting in a poor quality of life. Creating a sense of community within care homes and nurturing old and new relationships are important factors in addressing these issues.
- Admission to care is rarely anticipated in advance, leaving residents and their family caregivers with feelings of guilt and loss. Planning for care admission, and developing ways of enhancing choice in care placement, is beneficial. Threats to the financial viability of some care homes pose a barrier to choice and continuity of care.
- Care homes are increasingly places where older people die, with the percentage of deaths occurring in such institutions increasing year on year. However, older people in care homes tend not to be referred to specialist palliative care inpatient units proportionally to their needs for such care. This inequality needs urgent attention by policy-makers.
- The day-to-day care of people with palliative care needs is lacking in fundamental ways, despite the best efforts of care home staff and family caregivers, because of training, management and nursing and medical workforce issues. The policy rhetoric of partnerships between health and social services, and between the public, private and voluntary sectors, needs translating urgently into long-term initiatives to address this basic inadequacy.
- Collaborative relationships between care home staff and family caregivers have the potential to enhance the quality of care given to older people with palliative care needs.
- Care home staff, other residents and family caregivers may all need bereavement support following the death of a resident.

Note

1 These figures relating to deaths in nursing homes are approximate. The classification used by the ONS does not identify nursing homes as a separate category. It is likely that there are small numbers of nursing homes in the 'NHS hospitals and communal establishments for the care of the sick' category and similarly small

numbers of private hospitals providing acute care in the 'Non-NHS hospital and communal establishments for the care of the sick' category. Following Froggatt (1998), we are assuming that these unknown figures balance one another out.

References

Aday, R. H. and Shahan, D. R. (1995) Elderly reactions to a death education program in a nursing home setting. *Gerontology and Geriatrics Education*, 15(3): 3–18.

Addington-Hall, J. M., Fakhoury, W. and McCarthy, M. (1998) Specialist palliative care in non-malignant disease. *Palliative Medicine*, 12: 417–27.

Ade-Ridder, L. and Kaplan, L. (1993) Marriage, spousal caregiving and a husband's move to a nursing home: a changing role for the wife? *Journal of Gerontological Nursing*, 19(10): 12–23.

Aneshensel, C. S., Pearly, L. I., Mullan, J. T., Zarit, S. U. and Whitlach, C. J. (1995) *Profiles in Caregiving: The Unexpected Career*. San Diego: Academic Press.

Audit Commission (1986) *Making a Reality of Community Care*. London: The Audit Commission.

Audit Commission (1997) *The Coming of Age: Improving Care Services for Older People*. London: The Audit Commission.

Ballard, C., Fossey, J., Chithramohan, R. *et al.* (2001) Quality of care in private sector and NHS facilities for people with dementia: cross-sectional survey. *British Medical Journal*, 323(7310): 426–7.

Baltes, M., Neumann, E. M. and Zank, S. (1994) Maintenance and rehabilitation of independence in old age: an intervention program for staff. *Psychology and Ageing*, 9(2): 179–88.

Bartlett, H. (1993) *Nursing Homes for Elderly People: Questions of Quality and Policy*. Victoria, Australia: Harwood Academic Publishers.

Bartlett, H. and Burnip, S. (1998) Quality of care in nursing homes for older people: providers' perspectives and priorities. *Nursing Times Research*, 3(4): 257–68.

Beyleveld, J. (1997) *Marital Separation in Long-term Nursing Home Care*. Sheffield: Sheffield Community Health Council.

Black, D. and Bowman, C. (1997) Community institutional care for frail elderly people. *British Medical Journal*, 315: 441–2.

Blair, C. E. (1995) Combining behavior management and mutual goal setting to reduce physical dependency in nursing home residents. *Nursing Research*, 44(3): 160–5.

Bliesmer, M. and Earle, P. (1993) Research considerations: nursing home quality perceptions. *Journal of Gerontological Nursing*, 19(6): 27–34.

Bogo, M. (1987) Social work practice and family systems in adaptation to homes for the aged. *Journal of Gerontological Social Work*, 10(1/2): 5–20.

Bond, J. and Bond, S. (1987) Developments in the provision and evaluation of long term care for dependent old people. In P. Fielding (ed.) *Research on the Nursing Care of Elderly People*. New York: John Wiley.

Bowsher, J. E. (1994) A theoretical model of independence for nursing home elders. *Scholarly Inquiry in Nursing Practice*, 8(2): 207–24.

Brocklehurst, J. and Dickinson, E. (1996) Autonomy for elderly people in long-term care. *Age and Ageing*, 25(4): 329–32.

Butler, P. (2001) 'No question' of free personal care in England. *Guardian*, 26 January.

Cartwright, A., Hockey, L. and Anderson, J. L. (1973) *Life Before Death*. London: Routledge and Kegan Paul.

Casey, M. S. and Holmes, C. A. (1995) The inner ache: an experiential perspective on loneliness. *Nursing Inquiry*, 2(3): 172–9.

Cayton, H. (2001) Valuing long term care. In *Long Term Care for the Elderly: Planning for Change*, Conference proceedings, 23 January. London: Carers National Association.

Chen, K. and Snyder, M. (1996) Perception of personal control and satisfaction with care among nursing home elders. *Perspectives*, 20(2): 16–9.

Clark D. and Seymour J. (1999) *Reflections on Palliative Care*. Buckingham: Open University Press.

Clinical Standards Advisory Group (1998) *Community Health Care for Elderly People*. London: HMSO.

Cookman, C. A. (1996) Older people and attachment to things, places, pets, and ideas. *Image: Journal of Nursing Scholarship*, 28(3): 227–31.

Costello, J. and Kendrick, K. (2000) Grief and older people: the making or breaking of emotional bonds following partner loss in later life. *Journal of Advanced Nursing*, 32(6): 1374–82.

Cotter, A., Meyer, J. and Roberts, S. (1998) Humanity or bureaucracy: the transition from hospital to long-term residential care. *Nursing Times Research*, 3(4): 247–56.

Daley, O. E. (1993) Women's strategies for living in a nursing home. *Journal of Gerontological Nursing*, 19(9): 5–9.

Davies, S. (2001) Caring for older people with continuing care needs and their families. In M. Nolan, S. Davies and G. Grant (eds) *Working with Older People and Their Families: Key Issues in Policy and Practice*. Buckingham: Open University Press.

Davies, S. and Nolan, M. (2000) Relatives' experiences of nursing home entry. Unpublished final report to the General Nursing Council Trust, Sheffield.

DePaola, S. J. and Ebersole, P. (1995) Meaning in life categories of elderly nursing home residents. *International Journal of Aging and Human Development*, 40(3): 227–36.

Department of Health (1989) *Caring for People: Community Care in the Next Decade and Beyond*. London: HMSO.

Department of Health (1998) *Partnership in Action: New Opportunities for Joint Working between Health and Social Services*. London: HMSO.

Department of Health (2000a) *Community Care Statistics 2000. Residential Personal Social Services for Adults, England*. London: HMSO.

Department of Health (2000b) *The NHS Plan: A Plan for Investment, A Plan for Reform*. London: HMSO.

Department of Health (2000c) *The NHS Cancer Plan: A Plan for Investment, A Plan for Reform*. London: HMSO.

Department of Health (2001) *The National Service Framework for Older People*. London: HMSO.

Eve, A. and Higginson, I. (2000) Minimum dataset activity for hospice and palliative care services in the UK 1997/8. *Palliative Medicine*, 14: 395–404.

Expert Advisory Group on Cancer (1995) *A Policy Framework for Commissioning Cancer Services: A Report by the Expert Advisory Group on Cancer to the Chief Medical Officers of England and Wales* (The Calman-Hine Report). London: Department of Health and the Welsh Office.

Ferrell, B. A. (1995) Pain evaluation and management in the nursing home. *Annals of Internal Medicine*, 123(9): 681–7.

Finch, J. and Groves, D. (1980) Community care and the family: a case for equal opportunities. *Journal of Social Policy*, 9: 487–511.

Fleming, A. A. (1998) Family caregiving of older people with dementing illnesses in nursing homes: a lifeline of special care. *Australasian Journal on Ageing*, 17(3): 140–5.

Ford, P. and McCormack, B. (1999) The key attributes of a gerontological nurse specialist. *Elderly Care*, 11(4): 26.

Froggatt, K. (1998) 'Fading like a flower': understandings of death in a nursing home setting. Paper presented to the Social Context of Death, Dying and Disposal, Fourth International Conference, Glasgow, 3–6 September.

Froggatt, K. A. (2001) Palliative care and nursing homes: where next? *Palliative Medicine*, (15)1: 42–8.

Gerrish, K., Husband, C. and Mackenzie, J. (1996) *Nursing for a Multiethnic Society*. Buckingham: Open University Press.

Gillick, M. R. and Mendes, M. L. (1996) Medical care in old age: what do nurses in long-term care consider appropriate? *Journal of the American Geriatric Society*, 44(11): 1322–5.

Gilloran, A., McGlew, T., McKee, K., Robertson, A. and Wright, D. (1994) Measuring the quality of care in psychogeriatric wards. *Journal of Advanced Nursing*, 18(2): 269–75.

Gladstone, J. W. (1995) The marital perceptions of elderly persons living or having a spouse living in a long-term care institution in Canada. *The Gerontologist*, 35(1): 52–60.

Goffman, E. (1961) *Asylums: Essays on the Social Situation of Mental Patients and Other Inmates*. Harmondsworth: Penguin.

Grande, G. E., Addington-Hall, J. M. and Todd, C. J. (1998) Place of death and access to home care services: are certain patient groups at a disadvantage? *Social Science and Medicine*, 47: 565–79.

Hancock, C. (2001) The Christine Hancock column. The government should fund all the nursing care identified by the patient's nursing assessment, irrespective of who provides that care. *Nursing Standard*, 15(25): 26.

Hanson, L. C., Danis, M. and Garrett, J. (1997) What is wrong with end of life care? Opinions of bereaved family members. *Journal of the American Geriatric Society*, 45: 1339–44.

Harrington, C. (2001) Residential nursing facilities in the United States. *British Medical Journal*, 323: 507–10.

Henwood, M. (2001) *Future Imperfect? Report of the King's Fund Care and Support Inquiry*. London: King's Fund Publishing.

Herzberg, S. R. (1993) Positioning the nursing home resident: an issue of quality of life. *American Journal of Occupational Therapy*, 47(1): 75–7.

Hinton, J. (1972) *Dying*. Harmondsworth: Penguin.

Hockey, J. (1988) Residential care and the maintenance of social identity: negotiating the transition to institutional life. In M. Jeffreys (ed.) *Growing Old in the Twentieth Century*. London: Routledge.

Jack, R. (1998) Institutions in Community Care. In R. Jack (ed.) *Residential vs. Community Care: The Role of Institutions in Welfare Provision*. Basingstoke: Macmillan.

Kaplan, L. (1996) Sexual and institutional issues when one spouse resides in the community and the other lives in a nursing home. *Sexuality and Disability*, 14(4): 281–93.

Katz, J., Komaromy, C. and Sidell, M. (1999) Understanding palliative care in residential and nursing homes. *International Journal of Palliative Nursing*, 5(2): 58–64.

Komaromy, C. (2001) The sight and sound of death: the management of dead bodies in residential and nursing homes for older people. *Mortality*, 5(3): 299–315.

Laing, W. (1998) *A Fair Price for Care? Disparities between Market Rates and State Funding of Residential Care*. York: York Publishing Services.

Laing and Buisson (2001) *Care of Elderly People: Market Survey 2000*, 13th edn. London: Laing and Buisson (http://www.laingbuisson.co.uk). Accessed on 5 September 2001.

Laird, C. (1982) *Limbo: A Memoir of Life in a Nursing Home by a Survivor*. Novato, CA: Chandler and Sharp.

Lawton, M. P., Moss, M. and Dunamel, L. M. (1995) The quality of life among elderly care receivers. *Journal of Applied Gerontology*, 14(2): 150–71.

Lewyeka, M. (1998) *Finding and Paying for Residential and Nursing Home Care*, 2nd edn. London: Age Concern.

Lipsey, D. (2001) Paying for care. In *Long Term Care for the Elderly: Planning for Change*. Conference proceedings, London, January.

Liukkonen, A. (1995) Life in a nursing home for the frail elderly. *Clinical Nursing Research*, 4(4): 358–72.

McAuley, W. J., Travis, S. S. and Safewright, M. P. (1997) Personal accounts of the nursing home search and selection process. *Qualitative Health Research*, 7(2): 236–54.

McDerment, L., Ackroyd, J., Tealer, R. and Sutton, J. (1997*) As Others See Us: A Study of Relationships in Homes for Older People*. London: Relatives Association.

Maslin-Prothero, S. and Masterson, A. (1998) Continuing care: developing a policy analysis for nursing. *Journal of Advanced Nursing*, 28(3): 548–53.

Miller, A. and Gwynne, G. (1972) *A Life Apart*. London: Tavistock.

Morris, D. (1997) Palliation: shielding the patient from the assault of symptoms. *Academy Update*, 7(3): 1–11.

Murphy, K. P., Hanrahan, P. and Luchins, D. (1997) A survey of grief and bereavement in nursing homes: the importance of hospice grief and bereavement for the end-stage Alzheimer's disease patient and family. *Journal of the American Geriatrics Society*, 45(9): 1104–7.

Naleppa, M. J. (1996) Families and the institutionalised elderly: a review. *Journal of Gerontological Social Work*, 27(1/2): 87–111.

National Council for Hospice and Specialist Palliative Care Services (2000) *National Plan and Strategic Framework for Palliative Care 2000–2005* (Draft for consultation). London: NCHSPCS.

National Council for Hospice and Specialist Palliative Care Services (2001) *What Do We Mean by Palliative Care? A Discussion Paper*. Briefing, Number 9, May. London: NCHSPCS.

National Council of Social Service (1950) *Welfare Problems of Old People: Report of the Fifth National Conference on the Care of Old People*, The Dome, Brighton, 18–20 October. London: National Council of Social Service.

Nolan, M. and Caldock, K. (1996) Assessment: identifying the barriers to good practice. *Health and Social Care in the Community*, 4(2): 77–85.

Nolan, M., Davies, S. and Grant, G. (eds) (2001) *Working with Older People and their Families*. Buckingham: Open University Press.

Nolan, M. and Dellasega, C. (1999) 'It's not the same as him being at home': creating caring partnerships following nursing home placement. *Journal of Clinical Nursing*, 8(6): 723–30.

Nolan, M. R., Grant, G. and Keady, J. (1996) *Understanding Family Care: A Multi-dimensional Model of Caring and Coping*. Buckingham: Open University Press.

Nolan, M. R., Grant, G. and Nolan, J. (1995) Busy doing nothing: activity and interaction levels amongst differing populations of elderly patients. *Journal of Advanced Nursing*, 22(3): 528–38.

Norburn, J. E. K., Nettles Carlson, B., Soltys, F. G., Read, C. D. and Pickard, C. G. (1995) Long-term care organizational challenges and strategies: art vs. regulation. *Journal of Gerontological Nursing*, 21(8): 37–44.

Nystrom, A. E. and Andersson-Segesten, K. M. (1990) Peace of mind as an important aspect of old people's health. *Scandinavian Journal of Caring Sciences*, 4(2): 55–62.

Nystrom, A. E. and Segesten, K. M. (1994) On sources of powerlessness in nursing home life. *Journal of Advanced Nursing*, 19(1): 124–33.

Office of National Statistics (2000) *Mortality Statistics: General 1998*. Series DH31. London: ONS (last updated 28 September 2000).

Oleson, M., Heading, C., Shadick, K. M. and Bistodeau, J. (1994) Quality of life in long-stay institutions in England: nurse and resident perceptions. *Journal of Advanced Nursing*, 20(1): 23–32.

Patterson, B. J. (1995) The process of social support: adjusting to life in a nursing home. *Journal of Advanced Nursing*, 21(4): 682–9.

Pillemer, K., Hegerman, C., Albright, B. and Henderson, C. (1998) Building bridges between families and nursing home staff: The Partners in Caregiving Programme. *The Gerontologist*, 38(4): 499–503.

Powers, B. A. (1992) The roles staff play in the social networks of elderly institutionalised people. *Social Science and Medicine*, 34(12): 1335–43.

Raynes, N. V. (1998) Involving residents in quality specification. *Ageing and Society*, 18(1): 65–77.

Reed, J. and Morgan, D. (1998) From hospital to care home. Paper given at British Society of Gerontology Annual Conference, Sheffield, September.

Reed, J. and Payton, V. R. (1996) Constructing familiarity and managing the self: ways of adapting to life in nursing and residential homes for older people. *Ageing and Society*, 16(5): 543–60.

Reed, J., Payton, V. R. and Bond, S. (1998) The importance of place for older people moving into care homes. *Social Science and Medicine*, 46(7): 859–67.

Reynolds, C. (1992) An administrative program to facilitate culturally appropriate care for the elderly. *Holistic Nursing Practice*, 6(3): 34–42.

Robb, B. (1967) *Sans Everything: A Case to Answer*. London: Nelson.

Ross, H. M., Rosenthal, C. J. and Dawson, P. (1997) Spousal caregiving in the residential setting – visiting. *Journal of Clinical Nursing*, 6(6): 473–83.

Royal College of Nursing (1994) *An Inspector Calls*. London: Royal College of Nursing.

Royal Commission on Long Term Care (1999) *With Respect to Old Age*. London: HMSO.

Salgado, R., Ehrlich, F., Banks, C. *et al*. (1995) A mobile rehabilitation team program to assist patients in nursing-homes rehabilitate and return to their homes. *Archives of Gerontology and Geriatrics*, 20(3): 255–61.

Savishinsky, J. S. (1991) *The Ends of Time: Life and Work in a Nursing Home*. New York: Bergin and Garvey.

Seale, C. and Cartwright, A. (1994) *The Year Before Death*. Aldershot: Avebury.

Seymour, J. E. and Hanson, E. (2001) Palliative care and older people. In M. Nolan, S. Davies and G. Grant (eds) *Working with Older People and Their Families: Key Issues in Policy and Practice*. Buckingham: Open University Press.

Shemmings, Y. (1996) *Death, Dying and Residential Care*. Aldershot: Avebury.

Sommers, T. and Shields, L. (1987) *Women Take Care: The Consequences of Caring in Today's Society*. Gainesville, FL: Triad.

Standing Medical Advisory Committee (SMAC) and Standing Nursing and Midwifery Advisory Committee (SNMAC) (1992) *The Principles and Provision of Palliative Care*. London: HMSO.

Symonds, A. (1998) The social reconstruction of care: from the state to the 'community'. In A. Symonds and A. Kelly (eds) *The Social Reconstruction of Community Care*. Basingstoke: Macmillan Press.

Townsend, P. (1962) *The Last Refuge*. London: Routledge and Kegan Paul.

Victor, C. R. (1997) *Community Care and Older People*. Cheltenham: Stanley Thornes.

Walker, A. (1995) Integrating the family in the mixed economy of care. In I. Allen and E. Perkins (eds) *The Future of Family Care for Older People*. London: HMSO.

Walker, A. (1999) Older people and health services: the challenge of empowerment. In M. Purdey and D. Banks (eds) *Health and Exclusion: Victims and Collaborators in Health Care*. London: Routledge.

Warner, J. (1997) Bedtime rituals of nursing home residents: a study. *Nursing Standard*, 11(20): 34–8.

Webster, C. (1991) The elderly and the early National Health Service. In M. Pelling and R. M. Smith (eds) *Life, Death and the Elderly: Historical Perspectives*. London: Routledge.

Wilde, B., Larsson, G., Larsson, M. and Starrin, B. (1995) Quality of care from the elderly person's perspective: subjective importance and perceived reality. *Aging Clinical Experimental Research*, 7(2): 140–9.

Working Group on Terminal Care (1980) *Report of the Working Group on Terminal Care* (The Wilkes Report). London: DHSS.

World Health Organization (1990) *Cancer Pain Relief and Palliative Care*. Technical Report Series No. 804. Geneva: World Health Organization.

Wright, F. (1998) *Continuing to Care: The Effect on Spouses and Children of an Older Person's Admission to a Care Home*. York: York Publishing Services.

Zerzan, J., Stearns, S. and Hanson, L. (2000) Access to palliative care and hospice in nursing homes. *Journal of the American Medical Association*, 284(19): 2489–94.

2 Assessment of need in care homes

DEBORAH PARKER AND ALISON McLEOD

Assessing the palliative care needs of residents in aged care facilities and care homes is a major challenge, for palliative care professionals being asked to provide services, for those working in these facilities and more broadly for planners of health care services. In the final stages of their lives, residents in care homes are often suffering from one or more chronic degenerative diseases and these have a more unpredictable trajectory of dying than those people with cancer traditionally cared for by palliative care services.

This chapter examines the assessment process from two angles. First, we discuss the assessment of need for palliative care in aged care facilities at a population level; second, we look in detail at the assessment process as one of identifying the main areas of individual need.

Classification and policy

In Australia aged care facilities are increasingly places for older people to die (Maddocks and Parker 2001). The proportion of all deaths occurring in nursing homes rose from 1 per cent in 1960 to 20 per cent in 1990 (Hunt and Maddocks 1997). The percentage of separations by death in aged care facilities in Australia also increased steadily, from 70 per cent in 1993 to 81 per cent in 2000 (Australian Institute of Health and Welfare 1999, 2001). A similar trend has occurred in the United Kingdom, with an increase in deaths in residential and nursing homes from 13 per cent in 1990 to 18 per cent in 1995, and approximately 10 per cent of deaths in 1995 occurring in nursing homes (Office for National Statistics, cited in Froggatt 2000a). These figures indicate that although only a minority of the population die in aged care facilities, those who require this level of care will most probably die there.

The residential care system in Australia has been in a state of change since the introduction in 1985 of the Aged Care Reform Strategy. This strategy, formulated after four reviews and inquiries into aged care services, was intended to reform both community and residential care. It was designed to implement assessment strategies and provide a greater continuity between the different service sectors (Gibson 1998). The cost of nursing home care had become unsustainable and in an effort to curb this spending the number of nursing homes beds was to be gradually decreased, with a corresponding increase in service in the cheaper alternative care sectors: hostels and community care.

A system of regulation was introduced, with nursing homes and hostels required to meet national standards. All residents had to be assessed by a geriatric assessment team for entry eligibility, and funding for individual residents was to be based on assessment of dependency (Nay et al. 1999). Nursing homes provided the highest level of care. The person had to be assessed as highly dependent for activities of daily living and unable to be sustained by care in the community. Twenty-four-hour nursing care was provided. Hostels were available for individuals also unable to manage with existing community supports, but who were less dependent for activities of daily living and who did not require 24-hour nursing care.

In both settings funding was allocated according to assessments of resident dependency. Nursing homes were funded through the Resident Classification Instrument (RCI), which placed the resident in one of five dependency categories (one being the highest and five lowest). Hostels used the Personal Care Assessment Instrument (PCAI), which had three levels of payment: high, medium and low (AIHW 1997). As a consequence of this separate funding, residents in the hostels whose physical or mental deterioration warranted a higher level of care than that funded by the PCAI were forced to relocate into a nursing home. In some instances this was a relatively simple relocation, as many nursing homes and hostels are geographically co-located and administered. For others, where this was not the case it often meant moving outside the local area, posing the threat of increased social isolation. In situations where no beds were available in the nursing homes, staff within hostels struggled to meet the care requirements of the residents without reimbursement of the increased level of care required.

A change in government in 1996 and subsequent passage of the Aged Care Act 1997 heralded the implementation of the Structural Reform Package. Introduced in October 1997, it includes two major changes for residential care:

1 The collapsing of nursing homes and hostels under one umbrella to be known as residential aged care services. This was to facilitate residents

receiving the appropriate level of care regardless of location. The RCI and PCAI were replaced with one funding tool: the Resident Classification Scale (RCS).

2 The introduction of a new system of outcome standards and the replacement of government regulation by an industry based and independent accreditation system (AIHW 1997; Nay *et al.* 1999).

These changes have had important implications for palliative care. The RCS has eight dependency categories, of which one is the most dependent and eight is the least. The RCS has been extended to include 20 areas of assessment, with changes predominantly in the social and emotional support category. This was a result of complaints within the industry that the RCI did not account for the care needs of residents with dementia (AIHW 1997). In addition, a social and human need category for both the resident and family, which includes support for palliative care, was included for the first time. Unfortunately, the relative weightings, which determine the monetary value placed on social and human need, are very low in comparison to those for behavioural problems.

Monitoring and quality of assessment

As part of the Aged Care Reforms Strategy, an Outcome Standards Monitoring Program was implemented in Australian nursing homes and subsequently in hostels in 1991. There were 31 nursing home standards and 25 hostel standards covering broad areas such as health care, social independence, freedom of choice, home-like environment, privacy and dignity, variety of experience and safety. Assessment of whether these standards were appropriately met was by a Standards Monitoring Team which visited approximately on a two-year basis, and which was required only to give 24 hours' notice to the organization before a visit (Gibson 1998). Two standards of direct relevance for palliative care were that the nursing home practices support the residents' right to die with dignity and that all residents should be as free from pain as possible.

Under the 1997 Structural Reform Package the 31 nursing home and 25 hostel standards were replaced with 44 outcome standards encompassing four areas: management and organization; health and personal care; resident lifestyle; and environment. Under these new standards, 'freedom from pain' remained as an outcome measure. The outcome 'death with dignity' was subsumed under the standard 'palliative care', which was expanded to include: identifying and respecting the residents' wishes in relation to terminal care; designing individual palliative care programmes incorporating families; and accommodating cultural and religious beliefs (Department of Health and Aged Care 1999).

Studies conducted prior to the 1997 reforms examined the quality of palliative care given to residents in nursing homes (Clare and DeBellis 1996;

Maddocks *et al.* 1996) and highlighted the inability of the RCI to provide an appropriate level of funding for dying residents and their families. These studies also showed that for some residents 'death with dignity' or adequate pain control was not achieved.

Since the introduction of the new RCS in Australia, no studies have been conducted to explore whether it provides an appropriate level of funding for residents who require palliative care. However, as this instrument appears to be based upon principles and care areas similar to the RCI, the same criticisms identified by Clare and DeBellis (1997) and Parker and DeBellis (1999) may apply. Similarly, no studies are available to gauge the impact of the introduction of a specific palliative care standard which broadens outcomes beyond 'death with dignity'.

Standardized assessment in care homes

Under successive reform strategies residential care in Australia has become highly regulated compared to other sectors in the health care system. The RCS, the tool that dictates the level of funding available per resident, is based on the assessment of 'relative' care need. It is neither designed nor reflects a comprehensive tool to determine individual care provision. Instead, identification of individual need is dependent on a process of professional assessments. Current government guidelines advocate against the use of a single assessment instrument. Instead, eight key areas are suggested to provide a framework to guide the assessment process:

1 Behavioural assessment
2 Continence assessment and management
3 Gait/mobility
4 Nutrition/hydration
5 Pain assessment and management
6 Palliative care assessment
7 Psychological assessment
8 Sensory/communication (DHAC 1999).

For each there are suggestions of the types of issues that should be considered during the assessment. It is encouraging to note that two of the eight areas – pain and palliative care assessment – afford opportunities for residents requiring end-of-life care. Although the heading 'psychological assessment' would seem to offer a similar opportunity, guidelines clearly identify that the assessment is for those who require expert psychological assessment and not that of the nursing team members. Guidelines for 'pain assessment and management' highlight that pain is often under-recognized and poorly managed and a thorough assessment is stipulated, which may be done using a selected tool, form or flow chart. It is recommended that the 'palliative care assessment' should be informed by the resident's diagnosis, stage of illness and prognosis, the phase of care, symptom severity, effect of symptoms, dependency level, specific care needs, spiritual and emotional care needs of both the resident and family and expectations of care. The need for regular assessment, and often reassessment, is identified, as is documentation of the individual wishes of the resident. It also encourages consideration of the Australian Association for Hospice and Palliative Care Standards for Hospice and Palliative Care Provision (Palliative Care Australia 1999). The exact translation of these guidelines into practice is left to the discretion of the individual organization. Similarly, there are no mandatory rules for time frames of reassessment, although the RCS requires yearly completion, which would require a thorough assessment (DHAC 1999).

The Resident Assessment Instrument

The United States followed a similar reform process during the 1980s, but unlike Australia has adopted a more prescriptive and structured approach (Hawes *et al.* 1997). The result has been the development and implementation of the Resident Assessment Instrument (RAI). This has two components: the Minimum Data Set (MDS), which has over 300 items in 20 assessment domains; and 18 Resident Assessment Protocols (Redfern 1999; Achterberg *et al.* 2001). Completion of the MDS is based on observations, interviews and clinical assessments and takes approximately 30 minutes by an experienced nurse. Administration of the MDS is recommended at admission and then yearly, with a quarterly review using a condensed version to ensure that changes in individuals' status are identified. Certain scores on the MDS domains trigger the Resident Assessment Protocols, which then provide directives for assisting staff responding to that particular care issue (Achterberg *et al.* 2001).

Similar concerns regarding appropriate assessment in residential care have prompted other countries to adopt the RAI (Ribbe *et al.* 1997). In the United Kingdom, while it is not widespread, there has been some use of the RAI in residential and care home facilities (Redfern 1999). A number of studies have supported the use of the RAI to assess quality of care (Phillips *et al.* 1997), improving quality of coordination of care (Achterberg *et al.* 2001), its use for comparison of care across different countries and settings (Phillips *et al.* 1997; Ribbe *et al.* 1997), and its utility in calculating payments based on resident classification systems or to generate outcome indicators (Hawes *et al.* 1997).

However, not all reports of the RAI are positive. Beales *et al.* (2001), who interviewed directors of nursing from skilled nursing facilities in Virginia, found that almost half did not use the RAI in the day-to-day care of their residents and 43 per cent felt that it had no impact on the daily care of residents. They concluded that while it is a requirement that facilities use the RAI system, the complexity of its implementation in daily care restricts its usefulness. Few studies have reviewed the appropriateness of the RAI for terminally ill residents. Engle (1998) and Engle *et al.* (1998) argue that as the RAI is geared towards maximizing function it is not only inappropriate for terminally ill residents but in addition omits care needs such as pain, dyspnoea, spiritual or religious needs and bereavement care. A palliative care version of the RAI has been developed (Interrai 2000), which perhaps indicates that the original version does not adequately address palliative care needs.

Palliative care assessment

Australia has followed the United Kingdom's move towards distinguishing between the need for specialist palliative care services and a palliative care approach (Field and Addington-Hall 1999). However, current standards for palliative care provision exist only for specialist services. Standards for a 'palliative care approach' are still to be developed (PCA 1999) and limited work has been undertaken so far. While the specialist palliative care standards provide some framework for residential care they are premised on the accessibility of a multidisciplinary team, the existence of bereavement services and the patient and family as the unit of care.

In residential aged care facilities a further complicating factor in assessing the palliative care needs of this population is that of defining when a resident becomes 'palliative'. Who decides and what criteria should be used? Studies in both the United Kingdom and Australia have explored palliative care for residents within these settings, but there has been no consistent approach in defining palliative care (Maddocks *et al.* 1996; Clare and DeBellis 1997; Avis *et al.* 1999; Katz *et al.* 1999). In a survey by Clare and DeBellis (1997), South Australian nursing home directors were asked to define palliative care. These nursing directors used phrases such as quality of life, comfort or holistic care, pain management and psychosocial or emotional support for the resident and family indicating a good understanding of palliative care. However, when asked to provide a profile of their palliative care residents and reasons why they had been identified, emphasis was placed on the need for terminal care. Forty-four per cent of residents were categorized as approaching a terminal state, 41 per cent were in a terminal state and 15 per cent were asymptomatic, but 'terminal'. It appeared therefore that although nursing directors were able to define palliative care, the residents they identified were receiving terminal care. Most residents identified had days, weeks or at most months to live but were in a state of progressive decline (Higginson 1997). This distinction is important, as the palliative care needs of residents should not be restricted to those in the terminal phase.

Despite these difficulties there is some indication that there are two groups of residents who have been identified as appropriate for a palliative care approach and in some instances specialist palliative care services (Parker and DeBellis 1999; Froggatt 2000b).

Residents who require palliative care at admission

Residents who are identified as requiring palliative care on admission are most likely to be transferred from a hospice or hospital and have been labelled 'palliative' from the transferring institution. There may also be other newly admitted residents who are given this status following a nursing and medical assessment. These residents will probably have a defined terminal illness with a reasonably predictable trajectory such as cancer or motor neurone disease (Froggatt 2000b). Froggatt's (2000b) UK study estimated that such situations accounted for 9 per cent of all deaths in the nursing homes evaluated. Similarly, in the Australian study by Maddocks *et al.* (1996) nursing home staff identified 13 per cent of residents as terminally ill on admission. In turn, a review of the use of the Medicare Hospice Benefit by nursing facility residents in the USA found that 14 per cent of residents admitted to care homes either were receiving or had previously received the Hospice Benefit; the majority therefore were not classified as hospice type residents until after admission (Miller *et al.* 2000).

There are only a small number of palliative care residents transferred from hospitals to aged care facilities. In Australia during 1999, of all hospital transfers to residential care for patients over the age of 70 only 1 per cent or 376 patients were discharged under the category of palliative care. The majority had been discharged from the hospitals under the categories of acute care (78 per cent), non-acute care (13 per cent) and for rehabilitation (8 per cent) (AIHW 2000). These figures are also reflected in the average length of stay for residents, as only 8 per cent die within four weeks of admission to an aged care facility (AIHW 2001).

At present in Australia transfer of patients from hospices to aged care facilities or care homes is a rare occurrence. In the 1998 (PCA) palliative care census only 3 per cent of patients of palliative care services died in nursing homes. Southern Adelaide Palliative Services (SAPS) in South Australia has been a forerunner in developing a good working relationship with aged care facilities and care homes within its geographical area. Where appropriate, patients are transferred to these facilities. However, despite this arrangement only 13 patients over a three-year period were transferred from the hospice inpatient unit. Of these 13 patients, 12 (92 per cent) had a malignant diagnosis (SAPS 2000).

Residents who require palliative care following a period of general deterioration

The second group of residents are those who die following a period of general deterioration. These residents will be the majority considered by residential staff to be 'palliative'. They may, however, not be awarded this status until they are in the terminal stages of their conditions, or sometimes only in retrospect (Katz *et al.* 1999). Froggatt (2000b) identified that of all deaths in residential homes in her study 51 per cent were following a period of general deterioration. This term included common references to residents as 'going downhill', 'fading' or 'frail', and was reinforced by signs of physical, mental and social deterioration. In Australia, although 17 per cent of all deaths in residential care occur within three months of admission, for 41 per cent of residents death occurs after they have been in the facility between one and four years (AIHW 2001). These residents are more likely to have a non-cancer diagnosis and, while deteriorating slowly, may have a series of acute events, any one of which might indicate terminal care is required. For these residents we would agree with Froggatt (2000a) that specialist palliative care services may not be required as long as both the nursing and medical staff within the facility have adopted a palliative approach to care; this must include up-to-date education and training in order to manage individual residents' and their families' needs.

This section of the chapter has tried to identify the broader population-based issues of assessing palliative care needs in aged care facilities and care homes. In the next section we turn our attention to a discussion of individual need assessment, focusing first on what impact the assessment process has on identifying individual need. We then draw on experience with cancer patients to identify key areas in which residents' and their families' needs should be considered.

Individual needs assessment

Assessing the needs of individuals is a dynamic process influenced by the culture of the setting, its team members, the focus of care and the expected outcomes as perceived by the patient/resident and the team members. Therefore, the process of assessment that is appropriate to specialist palliative care services may fail to capture the needs of individuals within other settings.

Assessment differences between 'palliative care services' and 'care homes'

There are two significant defining features of specialist palliative care that affect the assessment process: a multidisciplinary approach to care; and a holistic approach that encompasses the physical, psychosocial and spiritual needs of the patient and family.

The assessment process undertaken by palliative care teams is well documented (Doyle *et al.* 1995; Woodruff 1999). The culture of specialist palliative care, whether community- or inpatient-based, is determined largely by the nature of the clientele (people dying from cancer), alongside a focus of care developed to ensure patients' symptoms are well controlled and they are ushered to a comfortable and if possible 'good' death. While attempts are made to promote and enhance living, there is always in the minds of the assessors the expected outcome. With 90 per cent of patients in palliative care services (PCA 1998) diagnosed with cancer there are pre-conceived ideas in the minds of the team as to the expected outcome. While many may be accepting chemotherapy, radiotherapy or other treatments considered 'acute', the long-term prospect for most patients on palliative care programmes is poor, with a steady deterioration leading to death. Such an expectation markedly affects the way in which patients are viewed and assessed. Health professionals working with this population are ever mindful of the tenuous nature of their general condition. The result is that health professionals working in palliative care are always a little cautious, anticipating decline and adopting a dynamic approach to the ongoing assessment process.

In contrast, residential care facilities and care homes are based on a philosophy of 'normalization' (Maddocks et al. 1996). Normalization is an expectation that the resident will continue to live an active life while the facility promotes the maintenance of independence and, where appropriate, rehabilitation, to improve quality of life (Abbey 1994).

This philosophy may have been appropriate for these facilities during the 1970s and 1980s, when admittance was often based on social rather than physical and/or functional need. Over the past ten years, however, facilities have seen a change in the demographics of their incoming residents. Government policy has seen a shift towards community support, enabling elderly people to remain in their homes longer, and the population now seen entering aged care facilities is older and has more complex physical needs relating to chronic degenerative disease. While recognition of the changing population is acknowledged within the aged care industry, organizations have failed to adjust and adapt the assessment process. Assessment therefore continues to concentrate on normalization, rehabilitation and maintenance of function, when in fact the assessors need in some areas to be considering the frailty of the resident and adopting a more palliative care approach.

'Multi' versus 'uni' disciplinary approaches to end-of-life care

Elderly people entering aged care facilities and care homes are admitted under the care of their existing general practitioner or one selected by the resident. General practitioners by default take responsibility for care, although they may or may not have the knowledge, skills or interest in palliative care to best meet the residents' needs (Seymour and Hanson 2001).

It is not expected that general practitioners will visit and assess their clients any more than every six weeks when the medication orders need to be rewritten. Residents are therefore only assessed in the interim when the nursing staff request a review. Such a request is usually heralded by some concern by the registered nurse about the resident's condition.

Input from allied health services varies significantly in aged care facilities and care homes. The allied health professionals employed by these facilities are physiotherapists and occupational therapists. They are not social workers or psychologists. This again emphasizes the promotion of physical health rather than psychological or social needs. Such professionals are contracted on an 'as needed' basis. It is not expected that allied health professionals will offer daily or weekly advice on residents' care.

While patients in palliative care services may present with co-morbidities, generally the diagnosis on which their assessment is being undertaken is cancer. The progression of the disease can often be clearly tracked and the symptoms a person is likely to experience in the advanced stages of malignant disease are generally well known. The same cannot be said of those in aged care facilities and care homes. Elderly residents have multiple medical problems. The trajectory of their diseases is more difficult to determine and a palliative care approach is rarely introduced until it is thought the resident is entering the final phase of life. The terminal phase is also at times difficult to determine, as a sudden or gradual decline in a resident's condition may well have a reversible cause. Registered nurses in aged care frequently identify this phenomenon as further complicating the introduction of a palliative care approach, and describe the need to take a systematic approach to the identification of reversible conditions.

What is frequently observed in elderly people is a gradual decline in the health status of residents. While there may be clinical indicators that lead health professionals to suspect death may be imminent, the most reliable indicators appear to be the residents' functional status. Therefore, in the absence of any other criteria, the determinant for shifting from an 'aged care' focus to a 'palliative care' focus in residential care is when nursing staff take the view that the resident is entering the terminal phase. These indicators include reduced mobility, reduced interest in food or fluids, increasing weight loss, being bed bound, an altered state of consciousness, social withdrawal, incontinence, the resident talking about dying, increasing pain, a marked increase in symptoms related to their clinical condition and the existence of a known terminal illness (Maddocks et al. 1996; Abbey 1999). Commonly expressed is a 'sense' that a resident is changing and perhaps dying, not particularly scientific but often intuitively accurate. Some signs may be gradual and only with adequate documentation of the progress of these changes can decisions be made as to whether they signal a terminal decline or are part of the natural ageing process (Abbey 1999).

Failing to recognize imminent death

The lack of regular and skilled input from medical officers or allied health services precludes any reasonable team approach to care. The onus of responsibility instead falls on registered nurses who may or may not have the knowledge, skills or attitudes required to provide appropriate palliative care assessment. Anecdotes suggest that patients are slipping into the terminal phase of life unnoticed and therefore not receiving the most appropriate end-of-life care. Lack of knowledge, time or power has been identified as a reason why residents are found to be in the last stage of life without the initiation of appropriate care (Maddocks *et al.* 1996, 1999).

Perhaps the difficulty lies in the failure to undertake ongoing assessment. It is known in palliative care that assessment is a continuous process, as patients' symptoms and needs change on a day-to-day basis. Aged care facilities place unskilled workers in the situation where they provide the same care daily. They do not question the care plan and are at times oblivious to the innuendo of death. Failure to assess these needs properly not only results in residents perhaps dying without adequate symptom management, but also leaves relatives and other health team members ill prepared.

Lefebvre-Chapiro (1998) argues for the development of palliative care principles for specialist gerontological clinical professionals to assist with assessment. However, many aged care facilities do not have access to specialist gerontological services without sending residents to outpatient clinics. It therefore needs to be recognized that the culture of aged care organizations and the difficulties of establishing a complete multidisciplinary team both affect the palliative care assessment process in care homes.

Assessing physical, psychosocial and spiritual needs among care home residents at the end of life

Studies involving relatives' and health care professionals' retrospective reports of patients' symptom problems in the last year of life have shown differences between cancer patients and those dying of non-malignant disease (Cartwright 1991; Seale 1991; Addington-Hall *et al.* 1998). Cartwright (1991) noted that those in residential care were more likely to have been confused, been constipated, experienced dribbling, been bad tempered and been incontinent. Other symptoms, such as pain, breathlessness, vomiting, drowsiness and dry mouth, were also frequently reported. The length of time the person had experienced these symptoms was greater for those in residential care. These findings highlight how inadequate assessment of symptoms in this population perpetuates their poor ongoing management.

An Australian study by Maddocks *et al.* (1996) provides some preliminary data regarding the prevalence of symptoms for residents in the last two weeks of life. In this sample of 37 residents, of whom 27 per cent had a cancer diagnosis, nursing staff made daily assessment of the presence and severity of 17 symptoms. Similarly, in previously reported studies, residents were reported to have pain, weakness, anorexia, constipation, anxiety and dysphagia. Three symptoms not as prevalent in this population were nausea, vomiting and dyspnoea. This study also showed that these residents were very dependent for activities of daily living and were most likely to be incontinent of urine and faeces.

In the absence of more prospective studies of symptoms of residents within aged care facilities it would seem reasonable to assume that many of the symptoms well known in those dying from cancer may be looked for when assessing the needs of these residents. However, it should be kept in mind when assessing these symptoms that the underlying cause of the symptom may be quite different from that of cancer patients, as may be the length of time the resident has experienced the symptom. A further limiting factor in aged care facilities is the percentage of residents with cognitive failure from dementia, stroke or other diseases affecting cognitive function, as well as those with other communication difficulties.

Psychosocial and spiritual needs

An entire movement has developed in response to the psychological impact of cancer, with self-help books, videos and organizations offered to work through coping with the experience of loss, anger, hopelessness and fear. There is recognition that psychological distress is interrelated with the physical, social and spiritual concerns of the person. There is less understanding of the psychosocial impact of disability and death in aged care facilities (Froggatt 2000a). Residents in aged care facilities have often already suffered many losses both prior to and since entering care (Froggatt et al. 2000; see also Chapter 3). Relocation from their home brings loss of material goods, loss of self-identity and for many what has been described as a social death (Mulkay 1993). While the person may have struggled within their own home they may have received visits from neighbours, family and care professionals on a regular basis and be surrounded by their possessions. Davies (2001) has termed care homes as 'islands of the old', referring to the limited contact with the outside world. It is common within aged care facilities to separate the dying from the living, further increasing their isolation (Hockey 1990).

How residents feel about death and dying is not a topic that is openly discussed during the usual routine of the day. In our society, while deaths of young people from cancer are considered tragic, not so are those of people who are older, are institutionalized, have difficulty with communication and are perceived to have no quality of life. Death for these individuals is often described as a 'blessing' by staff, families and in many instances other residents. Some residents may make passing remarks, as in Hockey's (1990) study, such as 'you can put me in there too' when a resident was watching staff empty the rubbish, indicating they have no worth left. These remarks are usually made into a joke as both sides remain powerless to change the silent reality of how many feel. It is important to address the aching spiritual need of such a remark.

The 'awareness of dying' movement, prompted by the work of Glaser and Strauss (1968) and a key principle for palliative care, may have been influential for cancer patients where a clear trajectory of dying is indicated. For those with other diagnoses, and in particular for residents in aged care facilities where the trajectory is less predictable, it is unlikely that discussions regarding prognosis will occur perhaps until it is obvious to everyone concerned that death is imminent (Addington-Hall *et al.* 1998). In such instances this will be too late. Education that has concentrated on raising the awareness of staff about the psychosocial needs of residents has been successful in encouraging staff, particularly untrained carers, to spend time talking with dying residents and their families (Avis *et al.* 1999; Katz *et al.* 1999; Maddocks *et al.* 1999; Froggatt 2000b).

Just as the psychosocial needs of patients with cancer are complex and individual, the needs of residents in aged care cannot be assumed to be any different. Assessment and management of psychosocial needs is as important as that of physical care needs, but with the current lack of research in this area it may remain a secondary concern, as was initially the case for cancer patients.

Increasing attention has been given to the individual's spiritual needs in palliative care. Traditionally, spiritual issues leave most health professionals thinking in terms of religion or belief systems (Wilson and Daley 1999). In care homes the spiritual profile of residents is often discussed in terms of beliefs, practices, pastoral requirements and specific death rites. Is it satisfactory to discuss spirituality in terms of religion or is there a need to provide staff who can better assess spirituality in terms of how life has held meaning for residents? Spiritual needs beyond this narrow framework are often left unassessed or unattended as we concentrate on the more tangible physical and psychosocial needs (see Chapter 4).

Needs of the family and other residents in the home

Just as the resident will need support and understanding when facing death, so too will family members. Both will experience many emotions of distress. The needs of families who are caring for someone within an aged care facility may be quite different from those of people providing care in the home. Depending on how long their relative has been a resident within the facility there may be issues of guilt, particularly if a resident dies within a short time of admission. In these instances staff may not have built up a good rapport with the family, further hampering their ability to provide adequate support (Maddocks *et al.* 1996). In other instances a spouse who has visited daily for years is likely to have difficulty adjusting to the emptiness after the resident dies.

Wilson and Daley (1999) provide us with important insight into the needs of families of residents dying in care homes. They identify three specific needs for families: caring staff behaviour, participation in the dying process and providing spiritual support. Families indicated that it was important that the staff treated their relatives as if they were family members. Good and appropriate communication with the family was essential, as was taking time to enter a resident's room and 'being there' while not being imposing or dominating. Listening to the family was appreciated, as well as the opportunity to be part of the decision-making process and being able to participate in the dying process. Meeting these needs requires staff to be skilled in guiding families through difficult decisions and providing accurate information on which to base decisions.

In South Australia, since the proclaiming of the Consent to Medical Treatment and Palliative Care Act in 1995 there has been more emphasis on identifying residents' needs in their terminal phase. Many aged care facilities include, in their admission package, an invitation to discuss with the resident and relevant family members their wishes at the end of life. This opportunity is often readily accepted by resident and family but conversely there are those families who choose not to enter into those discussions.

Unfortunately, the funding structure dictates the level of care that a resident is entitled to but it does not take into account time required by families (Maddocks and Parker 2001). This is not to say that as a resident moves into the terminal phase the needs of the family are not identified and attended to. However, the care of the family is often *ad hoc*, undertaken by those who recognize the need and/or feel comfortable caring for families at this time. In the authors' experience nurses and carers feel ill prepared and lack time to meet effectively the needs of families facing death.

Conclusion

A number of issues that impact upon the assessment of palliative care needs in residential facilities have been highlighted. In Australia two decades of aged care reform have dramatically improved the standard of care. The most recent of these reforms has promoted 'ageing in place' and acknowledged the need for good palliative care as an outcome measure. However, despite the prescriptive nature of most aspects governing care in residential facilities (i.e. RCS, Outcome Standards) the process of assessing residents' needs is not subject to outside scrutiny. While flexibility is welcomed in what might be considered an over-regulated environment, an emphasis on rehabilitation and normalization directs and informs the assessment process, resulting in a failure to recognize or acknowledge palliative care needs.

Attempts in the USA and other countries to overcome inadequate assessment of need have led to the development and implementation of the RAI. Although some encouraging results have been demonstrated with this instrument, for those nearing the end of life the evidence is less convincing. Adding to the complexity of understanding the palliative care needs in these facilities is the dilemma of recognizing the 'palliative' stage of an illness. We identify two broad groups of residents, those whose care is highlighted as 'palliative' on admission and those assigned such a status following a period of deterioration.

Assessing individuals is a dynamic process. In specialist palliative care services the existence of the multidisciplinary team and a holistic approach to care are the norm. In residential facilities assessment falls largely upon nursing staff and the general practitioner. They are faced with a clientele that often has an unpredictable care trajectory and for whom only limited research is available to identify possible symptoms that may require attention. Similarly, there is limited understanding of the psychosocial needs of residents who already suffer the loss of relocation and the possibility of social death prior to biological death. Families may have guilt associated with the placement of elderly relatives and under current funding arrangements staff are not afforded the time necessary to allay uncertainties and fears as changes in physical and mental condition signal decline. While staff in aged care facilities identify the emotional needs of families, the existing funding arrangement makes it extremely difficult to provide adequate staffing and expertise to provide the necessary support.

One of the key challenges facing the care of older people in care homes is the development of an assessment process that meets a variety of needs, on the one hand promoting life and normalization, but on the other managing and acknowledging dying in an open and caring way. The continuing use of assessment tools integral to funding promotes a model that inadequately assesses individual residents' needs on a daily basis. It would seem that until the two processes are separated the provision of palliative care will continue to be thwarted by systems that promote maintenance or improvement in well-being. Ultimately this will always lead to a failure to recognize the point at which residents require appropriate palliative care. Assessments that remain the responsibility of only one discipline are at risk of limiting the identification of needs in this complex group of people requiring expert end-of-life care.

Implications for practice

- Current assessment processes and instruments may fail to identify palliative care needs of care home residents.
- Assessment in palliative care services is undertaken by a multidisciplinary team underpinned by a holistic care philosophy, whereas assessment in

residential care is nursing-based and premised on the philosophy of normalization.

- Ongoing assessment is required to recognize changes in palliative care need among residents.
- Age and diagnosis appear to influence palliative care needs but evidence specific to this population is limited.
- Emphasis on the identification of physical need neglects psychosocial, spiritual and family needs.

References

Abbey, J. (1994) Terminal care in nursing homes – a nurse's reply. *Geriaction* 13(3): 42–4.

Abbey, J. (1999) Palliative care. In R. Nay and S. Garratt (eds) *Nursing Older People: Issues and Innovations.* Sydney: Maclennan and Petty.

Achterberg, W. P., Holtkamp, C. C., Kerkstra, A. *et al.* (2001) Improvements in the quality of co-ordination of nursing care following implementation of the Resident Assessment Instrument in Dutch nursing homes. *Journal of Advanced Nursing,* 35(2): 268–75.

Addington-Hall, J. (1996) Heart disease and stroke: lessons from cancer care. In G. Ford and I. Lewin (eds) *Interfaces in Medicine: Managing Terminal Illness.* London: Royal College of Physicians.

Addington-Hall, J. M., Fakhoury, W. and McCarthy, M. (1998) Specialist palliative care in non-malignant disease. *Palliative Medicine,* 12(6): 417–27.

Australian Institute of Health and Welfare (1997) *Australia's Welfare.* Cat. no. Aus–8. Canberra: AIHW.

Australian Institute of Health and Welfare (1999) *Nursing Homes in Australia 1992–1993, 1993–1994 and 1994–1995: A Statistical Overview.* AIHW cat. no. AGE 11. Canberra: AIHW and DHFS (Aged Care Statistics Series Supplement).

Australian Institute of Health and Welfare (2000) *Australian Hospital Statistics 1998–1999.* AIHW cat. no. HSE 11. Canberra: AIHW (Health Services Series no. 15).

Australian Institute of Health and Welfare (2001) *Residential Aged Care Facilities in Australia 1999–2000: A Statistical Overview.* AIHW cat. no. AGE 19. Canberra: AIHW (Aged Care Series no. 9).

Avis, M., Greening Jackson, J., Cox, K. and Miskella, C. (1999) Evaluation of a project community palliative care support to nursing homes. *Health and Social Care in the Community,* 7(1): 32–8.

Beales, J. L., Davis, A. and Cotter, J. J. (2001) The Resident Assessment Instrument is not useful in daily care of nursing home residents. *Journal of the American Geriatrics Society,* 49(4): s106.

Cartwright, A. (1991) Changes in life and care in the year before death, 1969–1987. *Journal of Public Health Medicine,* 13: 81–7.

Clare, J. and DeBellis, A. (1996) *The Nature, Extent and Evaluation of Palliative Care in South Australian Nursing Homes.* Adelaide: Australian Institute of Nursing Research.

Clare, J. and DeBellis, A. (1997) Palliative care in South Australian nursing homes. *Australian Journal of Advanced Nursing*, 14(4): 20–8.

Curtis, E. B., Krech, R. and Walsh, T. D. (1991) Common symptoms in patients with advanced cancer. *Journal of Palliative Care*, 7: 25–9.

Davies, S. (2001) The care needs of older people and family caregivers in continuing care settings. In M. Nolan, S. Davies and G. Grant (eds) *Working with Older People and Their Families. Key Issues in Policy and Practice*. Buckingham: Open University Press.

Department of Health and Aged Care (1999) *The Documentation and Accountability Manual*. Canberra: Aged and Community Care Division.

Doyle, D., Hanks, G. C. and Macdonald, N. (1995) *Oxford Textbook of Palliative Medicine*. Oxford: Oxford University Press.

Dunlop, G. M. (1989) A study of the relative frequency and importance of gastrointestinal symptoms and weakness in patients with far advanced cancer. *Palliative Medicine*, 4: 37–43.

Engle, V. F. (1998) Care of the living, care of the dying: reconceptualizing nursing home care. *Journal of American Geriatrics Society*, 46(9): 1172–4.

Engle, V. F., Fox-Hill, E. and Graney, M. J. (1998) The experience of living-dying in a nursing home: self reports of Black and White older adults. *Journal of the American Geriatrics Society*, 46(9): 1091–6.

Field, D. and Addington-Hall, J. (1999) Extending specialist palliative care to all? *Social Science and Medicine*, 48: 1271–80.

Froggatt, K. (2000a) Palliative care and nursing homes: where next? *Palliative Medicine*, 15: 42–8.

Froggatt, K. (2000b) *Palliative Care Education in Nursing Homes*. London: Macmillan Cancer Relief.

Froggatt, K., Hasnip, J. and Smith, P. (2000) The challenges of end of life care. *Elderly Care*, 12(2): 11–13.

Glaser, B. G. and Strauss, A. L. (1968) *Time for Dying*. Chicago: Aldine.

Gibson, D. (1998) *Aged Care: Old Policies, New Problems*. Cambridge: Cambridge University Press.

Hawes, C., Morris, J. N., Phillips, C. D. *et al.* (1997) Development of the nursing home Resident Assessment Instrument in the USA. *Age and Ageing*, 26(S2): 19–25.

Higginson, I. (1997) *Palliative and Terminal Care Health Care Needs Assessment*, 2nd edn. Oxford: Radcliffe Medical Press.

Hockey, J. (1990) *Experiences of Death: An Anthropological Account*. Edinburgh: Edinburgh University Press.

Hunt, R. and Maddocks, I. (1997) Terminal care in South Australia: historical aspects and equity issues. In D. Clark, J. Hockley and S. Ahmedzai (eds) *New Themes in Palliative Care*. Buckingham: Open University Press.

Katz, J., Komaromy, C. and Sidell, M. (1999) Understanding palliative care in residential and nursing homes. *International Journal of Palliative Care Nursing*, 5(2): 58–64.

Interrai (2000) http://www.interrai.org

Lefebvre-Chapiro, S. (1998) Special care for elderly patients. *European Journal of Palliative Care*, 5(5): 162–4.

Maddocks, I., Parker, D., McLeod, A. and Jenkin, P. (1999) *Palliative Care Nurse Practitioners in Aged Care Facilities*. Report to the Department of Human Services. Adelaide.

Maddocks, I., Abbey, J., Pickhaver, A. *et al.* (1996) *Palliative Care in Nursing Homes*. Report to the Commonwealth Department of Health and Family Services. Adelaide: Flinders University.

Maddocks, I. and Parker, D. (2001) Palliative care in nursing homes. In J. Addington-Hall and I. Higginson (eds) *Palliative Care for Non-cancer Patients*. Oxford: Oxford University Press.

Miller, S., Gozalo, P. and Mor, V. (2000) *Use of Medicare's Hospice Benefit by Nursing Facility Residents*. Report from the Center for Gerontology and Health Care Research, Brown University, March (htttp://www.aspe.hhs.gov/daltcp/reports/nufares.htm).

Mulkay, M. (1993) Social death in Britain. In D. Clark (ed.) *The Sociology of Death: Theory, Culture and Practice*. Oxford: Blackwell Science.

Nay, R., Garratt, S. and Koch, S. (1999) Challenges for Australian nursing in the International Year of Older Persons. *Geriatric Nursing*, 20(1): 14–17.

Palliative Care Australia (1998) *State of the Nation Report of National Census of Palliative Care Services*. Canberra: PCA.

Palliative Care Australia (1999) *Standards for Palliative Care Provision*, 3rd edn. Canberra: PCA.

Parker, D. and DeBellis, A. (1999) A profile of dying residents in South Australian nursing homes. *International Journal of Palliative Nursing*, 5(4): 162–70.

Phillips, C. D., Zimmerman, D., Bernabei, R. and Jonsson, P. V. (1997) Using the Resident Assessment Instrument for quality enhancement in nursing homes. *Age and Ageing*, 26(S2): 77–81.

Redfern, S. (1999) Continuing care in residential settings, in S. Redfern and F. M. Ross (eds) *Nursing Older People*. 3rd Edition. Edinburgh: Churchill Livingstone.

Ribbe, M. W., Ljunggren, G., Steel, K. *et al.* (1997) Nursing homes in 10 nations: a comparison between countries and settings. *Age and Ageing*, 26(S2): 3–12.

Seale, C. (1991) A comparison of hospice and conventional care. *Social Science and Medicine*, 32: 147–52.

Seymour, J. and Hanson, E. (2001) Palliative care and older people. In M. Nolan, S. Davies and G. Grant (eds) *Working with Older People and Their Families: Key Issues in Policy and Practice*. Buckingham: Open University Press.

Skilbeck, J., Mott, L., Page, H. *et al.* (1998) Palliative care in chronic obstructive airways disease: a needs assessment. *Palliative Medicine*, 12: 245–54.

Southern Adelaide Palliative Services (2000) *Statistics for the Year 1999/2000*. Adelaide: SAPS.

Wilson, S. A. and Daley B. J. (1999) Family perspectives on dying in long-term care settings. *Journal of Gerontological Nursing*, 25(11):19–25.

Woodruff, R. (1999) *Palliative Medicine: Symptomatic and Supportive Care for Patients with Cancer and Aids*. 3rd Edition. Oxford: Oxford University Press.

3 | Loss and change

JAN REED, GLENDA COOK
AND CHRIS BURRIDGE

This chapter discusses some of the key characteristics of life in care homes, and highlights the impact they have on those who live and die there. Anticipation, preparation and adaptation prior to and after the move to a care home by older people is also discussed. Such a move often occurs at a time of crisis and the older person is frequently marginalized from the decision-making process. This has been found to influence the older person's participation in crucial decisions about their experience in care homes. We therefore undertake a critical examination of the concept of personal autonomy in order to demonstrate that reconceptualization of personal autonomy is needed to develop practice and maximize the involvement of older people in important decisions about the end of their life. Inevitably, loss and death are features of daily life in care homes, yet death has been found to be made invisible and residents are unsupported in their grief. The chapter concludes with a discussion of the evidence of positive changes, and suggests ways to move practice forward.

Perceptions of care homes

Moving into a care home has been portrayed by many writers as a 'last resort', with older people and their families resistant to the idea. Policies are based on the assumption that older people will want to stay in their own homes, and many service initiatives focus on helping people to become and remain independent enough to do this. Part of this antipathy can be traced back to the history of care homes, and their original development through Poor Law provision (see Chapter 1), as well as the association that people have in their minds with the workhouse. Means and Smith (1998) have given an account of the history of care home provision which argues that the development of the care home sector has rarely been the result of proactive policy, but has arisen through accident, circumstance and reactions to the perceived 'problem' of older people needing care. They give an example of the hasty establishment of residential homes as a response to the problem of older people taking up space in air raid shelters during the Second World War. When hospitals were evacuated in preparation for war casualties, many older people were discharged home, only to find that their families had been evacuated to country areas, or were unable to care for them. In desperation, some older people began to live in air raid shelters, where they had company, warmth and food. This, of course, led to overcrowding when there was an air raid, so, in response, care homes were established for older people to move to.

Means and Smith (1998) present a number of examples of such *ad hoc* policy-making, which suggest that the development of services for older people has been founded on hasty responses to what has been seen as a problem. The notion of older people as a problem has been discussed by Macintyre (1977), who distinguishes two ways in which the problem can be formulated. The humanitarian formulation presents the problem of how best to provide the most appropriate services to make life more dignified and comfortable. The organizational formulation, however, defines the problem as being concerned with seeking the most economical and efficient response. It would appear that the organizational formulation has been most predominant (Means and Smith 1998). For older people, who have constantly seen themselves identified as an organizational problem that requires the cheapest and easiest response, any solutions developed, whether services or policies, may become tainted with the perception that they are developed through expediency rather than caring.

In addition to the negative associations of care homes, there is also the cultural importance attached to the notion of one's own home. The image of 'home sweet home' is replicated across society as a place where one can be oneself, free from external pressures, somewhere to relax. Threats to the home may need to be defended – an idea expressed in the description of the home as a 'castle'. Sixsmith (1986) has argued that for older people the home can be closely linked with a sense of self and identity. Home becomes a place which is significant because of the memories that it holds; significant events, such as births, deaths and celebrations, may have happened in the home. Memories of these events and the associated relationships are likely to be strongly linked with the sense of self and personal history that has been built up. Similarly, the neighbourhood, where the older person has engaged in many activities over the years and has developed relationships with friends, neighbours, shopkeepers and others, reflects a sense of personal identity. Home is not simply a building, but is symbolic of identity and biography. In these circumstances, moving from one's own home to a home shared with strangers represents a huge personal change.

Care homes and institutionalization

Other sources of concern come from 'exposés' of institutional life, which have pointed to the depersonalizing effect of this way of living. Perhaps the most famous portrayal of the negative effects of living in an institution is that produced by Goffman (1961). In his observational account of life inside the hospital, Goffman portrays an environment in which life was lived according to the routines of the institution, where personal choice was not allowed and where inmates became depersonalized – losing their sense of themselves as individuals rather than inmates. Since the publication of Goffman's work, the term 'institutionalization' has become a shorthand term for the processes that are thought to occur in a wide range of settings where people live as a group, from schools to prisons to care homes.

It is debatable whether Goffman's analysis can be applied to different types of settings today. However, the idea of groups of people living demeaning and depersonalized lives still remain. This, in particular, has been the case with care homes; where a combination of folk memories of workhouses, as well as research studies predicated on notions of institutionalization, have produced a literature depicting a move into a care home as one which is an experience surrounded by inevitable loss of identity and independence.

There is, however, some research which indicates that, while life in a care home may be different to life in one's own home, simply portraying the differences under the heading of institutionalization does a disservice to the complexity of the culture of the care home. Gubrium and Holstein (1999), for example, have developed an understanding of life in care homes as one which involves a range of different social practices for managing interactions and relationships which would not be necessary for someone living alone or with family or friends. Living with strangers requires careful negotiation and the development of rules and rituals if it is to be accomplished without conflict or discomfort. Baldwin *et al.* (1993) and Oldman and Quilgars (1999) have similarly challenged the notion of care homes automatically robbing residents of their independence and dignity.

Pathways to care homes

Making the move into a care home involves a huge life change. The evidence is, however, that older people are not always well prepared or involved in the process of moving, some playing little part in the decision to move into a care home, or the choice of which care home to move into. Nolan and colleagues (1996) contend that most admissions to care are made at a time of crisis and that the older person is often not involved in the decision-making process. Such a lack of preparation may result in 'relocation stress syndrome', where older people are adversely affected by the move into a care home (Morgan *et al.* 1997).

The authors' own research shows the multiple pathways to care and that the amount of involvement in this process of the person requiring care can vary tremendously. Some people have little or no opportunity to prepare for the move, particularly if it results from an acute episode of ill-health, where the older person is admitted to hospital in an emergency. From here, discharge planning may result in the decision that the older person would be unable to return home, and a care home place would be found (Reed and Payton 1996).

This picture, however, may be unduly negative. Older people have had lifelong experience in adapting to change, and are likely to have developed many successful coping methods. Parkes (1972) suggests that minor changes are often embraced, but major change is more usually resisted, with the person refusing to accept the change. Unfortunately, some older people may experience multiple losses – for example, loss of health, of a spouse, of a carer, of their home – and these may undermine their confidence and self-esteem, thereby reducing their ability to cope. Frankl (1984) suggests that it is not necessarily the nature of the trauma itself that affects the person's ability to cope, but the person's attitude to the trauma, since the symbolic meaning is broader than just the loss. In other words, assumptive worlds (Parkes 1972) and a lifetime of habitual existence are challenged, leading to a discrepancy between the internal construct of the world that 'should be' and the world that is (Parkes 1972).

Older people may be in a more or less continuous process of transition as their lives and circumstances change (Nilsson *et al.* 2000). These transitions are not short-lived events and if recognition is not given to these processes there is, as Schumacher *et al.* (1999) remind us, a risk of a transition taking place which is difficult or unsuccessful. The decision to move to a care home therefore requires a great deal of support, as this change is 'alien to any other experience of the lifetime' (Willcocks *et al.* 1987: 7).

Reed and Payton (1996) found that there were a range of strategies that older people could use when moving into a care home, in order to make the transition to communal life more manageable. Central among these strategies were 'constructing familiarity' and 'managing the self'. In the former, older people would identify features of the care home on which they could base a claim to familiarity; for example, they would say that they 'knew' a home because they had passed by the building frequently on the bus, or that they had known someone who had worked there when the building had been used for something else. This construction of familiarity could also include people living or working in the home – staff whom the resident 'knew' from community life or fellow residents who were known through past shared activities. In one case, one resident described a fellow resident as known because he had lived in a familiar street, even though the residents had never met before moving into the care home. Constructing familiarity was related to another strategy: 'managing the self', where people were very careful about how they behaved in the communal environment. People did not want to seem intrusive or desperate for company, and so they would 'keep themselves to themselves'. It was, however, more acceptable to talk to another resident if they were 'known', or it was possible to construct some familiarity with them.

Issues of individual autonomy in the communal environment

Living with others is one significant change in lifestyle for people moving into care homes. When this move is accompanied or precipitated by increasing frailty, which results in being dependent on others, then one of the key aspects of daily life affected can be personal autonomy, the ability to make and act on choices.

The way people make decisions and act according to their decisions to achieve personal goals and interests throughout their life may change with life experience and alteration in physical and mental abilities. Making decisions, however, does not just depend on general ability to think through possibilities, but may also depend on specific knowledge and abilities. For example, possessing numerical skills, it could be argued, is essential to making a choice between three complex financial investment plans. Therefore, lacking numeric abilities would diminish an individual's capacity to act autonomously. The lack of numerical skills, however, would have little impact on an individual's ability to state preferences for meals. Determining and developing the abilities needed to make decisions, therefore, are challenges faced by everyone in negotiating day-to-day activities.

The majority of definitions of autonomy refer to the capacity of the individual for self-rule, and make reference to particular characteristics of the context where the decision is made and carried out. For example, Beauchamp and Childress (1994) state that context is central to creating, maintaining or enhancing an individual's liberty to select and act according to their wishes. Autonomous action, therefore, can only occur when these two interdependent factors come together, and for older people this may be problematic. The (negative) social construction of old age within our society (Townsend 1981) militates against the freedom of older people to act autonomously. This can be exacerbated in long-term care settings such as care homes, where residents depend on others to listen to and carry out

Box 3.1   Collopy's polarities within autonomy

Decisional autonomy (*having preferences, making decisions*) versus executional (*being able to implement them or carry them out*)

Direct autonomy (*deciding or acting on one's behalf*) versus delegated (*giving authority to others to decide/act on your behalf*)

Competent autonomy (*reasonable and judgementally coherent choice/ activity*) versus incapacitated (*that which exhibits rational defect or judgemental incoherence*)

Authentic autonomy (*choices/actions which are constant with character*) versus inauthentic (*those which are seriously out of character*)

Immediate autonomy (*present or limited expression*) versus long range (*future or wide-ranging expressions*)

Negative autonomy (*choice/activity that claims a right only to non-interference*) versus positive (*that which claims positive entitlement, support, capacitation*)

Source: adapted from Peace *et al.* (1997).

their decisions. They are also reliant on the same people to create responsive relationships and practices in these environments.

Older people may experience a range of problems, such as reduced mobility and functional capacity and changes in mental abilities, that influence their decision-making capability. It could be argued that if these problems reduce the older person's ability to make independent decisions then older people would experience a loss of autonomy. This is a simplistic understanding of autonomy that is unhelpful to older people, who may retain abilities to negotiate some aspects of decisions while experiencing changes in their ability to make and carry out all aspects and all types of decisions. Collopy (1988) has made a useful distinction between types of autonomy (see Box 3.1) which points to different ways in which autonomy can be thought about. These distinctions are useful as they identify the specific changes to autonomy that are experienced while at the same time highlighting aspects of the older person's capacity to participate in decisions that govern their life.

It is evident from this discussion that reduction in functional capacity may increase dependence on others to *carry out* decisions, while not necessarily reducing the ability to *make* decisions. As well as changes in functional capacity, older people can experience restricted sensory abilities. This can make communication difficult and has been found to limit older people's ability to negotiate their preferences with those carrying out decisions

(McCormack 1998). Thus, those with multiple functional and sensory problems are caught in a double jeopardy – they have an increased need to negotiate their preferences and needs with others at a time when they may be least able to do so.

There is considerable evidence that care home staff assume that physical and mental impairments mean that residents cannot make decisions at all (Cohen 1998). Consequently, limited awareness of the residents' residual abilities contributes to a situation where they are denied opportunities to participate in decisions. Residents, however, might be capable of making decisions if offered the kind of assistance needed for utilizing the decisional abilities they possess. Even when residents attempt to make independent decisions, Baltes (1996) found that independent behaviours tended to be ignored by staff. The implication of this is that residents may feel powerless as they learn that, no matter how hard they try to take control of their lives, staff will continue to dictate what occurs under the guise of a professional helping role. These findings, among other similar research, have contributed to the emphasis in contemporary UK health and social care policy on the development of approaches in care homes that promote the involvement of the older person in their care and the tailoring of the environment of care to a preferred way of living (CPA 1984, 1996).

In care homes strategies have been developed to involve residents, such as residents' committees (Flower 1993), quality improvement activities and care home planning groups (Reed *et al.* 1999). Although these strategies create ways to enhance the older person's control over their lifestyle within a dependent living environment, they also serve to demonstrate that the process of negotiation with individual residents in care homes is not entirely straightforward. The outcomes arising from such activities reflect the views of the group or possibly the views of the dominant members of the group, and not individual residents. Care homes are group living settings; hence the nature of the environment places enormous constraints on the behaviours and preferences of individual residents (Oldman and Quilgars 1999).

The significance of the move as 'the end of the line'

Not only can a move into a care home be viewed as 'the last resort', it can also be seen as 'the end of the line' – a place where people go to die. For many people there are strong associations between care homes and dying. They may have known people who have moved into a care home and have since died. Within the context of palliative care, another set of choices is made as people make end-of-life decisions about care and treatment.

Fortner and Neimeyer (1995) suggested that higher levels of death anxiety are associated with being female, living in restrictive settings such as nursing homes and having lower scores on measures of ego integrity. In a subsequent review of 49 research studies concerning the relationship between death anxiety and a range of individual factors, Fortner and Neimeyer (1999) found that higher levels of death anxiety in older adults were related to lower levels of ego integrity, more physical problems and more psychological problems, and may have been related to institutionalization. These authors found that loss of a significant other in different life stages has an incremental effect on the fear of one's mortality. Furthermore, loss and recent loss are related to fear of personal death. They were, however, careful to point out that the relationship between loss and death anxiety is complex and multifaceted; caution should be exercised when interpreting these findings in the context of an individual's life. For example, studies were identified where those who had experienced early losses were more likely to attribute their fear to the loss of social identity, the consequences of death for their family and the loss of self-fulfilment.

It is inevitable that older people living in care homes will experience the loss of other residents. Relationships with other residents vary from cohabitation in the premises to various degrees of friendship. These friendships can be extremely close and intimate. Hence, when death occurs grieving for the loss of a close friend will take place. Sklar and Hartley (1990) explore the experience of the loss of a friend and suggest that survivor friends carry a burden, as society does not recognize their grief. Doka (1989: 4) defined disenfranchised grief as 'the grief that people experience when they incur a loss that is not or cannot be openly acknowledged, publicly mourned or socially supported.' Reed and Payton's (1996) study found that this was the case in care homes where residents had formed friendships with each other. The significance of the death on the friendships formed often went unrecognized, with the consequence that mourning the death was not recognized either. Staff often reported that residents did not seem to be distressed when someone died, and so the staff did not manage it in any overt way, preferring to 'carry on as normal'. The resultant invisibility of death, however, could be offensive and distressing to residents, reinforcing the idea that because the death did not matter, the person who died was of little importance. A lunch companion or someone who sat in the lounge could simply 'disappear' and no more was said.

The staff story was more complex than this. Some staff genuinely felt that the unemotional way in which residents greeted a death did indicate their feelings about death and their fellow residents. Others were aware of grieving, but felt uncomfortable about dealing with it. Some of the practical and procedural aspects of dealing with death made staff reluctant to be open. In one care home it was thought that witnessing the removal of bodies in body bags would be distressing to residents, and so it was hidden from them. For the residents, however, this secrecy indicated a lack of respect for and valuing of the person who had died.

Secrecy can be a problematic strategy for responding to death in care homes, particularly as these are close communities, where the activities of residents impact on each other. In order to demonstrate respect for residents, and acknowledge their personal significance, some public recognition of death and dying is necessary.

Developing practice to foster 'open awareness' amidst loss

Older people have been found to move to a care home to avoid dying alone at home (Reed and Payton 1996). Others have little choice but to move to care, which may be their final home. Such moves provide an indicator to the older person that their physical and mental abilities are declining and they are drawing nearer to death. Hence, alongside the need to adapt to new living arrangements, they have to confront their own mortality. As friendships are formed with fellow residents and those friends die, mortality is even more evident. It is therefore important that care staff recognize that dying and death are features of care homes that are acknowledged by residents. Staff may attempt to hide the reality of death in the home by 'carrying on as normal' or by following policies and procedures that provide a process for informing relatives and the appropriate authorities, and for removal of the body from the home. However, these activities do not enable residents and staff to grieve the loss of a friend or acquaintance. Instead, to minimize the distress, residents create ways of distancing themselves from others in the home by developing superficial rather than meaningful relationships. They also learn to avoid broaching the subject of their own death.

The reality of dying and death in care homes cannot be changed, but the way in which these circumstances are approached influences residents' anticipation and preparation for their own death and the death of others. In contrast to practices where discussion of death is avoided and the process of dying is cloaked, this stage of life could be approached with openness. This requires a whole new approach to care and its development for those at the end of life (see Chapters 9 and 10) and may promote 'a good death', where the dying person participates in decisions about care, treatment and death, while receiving optimal physical, emotional and spiritual care. Those who are in their final stages of life may lack the ability to carry out their decisions about care and treatment, yet they may still have the capacity to make such decisions.

Whitler (1996) argues that care staff have a moral obligation to promote the involvement of older people in decisions about their care and treatment by adopting assisting behaviours in their practice. These behaviours include: providing resources and creating supportive environments for the older person to make and carry out decisions; giving information to help the older person to realize the available options, while assessing the risks and benefits of different courses of action; providing suggestions and reasons to help the older person determine whether they will accept or reject a particular course of action; exploring the causes of diminished capacity; and intervening where necessary to enhance it. While there is abundant literature pointing to the marginalization of older people from decisions about their lives, the practices suggested by Whitler (1996) are practical and positively promote autonomy even at the end of life.

While taking the philosophical stance of involving residents in decision-making processes is laudable, it must also be achievable. The resident population of care homes in the UK is becoming older and increasingly frail, and a greater proportion of residents are terminally ill. In the same homes staffing levels have not changed as residents have become more dependent. The budget rather than the needs of residents determines staffing. There has also been a marked lack of involvement from the multidisciplinary team to support staff in care homes, particularly nursing homes, when their capacity is stretched. The promotion of optimal physical, emotional and spiritual care of those who are dying in care homes requires restructuring of the current funding arrangements to a system where the cost of care is driven by the personal, health and nursing needs of residents. Emerging health and social care policy (Department of Health 2001) is addressing the need to develop partnerships between the statutory, independent and voluntary sectors to promote resident-led services. The challenges of an ageing population require coordination across all health care sectors to ensure that those dying in homes receive optimal care.

The needs of those who live with those who are dying must also be considered. The evidence points to circumstances where strategies for identifying and supporting other residents through their experiences are undeveloped. Indeed, public recognition of their loss and grief may be unrecognized. In a care home where dying and death were openly discussed there would be opportunities to inform others that someone had deteriorated. This might be on an individual basis or in a public forum. If handled sensitively this could create a situation where residents discussed how they could be involved. For example, they might take part in visiting the dying person – an activity usually reserved for family. Supporting those who are losing friends requires consideration within the busy life of a care home. Rather than carrying out the day-to-day routine, time could be set aside to reflect on the life of their fellow resident and commemorate the death.

Staff also need the opportunity to mourn the loss of a resident. Staff–resident relationships vary. Some relationships are functional, whereas others take on the characteristics of friendships. The different types of relationships need to be recognized and a range of approaches used to support staff through their grief.

Conclusion

This chapter has discussed some of the changes facing older people moving into care homes. Some of these changes begin before the move is made, as older people adjust to changes in health and activity, but can be reinforced by moving into what is widely regarded across society as a 'last resort'. The perceptions of others, that the care home is a place which represents the end of active and fulfilling life, can be shared by staff both in and outside the home, as well as family and friends, and older people themselves. Alongside this notion is the idea that autonomy will be decreased as disability increases.

The chapter has gone on, however, to argue that this pessimistic view need not be the case and has explored different ways of thinking about autonomy. These ideas offer the possibility of working creatively with older people who may have health and activity problems, in order to recognize and enhance their active participation in daily life.

Issues of autonomy are also important when an older person is dying in a care home. While other chapters in this book discuss how open awareness of death/dying is important in facilitating discussions about end-of-life decisions, this chapter has described how, in many care homes, death is made invisible by the actions of staff. A lack of acknowledgement of the death of a resident may be justified by the argument that others have no wish to be made aware, and had only a superficial relationship with the dying person. This argument ignores the way in which residents do form relationships with each other that can be missed by staff and family, and that the failure to acknowledge the death of a resident can be interpreted by the others as a lack of respect and value, not only for the person who has died, but for the other residents as well. We concluded with a discussion on ways in which open awareness might be facilitated by staff, so that the deaths of residents can be acknowledged and marked by all those who have come to know them.

Implications for practice

- Although care homes can be viewed as 'the last resort' and 'the end of the line', it is argued throughout this chapter that these homes are complex, communal living environments where the full range of human existence takes place.
- The move to a care home is a time of considerable loss and change for older people. Living with others is one significant change in lifestyle. While this requires constant negotiation with others about every aspect of life, it also creates the opportunity to develop relationships with fellow residents and staff.

- While residents have an increased need to negotiate their preferences and needs with others, there is considerable evidence that they are often marginalized from decisions about their life. Older people may have reduced capacity to make and carry out decisions, yet there are strategies to enhance the older person's decisional capacity. These strategies can be applied to involve older people in decisions about their care, death and treatment.
- As fellow residents deteriorate and die, further loss is experienced. The evidence points to the conclusion that mourning the death of fellow residents by residents may go unrecognized by staff. Practices such as carrying on as normal may limit discussion of death and result in disenfranchised grief. It is suggested that a whole new approach to care is needed, where death is approached openly.

Acknowledgement

Thanks are due to Elsbeth Russell (Matron, Wordsworth House, Newcastle) who commented and advised on the chapter.

References

Baldwin, N., Harris, J. and Kelly, D. (1993) Institutionalisation: why blame the institution? *Ageing and Society*, 13: 69–81.

Baltes, M. M. (1996) *The Many Faces of Dependency in Old Age*. New York: Cambridge University Press.

Beauchamp, T. and Childress, J. (1994) *Principles of Biomedical Ethics*, 4th edn. Oxford: Oxford University Press.

CPA (1984) *Home Life: A Code of Practice for Residential Care*. Report of a working group sponsored and convened by the Centre for Policy on Ageing. London: Centre for Policy on Ageing.

CPA (1996) *A Better Home Life*. London: Centre for Policy on Ageing.

Cohen, E. S. (1998) The elderly mystique: constraints on the autonomy of the elderly with disabilities. *The Gerontologist*, 28 (suppl.): 24–31.

Collopy, B. J. (1988) Autonomy in long-term care: some crucial distinctions. *The Gerontologist*, 28 (suppl.): 10–17.

Dean, E. (1996) Sitting it out. In D. Dickenson and M. Johnson (eds) *Death, Dying and Bereavement*. London: Sage Publications, in association with the Open University.

Department of Health (2001) *National Service Framework for Older People*. London: HMSO.

Doka, K. J. (1989) *Disenfranchised Grief: Recognising Hidden Sorrow*. New York: Lexington Books.

Flower, J. (1993) Creating a forum. *Community Care*, 45(9): 20–1.

Fortner, B. V. and Neimeyer, R. A. (1995) Death anxiety in the elderly. In G. Maddox (ed.) *Encyclopaedia of Aging*, 2nd edn. New York: Springer.

Fortner, B. V. and Neimeyer, R. A. (1999) Death anxiety in older adults: a quantitative review. *Death Studies*, 23(5): 387–411.

Frankl, V. E. (1984) *Man's Search for Meaning.* New York: Washington Square Press.

Goffman, E. (1961) *Asylums.* Harmondsworth: Penguin.

Gubrium, J. F. and Holstein, J. A. (1999) The nursing home as a discursive anchor for the ageing body. *Ageing and Society*, 19: 519–38.

Kaufman, S. R. (2000) Senescence, decline, and the quest for a good death: contemporary dilemmas and historical antecedents. *Journal of Aging Studies*, 14(1): 1–3.

McCormack, B. (1998) An exploration of the theoretical framework underpinning the autonomy of older people in hospital and its relationship to professional nursing practice. Unpublished DPhil thesis, Department of Educational Studies, University of Oxford.

Macintyre, S. (1977) Old age as a social problem: historical notes on an English experience. In R. Dingwall, C. Heath, M. Reid and M. Stacey (eds) *Health Care and Health Knowledge.* London: Croom Helm.

Means, R. and Smith, R. (1998) *From Poor Law to Community Care: The Development of Welfare Services for Elderly People 1939–1971*, 2nd edn. Bristol: Policy Press.

Morgan, D., Reed, J. and Palmer, A. (1997) Moving from hospital into a care home – the nurse's role in supporting older people. *Journal of Clinical Nursing*, 6(5): 463–71.

Nilsson, M., Sarvimaki, A. and Ekman, S. L. (2000) Feeling old: being in a phase of transition in later life. *Nursing Inquiry*, 7: 41–9.

Nolan, M., Walker, G., Nolan, J. *et al.* (1996) Entry to care: positive choice or fait accompli? Developing a more proactive nursing response to the needs of older people and their carers. *Journal of Advanced Nursing*, 24(2): 265–74.

Oldman, C. and Quilgars, D. (1999) The last resort? Revisiting ideas about older people's living arrangements. *Ageing and Society,* 19: 363–84.

Parkes, C. M. (1972) *Bereavement: Studies of Grief in Later Life.* New York: Basic Books.

Peace, S., Kellaher, L. and Willcocks, D. (1997) *Re-evaluating Residential Care.* Buckingham: Open University Press.

Reed, J., Cook, G. and Stanley, D. (1999) Promoting partnership with older people through quality assurance systems: issues arising in care homes. *Nursing Times Research*, 4(5): 353–63.

Reed, J. and Payton, V. (1996) *Working to Create Continuity: Older People Managing the Move to the Care Home Setting.* Report 76. Newcastle upon Tyne: Centre for Health Services Research, University of Newcastle upon Tyne.

Schumacher, K. L., Jones, P. S. and Meleis, A. I. (1999) The older persons in transition: needs and issues of care. In E. A. Swanson and T. Tripp-Reimer (eds) *Life Transitions in the Older Adult: Issues for Nurses and Other Health Professionals.* New York: Springer.

Scrutton, S. (1995) *Bereavement and Grief: Supporting Older People through Loss.* London: Edward Arnold and Age Concern.

Sixsmith, J. (1986) The meaning of home: an exploratory study of environmental experience. *Journal of Environmental Psychology*, 6: 281–98.

Sklar, E. and Hartley, S. F. (1990) Close friends as survivors: bereavement patterns in the hidden population. *Omega*, 21: 103–12.

Townsend, P. (1981) *The Family and Later Life. Contemporary Issues in Education*. Buckingham: Open University Press.

Whitler, J. M. (1996) Ethics of assisted autonomy in the nursing home: types of assisting among long-term care nurses. *Nursing Ethics*, 3(3): 224–35.

Willcocks, D., Peace, S. and Kellaher, L. (1987) *Private Lives in Public Places*. Tavistock: London.

4

Spiritual care in care homes: perceptions and practice

HELEN ORCHARD

> Spiritual care is so much a fabric of all that we do in our home
> that it would be strange not to deliver spiritual care to our residents.
> Staff who do not have strong faith or no particular faith are always
> encouraged to refer any questions a resident may have and they are
> unable to answer to someone else. That person can be the handyman,
> the laundry lady or whoever can give spiritual support.
>
> (Home manager, private dual registered home, 40 beds)

> Spiritual care is not discussed as part of everyday working life.
> We assume care staff can deal with the spiritual needs of our
> residents, however our staff have not received any training in this
> area and rarely are spiritual needs addressed.
>
> (Home manager, local authority residential home, 36 beds)

> Many people today feel that spiritual matters have no place in life
> and are far from relevant, this transfers into the workplace because
> we bring our prejudices with us.
>
> (Home manager, private residential home, 31 beds)

Spiritual care is an area fraught with personal and interpersonal challenges, confronting the individual with matters of a profound and often disturbing nature – suffering, meaning, mortality, eternity. The boundaries and nature of the discipline are notoriously difficult to define and easily misunderstood. Its ambiguous status may mean it is viewed as an optional extra – something for a select group of religious residents – or delivered only by those who feel they would like, or are able, to participate. It is hardly surprising that attitudes and practices currently vary enormously between different care homes. But recent policy documents in the United Kingdom have made it clear that spiritual care is to be seen as an integral part of the

---

Box 4.1 The Trent survey

In the autumn of 2000, a survey-based piece of research was carried out in the Trent region of England. Trent has a population of 5.1 million which is heterogeneous in nature, containing pockets of deprivation and affluence, and some inner-city areas with large ethnic minority populations. The region has over 1,500 nursing and residential homes, containing some 47,500 beds; although the position is continually fluctuating as new homes open and existing ones go out of business. The study identified 1,572 homes and, after a pilot of 50 homes, postal questionnaires were sent to the remaining 1,522 homes to be completed by the home manager, matron or senior member of staff. A response rate of 42 per cent was achieved, representing 644 homes. Responding homes spanned all sizes, types and locations, making the data a fair representation of the population as a whole.

---

care that all older people living and dying in the residential sector can expect to receive. Both the *National Service Framework for Older People* (Department of Health 2001a) and the *Minimum Standards for Care Homes for Older People* (Department of Health 2001b) specify that spiritual needs must be attended to, particularly for those near the end of life. This chapter explores some of the issues involved in understanding and delivering such care. As well as drawing on the wider literature, it makes extensive use of a questionnaire survey on this subject undertaken among nursing and residential homes in the Trent Region of England, an area of over five million people. Box 4.1 provides a basic overview of the study.

Spiritual care: an emergent discipline

Thinking and writing in the area of spirituality in a health care setting has burgeoned in the past few years in the UK, as well as further afield. There is now a large number of definitions of spirituality in play, with David Aldridge (2000) categorizing over 20 in his *Spirituality, Healing and Medicine*. Most discussions allow for a distinction to be made between religion on the one hand and a more diffuse (perhaps non-theistic) spirituality on the other. Many make reference to an 'existential' element (Speck 1998). Indeed, understandings which focus on the search for meaning and purpose in life have remained very popular with the nursing profession, particularly within palliative care settings, where they are often still linked to concepts derived from Viktor Frankl (1964) which have proved influential within the hospice movement (Saunders 1988).

Within the context of care delivery, spiritual care is commonly recognized as one of the four quadrants comprising the holistic model, the others being physical, social and emotional care (McSherry 2000; Cobb 2001). Caregiving practice has traditionally been understood primarily within a counselling model (pastoral counselling, often with some religious component), although recent literature suggests that a plurality of practice is developing. Examples of different approaches now include the 'dreamwork' of Michael Kearney (2000), narrative and storytelling activities (Abels 2000) and therapeutic touch, drama and art therapy (Grainger 1995; Farrelly-Hansen 2000). Nevertheless, it is clear that the counselling model remains dominant at this time.

The development in thinking and practice in the area of spirituality is an extremely welcome counterbalance to the increasing mechanization of care and the depersonalization of patients within health care settings. However, most attention in this field has been focused on acute hospitals and hospices, with research and writing (Stoter 1995; Cobb and Robshaw 1998; Orchard 2001) as well as empirical studies (Orchard 2000; Wright 2001) engaging primarily with these sectors. Very little research of any kind has been carried out in care homes, with most that is relevant concentrating specifically on death and dying (Hockey 1990; Shemmings 1996; Sidell *et al.* 1997). It has been far from clear whether the increased profile of spiritual care has infiltrated or by-passed homes, and this was an important stimulus to the Trent survey.

Broaching the subject

This topic is still felt very taboo.

(Private dual registered home, 25 beds)

There is little doubt that, despite the increase in profile of diffuse and arguably less threatening (religious) concepts of spirituality, it remains a subject avoided by many within the care home sector. Research in this sensitive area is therefore difficult and often regarded with suspicion. Those making follow-up telephone calls to homes involved in the Trent survey were sometimes firmly told by home managers, 'There's no call for that here' or 'We're not really into that sort of thing.' Negative attitudes and a tendency to avoid the subject of spiritual care may have a variety of explanations, but perhaps relate in particular to the close association between religion and death. Spiritual care can seem doubly taboo in an environment where death is routinely minimized and denied (Field and James 1993; Clark and Seymour 1999). The literature therefore suggests that, despite the fact that the opportunity to discuss end-of-life issues is a key wish of older people (Robbins *et al.* 1992; Seymour and Hanson 2001), this remains unrecognized by home managers, with avoidance and subtle control mechanisms coming into play (Sidell *et al.* 1997). There may be spoken or unspoken rules about who can discuss these issues with residents. Avoidance may be justified by recourse to the 'private' or 'personal' nature of this area of care, as revealed in the following questionnaire comment: 'Not all staff, despite training, wish to be involved in what they see to be such a personal need. Death is not a subject everyone is comfortable with, coupled with a belief they do not hold.'

If attitudes and perceptions can render spiritual care 'the care that dare not speak its name', the reverse may also be the case. Home managers may see it as the care that is only too willing to speak its name, and this can become even more awkward. Staff with strong views on (principally religious) matters can be very difficult to manage, creating concern about when and how the subject should be raised: 'People often have fears that if spirituality is discussed or encouraged it is "influencing" people or imposing your own views/ideas/opinions on service users.' Staff may not recognize appropriate boundaries, and comments made to residents may be misconstrued. Rather than attempting to navigate such complexities, silence on the matter may seem a safer option for a home, particularly within the politically sensitive context of officialdom:

> While wishing to encourage residents in their spiritual needs I do not think proselytising would be welcomed by the Local Authority. Also I would not want anyone to try to impose their beliefs on residents as some faiths can be quite dogmatic.

While generalized statements about taboo, avoidance and mitigation may fit the commonly held assumptions of care in these homes, they perhaps paint a bleaker picture than is warranted. In particular, levels of awareness among home managers (as opposed to other staff) about the importance and intricacies of spiritual care may be higher than expected. For example, over 90 per cent of home managers in the Trent survey disagreed with the statement 'We find it better not to encourage residents to talk about God as this may lead to thoughts of death.' Similarly, 72 per cent disagreed with the practice of encouraging staff to refer questions about spiritual matters to the home manager or matron to be dealt with centrally. Rather than minimizing the difficulties in a 'no problems here' fashion, many respondents referred thoughtfully and candidly to the difficult nature of this area for staff, residents and families. Staff find talking about spiritual care 'embarrassing' and 'awkward', 'unnerving' and 'uncomfortable', 'difficult' and 'daunting'. Staff, residents and relatives alike may lack confidence and fear raising difficult issues. One home manager simply noted: 'staff themselves are frightened of death and dying'. Nevertheless, these issues are being recognized and named, pointing to a positive engagement, at least at a basic level, with the challenges of this area of care.

Perceptions of spiritual care

If nursing and residential homes are engaging with this agenda on some level, what views do they hold about what constitutes spiritual care and how it may be delivered? As we have seen, the little work carried out in this area has often focused more on end-of-life issues than more general perceptions and practices of spiritual care (Counsel and Care 1995). However, spirituality is very far from being solely an end-of-life issue and perceptions of it can significantly influence the ethos and living environment of residents on a long-term basis. The Trent survey explored perceptions of spiritual care by asking respondents to indicate which of eight different activities they considered to be spiritual care. It was felt that questions that focused on practical activities would be more accessible to participants than an approach which required them to make choices between definitions with subtly different nuances. The activities were carefully selected and included tasks which were obviously religious in nature, as well as others where the focus was more on social or emotional support. They are listed in Box 4.2.

The results are set out in Figure 4.1, which shows the percentage of home managers who considered each activity to be spiritual care ($n = 637$). We see in these data a broad, all-encompassing perception of spirituality on the part of home managers. All activities – be they religious, emotional, physical or social in orientation – are considered spiritual care by over 50 per cent of respondents. While it is hardly surprising that activities with religious connotations ranked highly, tasks connected with relationships and remembrance also featured strongly. In addition, comforting a resident worried about continence – an emotional issue of an intimate personal nature, but without any overt connection with spirituality – was also considered to have a spiritual dimension by 403 home managers. The two activities least frequently felt to be associated with spiritual care were more closely aligned

---

Box 4.2   Which of the following activities would you consider to be spiritual care?

- Saying a prayer with a resident when asked to do so.
- Taking the residents on a trip out to the countryside.
- Arranging for the local school to come and sing Christmas carols.
- Comforting a resident who is worried about continence issues.
- Ensuring a resident sees their favourite TV programme.
- Reading a resident an old letter they particularly treasure.
- Discussing with a resident their funeral wishes.
- Listening while a resident reminisces about their spouse.

Figure 4.1 Activities considered to be spiritual care

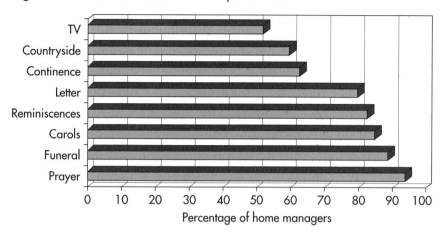

with the social sphere and could just as easily be viewed as entertainment. Nevertheless, significant numbers of home managers (over 300 in each case) still accorded them a connection with spirituality. If turning on the TV or discussing continence is considered spiritual care, the question that most readily presents itself is what types of activity are *not*, if any at all. One respondent explained the rationale for their views on this matter:

> When one of my staff asked why I considered a resident watching their favourite TV programme [spiritual], I was rather surprised. Most of our residents like to watch Songs of Praise and Coronation Street and others. Surely this is life, life is spiritual.

The understanding of spiritual care expressed here reflects a phenomenon evidenced in an increasing amount of literature on this subject; namely that spiritual care is synonymous with holistic care (Hopper 2000), or indeed *any* good quality care (Cressey and Winbolt-Lewis 1999). Viewed in this light, any action, however mundane, may be classified as spiritual care if it can be slotted into the holistic package, particularly if it contributes towards a 'feel better' outcome. While such broad conceptions of spiritual care render it more accessible and inclusive to both staff and residents without a specific religious affiliation, the separation of spirituality from concrete religious tradition has been berated by some as a dumbing down, which robs it of all that is distinctive and grounded, rendering spiritual care 'bespoke metaphysical marshmallow that is non-specific, unlocated, thin, uncritical, dull and un-nutritious' (Pattison 2001: 34). Others, however, may see this as simply another way of understanding spirituality, and perhaps parallels can be drawn with traditions which have a not dissimilar approach. Indeed, a Jew may have no hesitation in perceiving such straightforward physical tasks as turning on the TV as spiritual, understanding

Jewish spirituality to be worked out through simple, physical acts: 'It is the continual endeavour to turn the mundane into something sacred' (van den Bergh 2001: 161).

While home managers may feel that a significant amount of the care they provide can be categorized as spiritual, close associations with religion may not be that far below the surface. When asked whether they agreed with the statement 'spiritual care is primarily for those of our residents who have a religious faith', 32 per cent of respondents indicated they did, with a further 7 per cent not being sure. Set next to the results for the activities considered to be spiritual care, this figure seems to be high and perhaps suggests a reversion to more traditional understandings of spirituality once the word religious is introduced. For example, a number of the activities listed – reading a letter, listening to reminiscences – polled very highly, yet they are certainly not activities which in practice would be considered primarily for any specific group of residents, let alone the religious ones. This reveals a degree of confusion, or at least inconsistency, about what spiritual care is and who it is for.

Understanding the needs of residents

> Some elderly residents do not seem too bothered about their spiritual needs therefore the care staff are not.
>
> (Private dual registered home, 29 beds)

While on the surface it can appear as if broader notions of spiritual care have been adopted by care homes, they may not be very deep rooted. An underlying close association between spirituality and religion may surface in a number of ways, particularly when it comes to considering need and demand. The view that 'they're not bothered' is not uncommon among home managers and can result in either the sort of *laissez-faire* approach seen above or a reversion to the traditional assumption that where there are no religious needs, likewise there are no spiritual needs, as indicated by the following comment:

> My experience tells me that many of the residents have very little religious faith and demonstrate disillusionment with the concept of God as a being of a spiritual dimension to whom they can relate. The big difficulty to me is that they don't want it.

Alternatively, if religious expression is closely associated with the social dimension, 'spiritual care' may be viewed as just another social activity, which can be traded off against rival sources of entertainment:

> Many residents say they have no spiritual needs but enjoy carols by children, Lions etc. . . . . If they had the choice of playing bingo or going

to church service then bingo would be first choice, so we would see this as their need.

The sort of close association with religion indicated above makes the delivery (or non-delivery) of spiritual care relatively straightforward, as it is, in effect, reduced to simply getting residents to church. This simplified notion of spiritual care among staff may influence both the expression and the fulfilment of the needs of residents, as may the attitudes of other residents:

> It is not always easy for residents to discuss or acknowledge their spiritual needs (unless they are devoutly religious) in a communal setting. Non-believers can, intentionally or otherwise, influence 'middle of the road' believers who may find comfort from a specific religion now that they are in the winter of their lives.

For those who do view spiritual care as more than providing access to religious authorities, the challenge of understanding what residents really want and how best to supply it is a very real one. Identifying demand and choosing appropriate, personalized responses is extremely difficult in this very sensitive area. Staff may worry about saying or doing 'the wrong thing' and accidentally upsetting residents. A common anxiety is simply not knowing what to say when faced with difficult comments and questions about God, death or 'the point of it all'; all the while being conscious that such interactions must be highly tailored to the individual. Added to this is the fact that residents may be struggling themselves to speak about their concerns:

> Not all residents can express their wishes about their religious beliefs so it is sometimes difficult to know what is the best thing to do. People also have many different ideas on what happens at or after death so the wrong thing can be said without realising.

Personal knowledge of the residents' views is very important in order to facilitate suitable care. An appreciation of the beliefs of individual residents is the principal way of ensuring that 'the wrong thing' is not said.

Further complications arise when considering the needs of two specific groups of residents: the elderly mentally ill and those from ethnic and/or religious minority groups. The difficulties of providing care for residents with dementia who are confused or unable to express their needs makes the anticipation of spiritual need extremely challenging. Staff may rely heavily on guidance from families about 'what she would want' based on past experience. Alternatively, staff may resort to deciding for themselves: 'Frequently we have to second guess resulting in the resident receiving what we feel is appropriate action.' There is clearly a danger that those who are no longer able to express needs are assumed to have none, despite the fact that residents may have acute spiritual anxieties as their condition worsens. Froggatt and Shamy (1992: 18) describe this phenomenon in a person with the beginnings of dementia, whose very real concern was 'what will happen to my faith when I can no longer remember?'

The situation for ethnic minority residents is likely to be particularly fragmented. Very little is known about the ethnic characteristics of people in homes and the extent to which race and culture are important factors in determining care in later life (Peace *et al.* 1997). The concept of residential care is often regarded with abhorrence by members of African-Caribbean and Asian communities, who see it as a Western rejection of the responsibility for care of elderly relatives (Norman 1985). The belief that such groups 'care for their own', together with a resistance by the communities themselves to recognizing the needs of elders who cannot be cared for by the family, has precluded proper service provision (Firth 1999). Homes which cater specifically for residents from a particular cultural group are very thin on the ground. The result for many ethnic minority elders is that they are the only individual of their particular cultural or religious background living in the home. There is clearly a danger of significant isolation for such elders who live in homes populated by white residents and staff.

Identifying the care providers

The question of which party has responsibility for providing spiritual care is less straightforward for nursing and residential homes than it is for other care environments. While hospitals and hospices almost always have a chaplain in post who can function as a coordinator, adviser and deliverer of spiritual care, such posts do not extend to the care home sector. If access to 'professional' spiritual care is required, the home must rely on input from religious leaders within the local community, whose sense of commitment to the home may vary enormously, as may their interest or experience in working with older people. A key preliminary question for homes is where they feel the responsibility for providing spiritual care actually lies. Is it part of the remit of internal staff, or can they expect the external religious community or residents' friends and family to take a lead in this area? It would perhaps be expected that different types of home would reflect different views on this point. For example, homes which have a particular religious allegiance are likely to consider spiritual care an integral part of the package they are providing for the resident. It is likely to be stated clearly in their literature that the home is, for example, providing a 'Christian environment' for residents or is 'run on Christian principles'. Kenneth Howse suggests that, while homes with a religious foundation do not need to ask whether they have a duty to provide spiritual care, secular homes *should* be asking this question. Not only should they be asking whether it is incumbent on them to assist residents in maintaining contact with their religious community, but more specifically they should consider whether it is part of their role to assess and meet spiritual needs (Howse 1999). In particular, the question of whether *nursing* homes hold a different view from *residential* homes is a pertinent one. Nursing homes are staffed by nurses and have a specific remit to provide health care. It could therefore be expected that the spiritual dimension would be considered an integral part of the care package provided for residents in the same way that it would be for any other environment which provides health care, as the nursing process will naturally include some assessment and care planning of spiritual needs (Ross 1998; McSherry 2000). Residential homes, however, are in the business of social care and the intention is that those living in them should access health care in the same way as other people within the community. Despite the fact that many nurses work in residential homes, there is no specific requirement for input from this professional group and many homes will have no nursing presence. While it would be expected that residential homes would respond to particular requests by religious residents for access to faith leaders, their staff may not consider the identification of spiritual need in the broader sense to be part of their remit. Previous studies have actually suggested that while homes would call in ministers at the request of residents, they did not assess the potential spiritual needs of residents without a specific faith (Komaromy *et al.* 2000), although, as we will see, this is not always the case.

In the past, the regulatory framework for residential homes in the UK and codes of practice associated with it have given little steer on this question of responsibility and there have been minimal expectations levied on care homes in matters of spiritual care (Centre for Policy on Ageing 1984). However, the reform of the regulatory system and the establishment of a National Care Standards Agency has made the position clearer. As we have seen, newly developed minimum standards for care homes make specific reference to enabling service users to exercise choice in relation to religious observance within their routines of daily living, but also, at the time of death, to ensure 'spiritual needs, rites and functions' are observed (Department of Health 2001b: 13). These standards came into force in April 2002, making it mandatory for all homes – residential, dual and nursing; religious or secular in outlook – to assume responsibility for this aspect of a resident's care. In practice, many homes may already see this as a clear part of their remit. In the Trent study, home managers were asked where they thought the main responsibility lay both for providing spiritual care to their residents and for assisting residents to maintain contact with their religious community through attendance at church, social events and the like. Only 15 per cent of homes felt the responsibility lay entirely with a party other than themselves, and there was no significant difference between the views of nursing and residential providers on this matter. Most homes, in fact,

Figure 4.2 Responsibility for providing spiritual care and maintaining contact with religious community (*n* = 644)

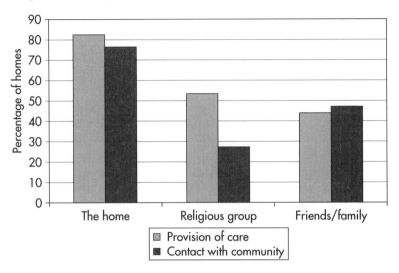

felt the responsibility was a shared one, with the principal participants being the home staff, residents' friends and family or members of the local religious community (e.g. clergy, temple or mosque members). The results are shown in Figure 4.2.

It is clear that most managers view responsibility for both care provision and maintenance of contact with the local religious community as resting with the home. While external religious leaders may be required to assist with the provision of care, there is less of an expectation that churches and other groups will be actively involved in retaining links with residents. This is despite the fact that corporate isolation is a key issue for nursing and residential homes (Seymour and Hanson 2000), resulting in social exclusion in the so-called 'islands of the old' (Reed 1988). Sustaining links with the wider community, as well as creating a sense of community within the home, has an important influence on quality of life for residents (Davies 2001). In addition, many homes in the Trent survey indicated they had practical problems in maintaining contact with the religious community, being unable to provide transport and escorts to church on a regular basis, and it would not have been surprising if they had expected the community to assist with this. Nevertheless, there was far less of an expectation that they should do so, with the responsibility resting with the home, or with friends and family. There is a greater expectation that family and friends will be involved in these practical arrangements than in actual caregiving. This perhaps indicates that the caregiving role is seen as something which should be provided in an official or specialist capacity, whereas practical aspects can draw in broader involvement. We now move on to look at the two principal caregiving groups in more detail.

External care providers: religious professionals

The type of care provided to homes by external religious leaders is fairly well defined and falls into two categories: regular services which are held in the home and specific visits to provide support for individuals, particularly those who are dying. In terms of the former, most homes will receive some kind of service (for example, Holy Communion) on a regular basis, even if this is fairly infrequent. In the Trent survey, 85 per cent of homes had a regular service, and while many simply had one service per month, 37 per cent were receiving input on a more frequent basis. Nevertheless, many homes felt their residents would benefit from a lot more input than they were getting and some homes had great difficulties in getting churches involved at all. It was generally recognized that clergy were very busy, but other reasons were also given for infrequent or inappropriate contact. Some expressed the view that churches were reluctant to expend energy on older people, preferring to focus on the young and hence contributing to the sense of social isolation within homes. Others felt ministers were not up to the job: 'Many ministers are not sufficiently equipped to care for frail elderly residents or those who are terminally ill and tend to adopt a "hail fellow well met" approach!' Another home manager agreed with this, commenting:

> Many clergy find it difficult to relate to confused residents who have difficulty conversing and may be disruptive during services. Visits usually dwindle to short visits to specific residents and an influx of well meaning groups at Christmas.

The challenges of providing communal services for residents with dementia are well recognized, although resources and advice for those attempting to offer them are on the increase (Austin 1999; Goldsmith 1999; Goodall 1999).

It is relatively common practice for homes to call out ministers to help to care for a resident who is thought to be dying. Many homes in the Trent study (67 per cent) felt residents benefited from such visits and 73 per cent had called out someone to visit a resident in those circumstances during the previous year. Nevertheless, some homes indicated they had had problems in accessing clergy even for dying residents:

> Our biggest problem is that local religious groups are reluctant to visit the home. If we ring and ask for a visit when someone suddenly deteriorates we are often told someone will call in, in a day or two. Often the resident dies in the meantime.

However, it may well be that in some homes, little input is received because of a lack of openness on the part of the homes, restricting clergy access (Sidell *et al.* 1997). Staff can act as gatekeepers to different types of care and interaction (Davies 2001) and home managers may exert personal views which have an impact on the ability of the religious community to provide care. Thus one home manager commented: 'I do not want to use the home for organized services, as spiritual care is carried out in private.'

Internal care providers: home staff

If homes view themselves as providing the bulk of the spiritual care required by their residents, how is this managed and who is involved in the task? While the general understanding of home managers may be that spiritual care is broader than simply religious needs, written policies generated by the homes often belied this. If a home has a policy which sets out how it aims to provide spiritual care (and less than half of the Trent respondents did), then this will often focus principally on religious practice, describing the different rituals associated with the main religions and providing instructions on how to treat the body after death and when to call a faith leader. Many policies are simply adjuncts to the policy for care of the dying and do not cover the broader aspects of what spiritual care is and how the home aspires to provide it. Some homes nevertheless have very definite expectations that staff should be involved in this area of care, without providing much guidance about what this means in practice. For example, the policy of one residential home stated: 'Every resident has a right to have their spiritual needs fulfilled. It is the care assistant's responsibility to ensure that these needs are met, either by herself or by informing the care manager.' Another stated: 'It is the policy of this Home to ensure each individual's spiritual and cultural beliefs are sought out, understood and catered for.'

The expectation that care assistants have a responsibility for this area raises the question of involvement by different groups of staff. Are all staff expected to participate and, if so, are they equipped to do this? The Trent survey asked home managers whether the main responsibility for providing spiritual care lay with *all* home staff or *some* home staff. Only 16 per cent of home managers felt the responsibility lay with particular groups or individuals (such as senior staff, managers), with most feeling the responsibility was shared across the home. Despite this figure, the reality may be quite different. The inclusion of spiritual care in the nursing role may enable nurses to feel equipped to deal with these issues, particularly for a resident who is dying (Danvers 2000). But care assistants working in this sector are largely low-paid and part-time, and have limited training (Field and James 1993). Lower grade staff may not be encouraged to respond to questions about death or religion at all. Even if they are able to they may not always feel confident enough to do so (Froggatt 2000), or may need to be given encouragement or permission in some circumstances, such as touching a dying resident (Counsel and Care 1995). In addition, the tendency in the minds of these staff to conflate spirituality with religion has the effect of 'professionalizing' the task, rendering it inappropriate for specific groups of people to deliver. One home manager illustrates this:

> Trained nurses have no real problems, it is an integral part of their role regardless of the patient's religion or creed. Care assistants, on the other hand, feel embarrassed or afraid to touch on many religious activities, including the care of the dying. They feel that it is a specialized subject, done by trained people, i.e. clergy, nurses etc.

Care assistants in this situation are unlikely to perceive themselves as able to act as spiritual carers, limiting their role, if any, to 'ticking church membership on a form' (Hudson 2000).

Challenges in care provision

Despite the majority of home managers considering that all staff had some responsibility for spiritual care, respondents provided a variety of reasons why specific groups of staff might be unable, or might find it particularly difficult, to do this. The reasons fell into several fairly distinct categories.

Limited understanding of spiritual care

Home managers may have a relatively broad understanding of this area of care, perceiving a distinction between spiritual and religious aspects, but other home staff may not share this. The 'definitional' vagaries prove problematic for care assistants in particular. They have often not had any training in this area and retain a very traditional understanding of spirituality, associating it entirely with religion. If such staff are not religious themselves, or have negative attitudes towards religion, they may view the entire area with suspicion and accord it a very low priority. Home managers in the Trent study were well aware that this was a problem, many feeling that one of the key priorities was simply defining what spiritual care actually is. However, overcoming this problem through training and awareness can also be difficult. Care assistants may be reluctant to participate in training even if it is offered, and hence will not be exposed to broader concepts of spirituality which help them to enlarge their views and understand aspects of this type of care that may be relevant to residents. As one home manager commented, 'Many staff do not have a faith and therefore find the subject difficult to approach. Staff do not always want to attend training sessions on spiritual care. I believe many feel it is not as important as physical care.'

A mismatch between the personal beliefs of staff and residents

Allied to the previous point is the perception that a mismatch between the beliefs of the resident and the beliefs of a staff member makes the provision of spiritual care problematic. The view that staff members need to be religious themselves to be able to offer spiritual care was evident in the Trent survey from comments such as:

> 'Most staff have no religious beliefs, so it's normally impossible for them to come alongside someone needing spiritual care.'

> 'Some staff who do not practice their religion or have no beliefs find it difficult to give spiritual care. It is like a taste of the unknown for staff.'

Staff may feel awkward or ignorant in attempting to provide something which they do not understand or have any experience of themselves. Conversely, if the mismatch is between staff who have strong views and residents who do not, this is also perceived to cause problems: 'Every staff member may have different views as to what they personally regard as spiritual care. Sometimes it can be difficult for staff to disregard their personal viewpoint to take on board residents' needs.'

While it is understandable that non-religious staff may find it difficult to negotiate this area with religious residents, and similarly religious staff with residents of a different or no faith, these comments do suggest an inability to identify the content and boundaries of the caregiving role. Furthermore, they point to a lack of recognition of the autonomy of the residents and proper respect for their practices and views within their own home.

The position of younger staff

A third area of difficulty for homes attempting to provide spiritual care is the increasing number of young care staff employed. These staff may feel awkward and embarrassed because they have not formed their own ideas about faith and religion. A typical comment from a home manager in the Trent survey demonstrated this: 'Many younger staff are unsure about their own views so find it hard to discuss spiritual issues with residents.' Other home managers recognized the importance of a degree of maturity in order to be able to respond to this element of residents' needs: 'Our staff are getting younger and consequently have not had enough experience of life to understand these deep and complicated issues.'

In addition to lack of maturity and unformed opinions, younger staff may have had very little exposure to church or other belief systems in a way that would have been common in the UK in the fairly recent past. They may have picked up some basic facts about the major religions from school, but have little familiarity with the currency of religious expression, such as rites and rituals and the language and practices of the church. For example, one home commented that non-Christian staff, although willing to read passages from the Bible to residents if they requested it, simply did not know how to approach this task and would just start at the beginning of the book. They had to be shown where to find 'comforting words' which residents would appreciate, rather than knowing automatically that, for example, something like Psalm 23 might be appropriate. Lack of experience in this area may also generate a lack of appreciation of the role spirituality plays in the life of the residents. One manager felt: 'Young new members of staff who have had no (or little religious) experience themselves seem to be less appreciative of the spiritual needs of the elderly.' Another added: 'Difficulties arise when care staff are young people who have no beliefs and have never attended church. They do not always appreciate how important religion has been in the lives of the elderly.'

A lack of suitable training

All three of the above issues point to a significant need for training in this area to overcome misunderstanding, ignorance and basic prejudice. Even when the reluctance of staff to be trained has been overcome, however, there is little training available that is suitable and a lack of clarity about how to access it. While hospitals and hospices usually have chaplains who are able to coordinate and deliver training, or at least act as a source of advice, the care home sector does not have this kind of specialist resource available. Advice and even training in some instances may be provided by members of the local faith community, but this is likely to be fairly *ad hoc* and to consist of parish clergy running the odd session. In addition, the specific needs of older people living in residential care mean that existing courses with relevant material (such as those dealing with palliative care or death and dying) may not be meeting the training needs of staff in this sector. A manager of a 52-bedded dual-registered secular home felt this was the case:

> All staff require training to recognize the broader aspects of spirituality and to be able to discuss religion, spirituality and death without embarrassment or fear. I have not yet found a suitable training course for this home. Most training sessions which cover spirituality do so only as part of death and dying. This is a great shame.

Another respondent echoed this view:

> Training in this area often involves solely visits to an undertakers and watching body preparation after death, which I personally do not feel is necessarily appropriate and does not help the staff to understand the spiritual needs.

The lack of training opportunities was the most common problem associated with spiritual care cited by home managers in the Trent survey – training that was relevant to the needs of residents, appropriate for younger staff and accessible enough for the reluctant to be able to cope with.

Conclusion

Homes like ours have to operate on minimum staffing levels which are inadequate, so residents' needs have to be prioritized and physical care always comes first – this is what the relatives want. We try to give holistic care but there is never enough time. There is no training on this issue that I am aware of. Churches don't support us really – communion once a month and carol singers at Xmas. Also 95 per cent of my staff have no religious beliefs and don't think of spirituality as a care need.

(Home manager, private residential home, 30 beds)

This comment encapsulates many of the problems faced by care homes which have been considered above:

• misconceptions among staff about spiritual care and the need for it;
• insufficient resources, in terms of both staffing and time;
• the low prioritization of spiritual care, particularly compared to physical care;
• a lack of practical support from external faith groups;
• an absence of training opportunities.

Despite these difficulties, there is evidence that nursing and residential homes are beginning to recognize the importance of spiritual issues as part of the overall package of care provided for residents. How might the level of interest and commitment be encouraged in order that spiritual care is better delivered in care homes in the future? From the challenges discussed above it is fairly clear that the key elements required for improving care provision are an increased level of input by spiritual care professionals, coupled with more appropriate training and profile raising for home staff. Both areas are problematic, demanding additional financial and personnel resources. However, creative partnerships can sometimes generate opportunities for input with relatively little additional cash. Within a particular parish in the Trent region, a group of churches from different denominations who were cooperating in an ecumenical fashion on a number of fronts had managed to fund a part-time post of Worker with Older People. The remit of the post was, among other things, to liaise closely with care homes in the area, visiting residents of any denomination, talking with staff, bringing together groups of care home managers and generally being available as a resource on spiritual care. Unsurprisingly, the scheme was well received, with a lot of demand from the homes involved. Examples of religious communities recognizing and responding to the needs of older people in care in this way do not appear to be common, but represent one way forward. It is easy to extract negative perceptions of the quality of care in homes from the literature. Damning reports have been produced on poor environments, substandard care and the depersonalization of residents (Royal College of Nursing 1992; Nolan *et al.* 1996). Faced with such challenges in physical and social care, it might perhaps be assumed that spiritual care is a fairly low priority for care homes. This chapter has tried to establish that the picture is not as clear cut as might have been assumed and that, while the task of equipping staff to respond appropriately to the needs of residents remains an ambitious one, this is an area with which nursing and residential homes may be more than willing to engage.

Implications for practice

- Understanding of the needs of residents in care homes must also include that of spiritual needs, and special attention is required in the case of those who are mentally ill, as well as those who belong to a religious and/or ethnic minority.
- Greater clarity is needed on the question of who is responsible for providing spiritual care in care homes.
- If staff within (rather than from outside) the homes are seen as taking the main responsibility for spiritual care of residents, then it is important to be clear about who is involved.
- This raises questions about the need for appropriate understanding, beliefs, aptitude, training and life experience among the staff involved in giving spiritual care.

References

Abels, S. L. (2000) *Spirituality in Social Work Practice: Narratives for Professional Helping.* Denver, CO: Love Publishing.

Aldridge, D. (2000) *Spirituality, Healing and Medicine.* London: Jessica Kingsley.

Austin, C. M. (1999) Joy in the moment: immediacy and ultimacy in dementia. In A. Jewell (ed.) *Spirituality and Ageing.* London: Jessica Kingsley.

Centre for Policy on Ageing (1984) *Home Life: A Code of Practice for Residential Care.* London: Centre for Policy on Ageing.

Clark, D. and Seymour, J. (1999) *Reflections on Palliative Care.* Buckingham: Open University Press.

Cobb, M. and Robshaw, V. (eds) (1998) *The Spiritual Challenge of Health Care.* Edinburgh: Churchill Livingstone.

Cobb, M. (2001) *The Dying Soul*. Buckingham: Open University Press.

Counsel and Care (1992) *From Home to a Home*. London: Counsel and Care.

Counsel and Care (1995) *Last Rights*. London: Counsel and Care.

Cressey, R. W. and Winbolt-Lewis, M. (1999) The spiritual nature of quality care. *Journal of Health Care Chaplaincy*, 2: 4–8.

Danvers, M. (2000) Time to go. *Elderly Care*, 12: 29.

Davies, S. (2001) The care needs of older people and family care-givers in continuing care settings. In M. Nolan, S. Davies and G. Grant (eds) *Working with Older People and Their Families: Key Issues in Policy and Practice*. Buckingham: Open University Press.

Department of Health (2001a) *National Service Framework for Older People*. London: Department of Health.

Department of Health (2001b) *Minimum Standards for Care Homes for Older People*. London: HMSO.

Farrelly-Hansen, M. (ed.) (2000) *Spirituality and Art Therapy*. London: Jessica Kingsley.

Field, D. and James, N. (1993) Where and how people die. In D. Clark (ed.) *The Future for Palliative Care: Issues in Policy and Practice*. Buckingham: Open University Press.

Firth, S. (1999) Spirituality and ageing in British Hindus, Sikhs and Muslims. In A. Jewell (ed.) *Spirituality and Ageing*. London: Jessica Kingsley.

Frankl, V. E. (1964) *Man's Search for Meaning: An Introduction to Logotherapy*, rev. edn. London: Hodder and Stoughton.

Froggatt, A. and Shamy, E. (1992) *Dementia: A Christian Perspective*. Occasional Paper No. 5. London: Christian Council on Ageing.

Froggatt, K. (2000) *Palliative Care Education in Nursing Homes*. Abridged Report of an Evaluation for Macmillan Cancer Relief. London: Macmillan.

Goldsmith, M. (1999) Dementia: a challenge to Christian theology and pastoral care. In A. Jewell (ed.) *Spirituality and Ageing*. London: Jessica Kingsley.

Goodall, M. (1999) Worshipping with those who have dementia. In A. Jewell (ed.) *Spirituality and Ageing*. London: Jessica Kingsley.

Grainger, R. (1995) *The Glass of Heaven: The Faith of the Dramatherapist*. London: Jessica Kingsley.

Hockey, J. L. (1990) *Experiences of Death: An Anthropological Account*. Edinburgh: Edinburgh University Press.

Hopper, A. (2000) Meeting the spiritual needs of patients through holistic practice. *European Journal of Palliative Care*, 7: 60–3.

Howse, K. (1999) *Religion, Spirituality and Older People*. London: Centre for Policy on Ageing.

Hudson, R. (2000) Death and dying in a nursing home: personhood, palliation and pastoral care. *St Mark's Review*, 182: 6–12.

Kearney, M. (2000) *A Place of Healing: Working with Suffering in Living and Dying*. Oxford: Oxford University Press.

Komaromy, C., Sidell, M. and Katz, J. T. (2000) The quality of terminal care in residential and nursing homes. *International Journal of Palliative Nursing*, 6: 192–200.

McSherry, W. (2000) *Making Sense of Spirituality in Nursing Practice*. Edinburgh: Churchill Livingstone.

Nolan, M., Grant, G. and Keady, J. (1996) *Understanding Family Care*. Buckingham: Open University Press.

Norman, A. (1985) *Triple Jeopardy: Growing Old in a Second Homeland*. London: Centre for Policy on Ageing.

Orchard, H. (2000) *Hospital Chaplaincy: Modern, Dependable?* Sheffield: Sheffield Academic Press.

Orchard, H. (ed.) (2001) *Spirituality in Health Care Contexts*. London: Jessica Kingsley.

Pattison, S. (2001) Dumbing down the spirit. In H. Orchard (ed.) *Spirituality in Health Care Contexts*. London: Jessica Kingsley.

Peace, S., Kellaher, L. and Willcocks, D. (1997) *Re-evaluating Residential Care*. Buckingham: Open University Press.

Reed, J. (1988) Gerontological nursing research – future directions. Paper given to the RCN Gerontological Nursing Research Seminar, Regents College, London.

Robbins, I., Lloyd, C., Carpenter, S. and Bender, M. P. (1992) Staff anxieties about death in residential settings for elderly people. *Journal of Advanced Nursing*, 17: 548–53.

Ross, L. (1998) The nurse's role in spiritual care. In M. Cobb and V. Robshaw (eds) *The Spiritual Challenge of Health Care*. Edinburgh: Churchill Livingstone.

Royal College of Nursing (1992) *A Scandal Waiting to Happen?* London: Royal College of Nursing.

Saunders, C. (1988) Spiritual pain. *Hospital Chaplain*, March: 3–7.

Seymour, J. E. and Hanson, E. (2001) Palliative care and older people. In M. Nolan, S. Davies and G. Grant (eds) *Working with Older People and Their Families: Key Issues in Policy and Practice*. Buckingham: Open University Press.

Shemmings, Y. (1996) *Death, Dying and Residential Care*. Aldershot: Avebury.

Sidell, M., Katz, J. T. and Komaromy, C. (1997) *Death and Dying in Residential and Nursing Homes for Older People: Examining the Case for Palliative Care*. Unpublished Department of Health report, London.

Speck, P. (1998) The meaning of spirituality in illness. In M. Cobb and V. Robshaw (eds) *The Spiritual Challenge of Health Care*. Edinburgh: Churchill Livingstone.

Stoter, D. (1995) *Spiritual Aspects of Healthcare*. London: Mosby.

van den Bergh, M. (2001) Jewish spirituality: the impact on healthcare. In H. Orchard (ed.) *Spirituality in Health Care Contexts*. London: Jessica Kingsley.

Wright, M. (2001) Chaplaincy in hospice and hospital: findings from a survey in England and Wales. *Palliative Medicine*, 15: 229–42.

5

Caring for people with dementia at the end of life

SYLVIA COX AND AILSA COOK

Much of the research on dementia has focused on medical aspects of care and problems of service delivery. This focus is indicative of the medicalized and problematicized approach to dementia prevalent in the 1980s and 1990s, which has been widely critiqued. These critiques have led to the adoption of a social disability model of dementia, which has encouraged a greater emphasis on quality of life and the experience of living with dementia. The experience of dying with dementia, however, has been largely excluded from these developments. Similarly, palliative approaches to end-of-life care, at least in the United Kingdom, have, in the main, ignored the needs of people with dementia.

In this chapter we argue that by extending a 'person-centred approach' to people with dementia who are dying, while drawing on the expertise from palliative medicine, people with dementia can be afforded 'a good death'. We introduce the background to dementia by looking at the changing ideation of dementia. Research on dying and dementia is then reviewed and three case studies are presented.

About dementia

Dementia is an 'umbrella' term used to cover a range of progressive disorders that lead to the loss of intellectual and cognitive functions, such as remembering, reasoning and thinking. The most common forms of dementia are Alzheimer's disease, vascular dementia and dementia with Lewy bodies. The risk of dementia increases with age. However, younger people can be affected, and some people have a greater risk of developing dementia, for example those with Down's syndrome.

People with dementia commonly experience difficulties with memory, orientation, communication, completing physical tasks such as dressing, and sequencing and initiating tasks. Someone with advanced dementia may, therefore, become dependent on others to complete the tasks of everyday living, such as washing, dressing and eating. Furthermore, communication may be impaired to the extent that the person with dementia is unable to verbalize even the simplest of requests. Frustration and confusion resulting from these problems may manifest themselves in so-called challenging behaviour. Although the progressive nature of the dementia will ultimately result in death, many people will die from some other condition, such as cancer, before this stage is reached. The wide range of needs thus described results in a complex set of individual circumstances which shape the dying process.

As we have seen in Chapter 1, people with dementia form a significant proportion of residents in mainstream care homes. In the UK few people with dementia live in specialist dementia care or palliative care settings such as hospices. At present many people with advanced dementia are admitted to care homes and long-stay geriatric and psychogeriatric wards (NCHSPCS and SPAPCC 2000). There is evidence of a range of unmet needs in long-stay ward settings, including inadequate or non-existent palliation for symptoms such as shortness of breath, pain (including from pressure sores) and pyrexia (Lloyd-Williams 1996). We suggest that people with dementia are *doubly disadvantaged* in that they are at risk of being marginalized and excluded from the extension of more positive approaches to care at the end of life, due to ageism and stigma.

Changing understandings of dementia

Until the early 1990s, the biomedical model of dementia, which links all the changes in the person with dementia directly to the damage in the brain, had dominated health and social service responses to the provision of care. This model located the problem of dementia securely in the realm of the individual and offered little in the way of solution to the problems of dementia, aside from containment of the 'sufferers' in long-term care or an emphasis on the 'burdens' of carers. This model has been criticized for emphasizing a negative view of the person with dementia, with writers describing the condition as a 'living death' (Woods 1989). The biomedical model has also been criticized for distancing us from those who are old, from those who are dying and from those who behave in ways that frighten us (Cheston and Bender 1999). Researchers have stressed that a purely biomedical understanding of dementia may lead to the devaluing of those who have the condition and those who care for them. There is some evidence that people with cognitive impairment are aware of these attitudes (Lyman 1989; Post 1995; Barnett 2000).

These critiques of the medical model have led to a large body of researchers and practitioners advocating the adoption of a social disability model of dementia. The social disability model acknowledges that social and physical barriers rather than individual neuropathology contribute to impairment. These barriers will be influenced by socio-cultural factors, such as the person's class, gender and ethnic background (Downs 2000). It is also important to remember that older people with dementia are coping with a stage in life where death can be expected and where there have already been multiple losses of friends and family (Slater 1995). A sociological model of dementia therefore sees individual experiences within a context of wider political, social and economic worlds and 'the meaning dementia has for the individuals and the struggle they experience to be included as citizens of their societies' (Bond 2001: 48).

Psychological approaches to dementia have often been expressed within the biomedical model. However, the contribution of Kitwood and colleagues has emphasized a new culture of dementia care that puts people at the centre and proposes positive approaches to improve quality of life (Kitwood and Benson 1995; Kitwood 1997). These understandings have been encapsulated most notably by the concept of 'personhood'. This term encompasses the essence of the whole person: a person's unique life history and experiences; family and social networks; current interests, enjoyments and preferences. The term is often used in the context of preserving and maintaining well-being. This person-centred approach to care sets out a value base that is focused on the worth and dignity of all human beings and affirms their uniqueness and individuality regardless of age, disability or illness (Kitwood 1997). Human dignity includes the dignity of the body: 'one's living body is intrinsic to one's personhood' (Finnis 1992: 194). The principles of person-centred care (Maciejewski 2001) may be briefly summarized as:

- respecting the dignity and needs of the whole person;
- equal membership of the human race as of right;
- clear understanding of the person's life history, values, spirituality, tastes and preferences;
- empathy.

The shift in focus by researchers, policy-makers and practitioners from a medical to a social understanding of dementia has done much to improve the quality of life of people with dementia. There has, however, been relatively little focus on the quality of death of people with dementia in the UK and the research that has been carried out in the USA has tended to focus on those with advanced dementia in specialist dementia units or hospice programmes. The following section provides an overview of this body of research and is followed by three case studies that illustrate the interplay between social and medical considerations when caring for people with dementia.

What does the research tell us about dying and dementia?

The particular needs of people with dementia at the end of life have been raised by a number of writers (Hanrahan and Luchins 1995; McCarthy *et al.* 1997), but often in the context of highlighting problems for service providers and health and social care systems rather than the experience of the individual. Specialist studies on dementia care have understandably tended to emphasize quality of life issues as opposed to the dying stage, partly as a response to the nihilistic attitudes that have been sustained for so long. However, there are some developments in our understanding of the provision of optimum palliative and terminal care for people with dementia (Cox 1996; Wilson *et al.* 1996; Solomon and Jennings 1998).

Clinical issues

There has been fairly extensive research in the USA with a particular focus on 'end stage' or advanced dementia. There are suggestions that this emphasis is because of funding systems that govern access to programmes of care in the USA and the more widespread use of advance directives (NCHSPCS and SPAPCC 2000). This body of work provides useful information about the medical and social care needs of people with dementia and their family carers at this stage. Clinical and care challenges in 'end stage' dementia are frequently complicated by poor mobility, often due to osteoarthritis and cardiovascular problems (Hanrahan *et al.* 2001). Some impairments affect functional capacity to engage in ordinary activities and activities of daily living. In addition staff report behavioural problems, such as apathy, agitation and aggression. Delusions and hallucinations may be associated with other behaviour problems, and it is reported that apathy and disinhibition may get worse as the condition advances (Hanrahan *et al.* 2001).

Much of the research in the USA centres on the fact that many people with very advanced dementia continue to receive aggressive interventions in the terminal stages, and there is a wish to demonstrate alternative approaches (Morrison *et al.* 1998). Recognition that death is approaching through the use of predictive ratings (Volicer *et al.* 1993) may assist in anticipating treatment decisions and in supporting people with dementia and their family carers. On the other hand, carers and professional staff in the American studies have voiced concerns that people with dementia do not receive active treatment even though this may be indicated (Luchins and Hanrahan 1993).

Ensuring that any medical conditions are managed effectively is vital because, if neglected, these may exacerbate confusion already present in people with dementia. For example, acute infection, dehydration and constipation, pain and depression may all result in excess confusion and

Table 5.1   Most common symptoms identified during the last year of life among people with dementia (percentages)

Mental confusion	83
Urinary incontinence	72
Pain	64
Low mood	61
Constipation	59
Loss of appetite	57

Source: McCarthy *et al.* (1997)

disability. Both the American and UK studies show such symptoms to be prevalent in nursing homes (Luchins *et al.* 1997; McCarthy *et al.* 1997). The retrospective survey by McCarthy and colleagues (1997) in the UK compared cancer patients to people with dementia, showing that the latter experienced symptoms for longer and were much more likely to have lived in residential care (67 per cent) during their last year. These findings have to be interpreted cautiously, as very few people who die with dementia have this factor recorded on the death certificate (Morgan and Clarke 1995) and the study may reflect the more severe end of the spectrum of need. Forty-three per cent of this relatively large sample had lived (and 41 per cent had died) in a nursing or residential home. Dementia patients saw their GP less than patients with cancer, and 67 per cent had a hospital stay during their last year, with 26 per cent in hospital for more than three months. Table 5.1 lists the most common symptoms identified during the last year of life among people with dementia.

Service provision and models of care

In the UK there appear to be no evaluations of alternative care models apart from the acceptance that hospices currently care for few older people, especially those with dementia, even if they have a cancer (NCHSPCS and SPAPCC 2000). Yet a number of predominantly North American studies have highlighted the relevance of the hospice approach for the care of terminally ill people with dementia (Volicer 1986; Luchins and Hanrahan 1993) and some have argued for the potential benefits of developing a hospice household model within a specialist dementia care setting with little additional cost (Wilson *et al.* 1996). A survey of professionals and family members involved with dementia care in the USA (Luchins and Hanrahan 1993) suggested that there were positive attitudes to hospice approaches but very limited knowledge of available hospice programmes.

As seen in Chapter 3, moving to a new care environment such as a care home is problematic for anyone. It is especially so for a person with dementia and can lead to 'wandering' behaviour, rummaging, problems with continence and excess confusion. In Australia, the USA and some European countries, people with dementia will move between different kinds of provision as their needs change in order to provide care for a relatively 'homogeneous' population within a particular care environment. In the UK there has been more emphasis on a 'home for life' model (Marshall 2001a). Continuity of care remains an important core value of person-centred care (Cox *et al.* 1998) and is central to a person-centred approach.

Staffing, as in a hospice, is the most expensive cost incurred by care homes, though the design and availability of single rooms is also a factor. Issues of staffing ratios cannot be discussed without looking at the differing needs of residents and the particular skills, knowledge and expertise required (Marshall 2001a).

User views

It is thought that people with dementia are likely to vary greatly in their attitude to and awareness of death. There are indications that despite their dementia some people retain awareness of approaching death (Cox 1996). However, anxiety may manifest itself differently; for instance, by stopping eating rather than expressing emotion (Barnett 1996). None the less, such fears and anxieties may be balanced by others who anticipate death as a painless release (Barnett 1996).

Much has been written about the specific psychosocial aspects of the experience of dying, the medical symptoms common in the dying experience and matters of service provision and the most cost-effective and appropriate models of care. Yet there has been little consideration of the ways in which a person-centred approach to dementia care can inform the management of dying (Marshall 2001b), though the relevance of the concepts of person-centred care and personhood to all older people who are dying has been noted (Seymour and Hanson 2001). The next section considers the care of people with dementia who are dying.

Caring for people with dementia who are dying in a care home

End of life may come at any point in the journey through dementia and it is possible to highlight three distinct groups of people with dementia end-of-life care needs. These are:

- people who reach the end of life with dementia but die from some other identifiable condition (e.g. cancer) at some point in the pathway through dementia;

- people who reach the end of life due to a complex mix of mental and physical problems but where the effect on brain functioning is not as advanced;
- people who reach the end of life and die of the complications of dementia, such as end stage dementia.

These three different groups of people with dementia approaching the end of life may have very different care needs and may find themselves in quite different caring environments. Just as the lived experience of dementia varies considerably with individual personality, social circumstances and the biology of the disease, so too the experience of dying with dementia will vary. However, all people with dementia approaching the end of life, regardless of the cause, are united by their need for appropriate medical, psychosocial and spiritual care. There is a large body of expertise related to providing appropriate medical care to people who are dying. There is also a growing body of knowledge informing our provision of person-centred care to people living with dementia. The challenge for those caring for people with dementia who are dying is to extend person-centred care while at the same time drawing on expertise from palliative care to ensure that medical nursing needs are met appropriately.

The following case studies illustrate three very different deaths from dementia and the specific medical and psychosocial needs of each person. The ways in which these needs were addressed are discussed, along with suggestions as to how things might have been done better. Case study 1 describes the situation of Thelma and the management of her death from bowel cancer in a specialist palliative care setting. Case study 2, concerning George, highlights the importance of meeting the person's acute medical *and* psychosocial needs in an appropriate environment. Finally case study 3, on Helena, is a semi-fictitious case study of a 'good death' and illustrates how death from late stage dementia can be a positive experience for both the person with dementia and those around them.

Case study 1: Thelma

Thelma, a retired health professional, was diagnosed with dementia and subsequently developed bowel cancer in her early eighties. Thelma was eventually admitted to a continuing care ward as her rectal tumour became worse, and she had developed a Grade 1 pressure sore. From here the consultant referred her to the local hospice. At this stage she was described as 'very demented'; disoriented regarding time, place and person; restless and agitated with difficulty in communicating verbally.

Her communication problems meant that the admitting consultant at the hospice found it difficult to assess her needs, although her family were able to provide details of her personal history and 'likes and preferences'. The hospice was aware from its experience of other patients with the same condition that she must be in pain, but staff were unable to assess her pain using common pain assessment tools. They therefore developed a behavioural chart, detailing changes in patterns of behaviour and facial expressions, to try to monitor her needs.

Thelma was very frail and moaned when she was moved. She would also hit out at staff when they intervened to turn or bathe her, but she tended to settle quickly. She did call out sometimes and staff endeavoured to respond to simple needs like food, drink, warmth, comfort and reassurance before resorting to additional medication. She was on an opioid prior to admission, taken orally every 12 hours, as well as night sedation and an inhaler. The hospice consultant reduced the night sedation and prescribed a 24-hour opioid.

After about three months Thelma's physical condition deteriorated and she became more agitated. She could still speak but it was difficult for staff and family to make sense of what she said. She could still swallow, eat and drink but swallowing medication became more difficult. The decision was made to use a syringe driver as she became weaker. The physiotherapist gave gentle massage, and music seemed to calm her.

Thelma remained on the syringe driver for about four weeks. A few days before she died she managed to eat a proper meal. In the last week she just took fluids and ice cream. Over the last two days her family stayed with her and were there when she died, peacefully.

The case of Thelma clearly illustrates the problems faced by specialist palliative care staff trying to make her death from a painful cancer as peaceful as possible. Although the staff were aware that Thelma was in pain and gave her medication to help manage this, their difficulty in communicating with Thelma meant that their management of her pain was based on guesswork, and, as a result, Thelma still experienced pain, at least on movement. This pain would cause her to hit out at staff when she was being moved and made the job of caring for her more difficult.

There is a substantial body of evidence to suggest that Thelma is not alone in her experience of pain and that many older people with dementia living in institutions experience pain which is not adequately treated (Bernabei *et al.* 1998; Horgas and Tsai 1998). Furthermore, Thelma's case illustrates how serious an issue pain is in the care of people who are dying of dementia. Research (Cohen-Mansfield and Marx 1993; Hallberg *et al.* 1993) has shown that being in pain is associated with the presence of so-called 'challenging behaviour', such as the hitting, calling out and agitation manifested by Thelma. Pain is also associated with increased depression and confusion, both of which exacerbate the effects of the person's existing cognitive impairment (Cohen-Mansfield and Marx 1993; Duggleby and Lander 1994; Chatten 1995).

Two key reasons have been identified for the poor treatment of pain among older people with dementia. The first is that people with dementia, such as Thelma, are less able to report pain, particularly in response to standard pain assessment measures (Ferrell *et al*. 1995). Second, health care professionals are not always aware that those in their care are experiencing pain (Marzinski 1991; Sengstaken and King 1993) and are poorly trained at pain management (American Geriatrics Society 1998).

Thelma was fortunate in that she was in a hospice being cared for by staff who were very aware that someone with her condition was likely to experience pain and were expert at managing it. In this case, her pain management was hindered by her difficulties in communicating with staff and the problems they had in understanding her. In particular, staff were frustrated by their inability to assess pain using a standard pain assessment measure. These frustrations were overcome, to a degree, by careful monitoring of Thelma's behaviour for signs of pain and discomfort. However, a more comprehensive behavioural pain assessment tool is now available (Lefebvre-Chapiro 2001).

Review of pain assessment tools has shown that many people with dementia are unable to use those which require comprehension of writing or speech and abstract thought, all of which are commonly impaired in dementia (Cook *et al*. 1999b) Furthermore, dementia has been found to be associated with a wide range of communication problems, such as faulty linguistic reasoning, and problems with word generation that will hinder the communication of meaning (Bourgeois 1991). There is, however, a growing body of evidence to show that people with dementia can circumnavigate these communication problems, but that this requires careful listening on the part of the carer (Killick and Allan 2001). Pilot research has shown that people with even very advanced dementia are able to report pain when interviewed in a very informal and person-centred manner. People with less advanced dementia were also able to use pain assessment tools, but it was not possible to predict which tool a participant could use based on the extent of their cognitive impairment alone (Cook *et al*. 1999a).

It is possible that through person-centred pain interviews the staff may have been able to assess, and therefore manage, Thelma's pain more effectively. In this way her agitation and aggression may have been reduced, making her time in the hospice more pleasant for all involved. As it was, the good relationship the staff developed with Thelma over time enabled them to anticipate many of her needs. Thelma was fortunate that the specialist palliative care staff in this setting were committed to providing her with person-centred care and that this care, combined with their specialist medical knowledge, afforded her a relatively peaceful and pain-free death.

Case study 2: George

George was a retired headmaster in his late seventies who lived alone after his wife died. He developed both Alzheimer's and vascular dementia, which, alongside hypertension and late onset diabetes, eventually necessitated moving to a nursing home. He settled well into the nursing home, and his diabetes was well controlled, though his blood pressure continued to be problematic. While still able to enjoy conversations, outings and daily walks, he was nevertheless agitated and anxious about his memory problems.

After about a year in the nursing home George was diagnosed with severe left ventricular failure and was sent to the accident and emergency ward of his local hospital. Staff from the home stayed with him as he was moved to the acute admissions ward where they gave a full history on admission. However, it became clear that some of the hospital staff were unaware that his confusion was due to dementia. A move to another ward followed, and because he was in severe heart failure, plans were made for admission to the high dependency unit. This did not happen and George became more stable on oxygen, with the presence of family members and staff to comfort him.

However, the ward was noisy, with other patients crying out, and this was unsettling for George and his relatives. He had always been fond of his food but tended to have smaller, more frequent meals in the nursing home. In the hospital, against the advice of the nursing home staff and relatives, George tucked into a very large meal, and became very breathless and distressed. It was clear that neither George nor his family wanted there to be aggressive intervention to prolong his life. The family wanted him to return to the nursing home but medical staff thought he should remain in hospital. The oxygen mask was becoming very distressing for George, who kept trying to remove it and became more and more agitated.

After three days in hospital George was discharged back to his own room in the nursing home. George showed by his behaviour and facial expressions that he was happy and contented. He was alert some of the time and could still say a few words. Medication was assessed daily to ensure that he was comfortable and his pain and symptoms were well controlled. Morphine was prescribed via a syringe driver (borrowed from a local hospice) to ease breathlessness. George died peacefully in the company of family and the staff in the home.

George is a further example of the importance of meeting complex medical and psychosocial needs in a person-centred way. For George, the move to hospital was beneficial in that it enabled the eventual provision of the appropriate medical care in his own bed in the nursing home. However, the move caused George a great deal of distress and confusion, which manifested itself in agitation. Although staff and family were present during the admission procedure, and for much of the rest of his stay, he was agitated by the change in circumstances. Sufficient information was not handed on by the hospital staff to even begin to manage this. This poor management of his psychosocial needs made dealing with his medical needs more difficult, as George did not comply with aspects of his care.

The eventual move back to the nursing home enabled the essential medical care to be provided in a familiar and 'dementia-friendly' environment. There is general acceptance of the importance of therapeutic design for people with dementia that not only reduces 'excess disability' but also positively contributes to quality of life (Calkins 1997; Marshall 2001a). The built environment also has an impact on the morale and ability of staff to provide person-centred care – for example, privacy in bathing and toilet areas, appropriate equipment for lifting and transfer, acceptable levels of personal space (Calkins 1997). In this case, the built environment of the nursing home enabled the staff to provide better person-centred care (Marshall 2001a). George had his own room and therefore was not agitated by other noise and, when calm, could be encouraged by staff to use oxygen.

Despite the fact that neither George nor his family wanted aggressive intervention to prolong his life, he still had to endure a stressful stay in hospital during the last week of his life. Although his eventual death was a positive experience for all involved, better communication and planning between medical care and nursing home staff might have averted this hospital stay and in doing so would have maintained the good quality of life George enjoyed in the nursing home to the end (Cox 1996; Barclay 2001).

Case study 3: Helena

Helena had been living in the nursing home for five years, having moved to the home after her family and doctors became more concerned about the possible consequences of her frequent wandering. It had taken Helena a while to settle into life there. Her dementia meant that she frequently forgot where she now lived and would try to leave the nursing home after meal times. Over time, however, she came to feel more at home in the nursing home, and formed good relationships with the staff, who worked hard to reassure her and make her feel like she belonged.

Over the years Helena's dementia advanced and she became more frail. She could still eat and move round the home, but she could no longer manage to dress or wash herself and most of the time communicated non-verbally. Helena had made an advance directive that no aggressive medical intervention be taken to prolong her life. Her wishes had been discussed with her relatives and her GP, and had been noted fully in the care plan. However, when she contracted a series of chest infections the staff, after discussion with the GP and relatives, thought she had a good chance of a full recovery and treated them with antibiotics.

After living in the home for five years, Helena was very frail, was no longer able to walk about and was very withdrawn. She did, however, seem to enjoy the company of others, even though she was unable to contribute to what was going on. Eventually she contracted pneumonia, and the care team and her family, recognizing her advance directive, decided not to treat her with antibiotics. A decision was made to make her death as peaceful and as pleasant as possible. They did not try to feed her meals, but offered her a few sips of water or ice cream at meal times. They also brought her through to the lounge of the home in a bed, where there was a fantastic view of the sea. There a member of staff would sit with Helena holding her hand, while keeping an eye on the other residents in the lounge. Helena died peacefully a week after contracting the pneumonia.

This last case study shows that death from dementia can be a calm and simple event. As Helena gradually became more frail, the agreed care plan, that incorporated her wishes, enabled the care staff, with the support of the primary care team and family members, to take the decision to allow her to die peacefully when the time was right. She was fortunate in that she needed no specialist medical intervention to ensure a peaceful death. She was pain-free, and as she had drunk so little over the previous few days, she suffered none of the distressing 'death rattles' that often accompany death.

The remarkable aspect of Helena's death was the way that it was managed in the public spaces of the home. Allowing her to spend time in the nursing home's sitting room, even though she was dying, served two key functions. Helena was allowed to spend her last days in a pleasant, homely environment, looking out at a view she had come to love. More importantly, by providing care to her in the public spaces of the home the staff played an important role in reinforcing Helena's positive sense of self and integrity. Sociological understandings of self indicate how a sense of self is intimately tied up with the perceptions others have of us (Blumer 1969). If, therefore, someone with dementia who is dying is seen by others as someone to fear and withdraw from, the person with dementia's sense of self will be under threat. Norberg and colleagues (1986) have shown how susceptible those with even very advanced dementia can be to other people's responses to them, and how easily their 'integrity' may be threatened in this way. In this case the staff and residents of the home, by their act of accepting Helena in the public spaces of the home when she was dying, gave her the message that she was still a valued member of their community. It also provided an 'openness' about dying; that death was not something to be feared and shut behind closed doors but something in which staff in the home were dynamically involved.

These case studies show that by providing appropriate medical, nursing and social care within a person-centred framework, people with dementia can have a good death. However, the case studies also serve to illustrate the many ways in which the 'good death' may be jeopardized. There is an urgent need to develop more holistic ways of planning for the care of people with dementia who are dying. In doing so it is important to learn from the expertise developed through the hospice movement without losing sight of the goals and values of person-centred dementia care.

Towards better care and support

Dementia may be regarded medically as a terminal condition. Yet the emphasis in dementia care has now shifted from despair and negativity to exploring the remaining capacity for well-being and even creativity. This is further enhanced by greater readiness to diagnose at an earlier stage and the availability of more effective drug treatment.

For some people with dementia, as well as families, staff and professionals, the use of the word 'palliative' with its connotations of cancer and death may not seem appropriate, even though the 'palliative care approach' is defined as holistic care as opposed to curative care. As we have seen in the case studies, active medical intervention may be appropriate at different stages of the person's journey through dementia, and the emphasis on improving 'quality of life' and 'quality of care' needs to encompass quality of death within it.

The shift from 'living' to 'dying' may be more difficult to ascertain for people with dementia depending on their particular situation. However, when the person is known well, staff appear to sense that a shift has taken place. This does not necessarily mean that there needs to be preoccupation with predicting death. One of the advantages of dying in a care home which upholds the philosophy and practice of person-centred care is that death can come at the right time, 'neither hastened nor postponed' (WHO 1990).

However, it is clear that the person-centred approach to care may not be enough as the person with dementia moves towards the end of life. The knowledge and skills built up in the field of palliative care, such as management of fever, sickness, oral care, pain management, spiritual care, support for families and loved ones, supervision and support for staff, can all be translated into the 'language' of dementia care practice. It is as if the life of the person with dementia needs to be illuminated through the prism of both specialist palliative care and person-centred care. This is made easier because the principles and values of person-centred care and palliative care are very close, with an emphasis on holism, dignity and respect for the individual as a person with rights (Seymour and Hanson 2001).

The case studies presented here have identified the problems faced by staff in three different settings. They each illuminate how care of people with dementia at the end of life may be improved. Ideally this is about providing appropriate care to people where they are currently living, rather than by transfer to another setting.

In extending the person-centred approach of dementia care to those who are dying, care staff are more likely to understand and respond to pain, discomfort and difficult behaviour by trying to understand the person's behaviour as a means of communication. By drawing on expertise developed in specialist palliative care, staff can develop skills and knowledge of caring that are appropriate and so augment the knowledge already gained in looking after people with dementia.

Like others, people with dementia would prefer a homely and peaceful death. Legislation, policy and regulation in the UK emphasize the need for inclusion in society and a reduction in marginalization. Care homes that can provide a breadth of styles and types of care without developing systems that give or withdraw care according to categories (the tendency in the USA) provide a great opportunity to continue 'integrity-promoting care' as the person draws to the end of life. Ideally, we would wish to avoid moving people to other settings at crucial points in their care, and instead support the carers who know the person best. The person with dementia has a right to appropriate interventions at the end of life.

Many challenges remain. Some need to be tackled as part of the wider issues about death in care homes. For people with dementia the issues of pain and communication are central. Research and evidence-based practice are beginning to have an impact, but more work is needed. An important message for all those involved in this type of care is that the death of a person with dementia is not so different, though people may express their fears and hopes in different ways. The most likely process is a gradual decline and death from the 'old man's friend', pneumonia. 'No bitterness or anguish, all loving-kindness. Now the evening is coming to its end for me. You can't barge it or dish it – all of it was everwell' (Killick and Allan 2001: 277).

Conclusion

The experiences and needs of people with dementia who are dying are beginning to be explored. Work in the USA has many useful lessons, but the focus on advanced dementia and specialist care, combined with different funding systems and legal frameworks, affects transferability to the UK.

People with dementia may become terminally ill at any stage through the journey of dementia. The shift from the purely biomedical model to the social disability model, combined with the values and practice of a person-centred approach, provides an opportunity to improve the quality of the dying process in care homes. People with dementia have a wide range of needs resulting from the impact of dementia on their individual needs and circumstances. There is a lack of research in the UK about optimal levels of health and social care for this range of need.

The achievement of a 'good death' may be compromised by a number of factors, not least the issues of communication and the assessment and management of pain. The case examples explore these challenges in relation to care practice but also shed light on policy implications. Those commissioning, regulating and managing care homes should recognize that implementing the principles and practice of person-centred care is more likely to result in end-of-life care that meets the needs of particular individuals and their families. Training, staff support and service improvement need to take place in all parts of the system.

Bringing together the values and approaches of person-centred and palliative care involves effective partnership between those working in care homes, elderly care teams, primary care teams and community and specialist palliative care teams. Such partnerships must ensure that people with dementia and their family carers are consulted and involved in this process.

Implications for practice

- People with dementia may die at any stage through the journey of dementia.
- Like other people, people with dementia would prefer a homely and peaceful death.
- The shift from the purely biomedical model to the social disability model, including the values and practice of a person-centred approach, provides an opportunity to improve the quality of care.
- The knowledge and skills built up in the field of palliative care can be translated into the 'language' of dementia care practice.
- Ensuring that any medical conditions are managed effectively is vital because, if neglected, these may exacerbate confusion already present in dementia.
- By extending the person-centred approach to those who are dying, care staff are more likely to understand and respond to pain, discomfort and difficult behaviour by trying to understand the person's behaviour as a means of communication.
- Whenever possible it is best to avoid moving people to other settings at crucial points in their care, and instead to provide support to the carers who know the person best.
- Effective partnerships between those working in care homes and community, elderly, primary and palliative care teams are needed if care is to improve. People with dementia and their family carers should be consulted and involved in this process.

Acknowledgement

We would like to thank and acknowledge the families and staff who have helped in the presentation of two of the case studies.

References

American Geriatrics Society (1998) The management of chronic pain in older persons. The American Geriatrics Society Panel on Chronic Pain in Older Persons. *Journal of the American Geriatrics Society*, 46: 635–65.

Barclay, S. (2001) Palliative care for non-cancer patients: a UK perspective from palliative care. In J. M. Addington-Hall and I. J. Higginson (eds) *Palliative Care for Non-cancer Patients*. Oxford: Oxford University Press.

Barnett, E. (1996) 'I need to be me': a thematic evaluation of a dementia care facility based on the client perspective. Unpublished PhD thesis, University of Bath.

Barnett, E. (2000) *Involving People with Dementia in Designing and Delivering Care: 'I Need to Be Me!'* London: Jessica Kingsley.

Bernabei, R., Gambassi, G., Lapane, K. *et al.* (1998) Management of pain in elderly patients with cancer. *Journal of the American Medical Association*, 279: 1877–82.

Blumer, H. (1969) *Symbolic Interactionism: Perspective and Method*. Berkeley: University of California Press.

Bond, J. (2001) Sociological perspectives. In C. Cantley (ed.) *A Handbook of Dementia Care*. Buckingham: Open University Press.

Bourgeois, M. S. (1991) Communication treatments for adults with dementia. *Journal of Speech and Hearing Research*, 34: 831–44.

Calkins, M. P. (1997) A supportive environment for people with late-stage dementia. In C. R. Kovach (ed.) *Late-stage Dementia Care: A Basic Guide*. Washington, DC: Taylor & Francis.

Chatten, C. (1995) Break up the pain chain. *Journal of Dementia Care*, September/October: 26–7.

Cheston, R. and Bender, M. (1999) *Understanding Dementia: The Man with the Worried Eyes*. London: Jessica Kingsley.

Cohen-Mansfield, J. and Marx, M. S. (1993) Pain and depression in the nursing home: corroborating results. *Journal of Gerontology*, 48: 96–7.

Cook, A. K. R., Niven, C. A. and Brodie, E. (1999a) Self report of pain by people with cognitive impairment: a pilot study. Proceedings of the British Society of Gerontology Annual Conference, Bournemouth, 17–19 September.

Cook, A. K. R., Niven, C. A. and Downs, M. G. (1999b) Assessing the pain of people with cognitive impairment. *International Journal of Geriatric Psychiatry*, 14: 421–5.

Cox, S. (1996) Quality care for the dying person with dementia. *Journal of Dementia Care*, July/August: 19–20.

Cox, S., Anderson, I., Dick, S. and Elgar, J. (1998) *The Person, the Community and Dementia: Developing a Value Framework*. Stirling: Stirling Dementia Services, Development Centre, University of Stirling.

Downs, M. (2000) Dementia in a socio-cultural context: an idea whose time has come. *Ageing and Society*, 20(3): 369–75.

Duggleby, W. and Lander, J. (1994) Cognitive status and postoperative pain: older adults. *Journal of Pain and Symptom Management*, 9: 19–27.

Ferrell, B. A., Ferrell, B. R. and Rivera, L. (1995) Pain in cognitively impaired nursing home patients. *Journal of Pain and Symptom Management*, 10: 591–8.

Finnis, J. (1992) Economics, justice and the value of life. In L. Gormally (ed.) *The Dependent Elderly: Autonomy, Justice and Quality of Care*. Cambridge: Cambridge University Press.

Hallberg, I. R., Edberg, A., Nordmark, A., Johnsson, K. and Norberg, A. (1993) Daytime vocal activity in institutionalized severely demented patients identified as vocally disruptive by nurses. *International Journal of Geriatric Psychiatry*, 8: 155–64.

Hanrahan, P. and Luchins, D. (1995) Access to hospice programmes in end-stage dementia: a national survey of hospice programmes. *Journal of American Geriatric Society*, 43: 56–9.

Hanrahan, P., Luchins, D. J. and Murphy, K. (2001) Palliative care for patients with dementia. In J. M. Addington-Hall and I. J. Higginson (eds) *Palliative Care for Non-cancer Patients*. Oxford: Oxford University Press.

Hanrahan, P., Raymond, M., McGowan, E. and Luchins, D. (1999) Criteria for enrolling dementia patients in hospice: a replication. *American Journal of Hospice and Palliative Care*, January/February: 395–400.

Horgas, A. L. and Tsai, P. (1998) Analgesic drug prescription and use in cognitively impaired nursing home residents. *Nursing Research*, 47: 235–42.

Killick, J. and Allan, K. (2001) *Communication and the Care of People with Dementia*. Buckingham: Open University Press.

Kitwood, T. (1997) *Dementia Reconsidered: The Person Comes First*. Buckingham: Open University Press.

Kitwood, T. and Benson, S. (1995) (eds) *The New Culture of Dementia Care*. London: Hawker Publications.

Levebvre-Chapiro, S. (2001) The DOLOPLUS 2 scale – evaluating pain in the elderly. *European Journal of Palliative Care*, 8(5): 191–4.

Lloyd-Williams, M. (1996) An audit of palliative care in dementia. *European Journal of Cancer Care*, 5: 53–5.

Luchins, D. J. and Hanrahan, P. (1993) What is the appropriate level of health care for end-stage dementia patients? *Journal of the American Geriatrics Society*, 41: 25–30.

Luchins, D. J., Hanrahan, P. and Murphy, K. (1997) Criteria for enrolling dementia patients in hospice. *Journal of American Geriatrics Society*, 45(9): 1054–9.

Lyman, K. A. (1989) Bringing the social back in: a critique of the biomedicalization of dementia. *Gerontologist*, 29(5): 597–605.

McCarthy, M., Addington-Hall, J. and Altmann, D. (1997) The experience of dying with dementia: a retrospective study. *International Journal of Geriatric Psychiatry*, 12: 404–9.

Maciejewski, C. (2001) Psychological perspectives. In C. Cantley (ed.) *A Handbook of Dementia Care*. Buckingham: Open University Press.

Marshall, M. (2001a) Care settings and the care environment. In C. Cantley (ed.) *A Handbook of Dementia Care*. Buckingham: Open University Press.

Marshall, M. (2001b) Promoting person-centered care for people with advanced dementia. In M. Z. Solomon, A. L. Romer and K. S. Heller (eds) *Innovations in End-of-life Care: Practical Strategies and International Perspectives*, Volume 1, 2000 Series. Newton Massachusetts, MA: Education Development Centre.

Marzinski, L. R. (1991) The tragedy of dementia: clinically assessing pain in the confused nonverbal elderly. *Journal of Gerontological Nursing*, 17: 25–8.

Morgan, K. and Clarke, D. (1995) To what extent is dementia under-reported on British death certificates? *International Journal of Geriatric Psychiatry*, 10(11): 987–90.

Morrison, R. S., Ahronheim, J. C. and Morrison, M. (1998) Pain and discomfort associated with common hospital procedures and experiences. *Journal of Pain and Symptom Management*, 15: 91–101.

NCHSPCS and SPAPCC (2000) *Positive Partnerships: Palliative Care for Adults with Severe Mental Health Problems*. Occasional Paper 17. London: National Council for Hospice and Specialist Palliative Care Services; and Scottish Partnership Agency for Palliative and Cancer Care.

Norberg, A., Melin, E. and Asplund, K. (1986) Reactions to music, touch and object presentation in the final stage of dementia: an exploratory study. *International Journal of Nursing Studies*, 23(4): 315–23.

Post, S. (1995) *The Moral Challenge of Alzheimer's Disease*. Baltimore and London: The Johns Hopkins University Press.

Sengstaken, E. A. and King, S. A. (1993) The problem of pain and its detection among geriatric nursing home residents. *Journal of the American Geriatrics Society*, 41: 541–4.

Seymour, J. E. and Hanson, H. (2001) Palliative care and older people. In M. Nolan, S. Davies and G. Grant (eds) *Working with Older People and Their Families: Key Issues in Policy and Practice*. Buckingham: Open University Press.

Slater, R. (1995) *The Psychology of Growing Old*. Buckingham: Open University Press.

Solomon, M. Z. and Jennings, B. (1998) Palliative care for Alzheimer patients: implications for institutions, caregivers and families. In L. Volicer and A. Hurley (eds) *Hospice Care for Patients with Advanced Progressive Dementia*. New York: Springer Publishing Company.

Volicer, B. J., Hurley, A. and Fabiszewski, K. J. (1993) Predicting short-term survival for patients with advanced Alzheimer's disease. *Journal of the American Geriatrics Society*, 41: 535–40.

Volicer, L. (1986) Need for hospice approach to treatment of patients with advanced progressive dementia. *Journal of the American Geriatrics Society*, 34: 655–8.

WHO Expert Committee (1990) *Cancer Pain Relief and Palliative Care*. Technical Report Series No. 804. Geneva: World Health Organization.

Wilson, S., Kovach, C. and Stearns, S. (1996) Hospice concepts in the care for end-stage dementia. *Geriatric Nursing*, 17(January/February): 6–10.

Woods, R. T. (1989) *Alzheimer's Disease: Coping with a Living Death*. London: Souvenir Press.

6 The role of the physician in nursing home care in The Netherlands

FRANS BAAR AND
HERMAN VAN DER KLOOT MEIJBURG

The motto of the Dutch Association of Nursing Home Physicians is 'to comfort always; always to relieve pain and discomforts; to cure if possible'. This motto reflects an insight gained from the developments in medicine after the Second World War, when medical knowledge exploded and all sorts of new treatments and interventions were made available to patients. These developments suggested that illnesses affect patients only temporarily and that cure is possible in most instances, and if cure is not possible, then discomforts can be minimized, and the dying process delayed. The focus of medical attention was on diagnosis and treatment; care meant cure. We might say that when cure was not possible the medical profession lost interest in 'the case' and the attending physician would happily refer the patient to the chaplain: a sure sign for all parties concerned that death was imminent. The history of the role of the nursing home physician in The Netherlands is therefore the history of how the medical profession started to understand that cure could also mean care. This option meant that physicians had to reassess their contributions to the well-being of patients in the last phases of life. For at this phase of life, medical presence is no longer required in terms of treatment but is necessary in terms of understanding the needs of the patient and facilitating the dying process by helping to care for the patient from a medical point of view.

To understand this reorientation in medical practice it is necessary to describe the context that brought this change about, a context which is strongly related to developments in nursing home care in The Netherlands. We illustrate these developments through a description of work which took place at Antonius IJsselmonde, one of the first health care institutions in The Netherlands specifically built as a nursing home in the early 1970s.

Nursing homes in The Netherlands

The development of special facilities in Holland for the care of the dying, the chronically ill and those among the elderly in need of rehabilitation started early in the 1960s. The image of the modern hospital was related to advancements in medical knowledge and there was a sense in which, within this new profile, the position of the chronically ill and the dying became problematic. The chronically ill and the dying also represented an extraordinary expense for a hospital to have to sustain. Yet there was a growing awareness that because of the ageing of the population, other measures had to be taken regarding the care of those citizens who suffer chronic disease. Early in the 1960s, therefore, some 'homes for the elderly' had already decided to employ their own physician and a number of physiotherapists. Nuns, together with nursing aids, usually provided daily care. Consequently the government and those involved started to look for other types of institutional solutions to deal with these categories of patients. It was at this time that the idea of nursing homes for the chronically ill and the dying emerged. Financially this was made possible by the AWBZ (Exceptional Medical Expenses Act) of 1967, which provided every citizen in The Netherlands with the assurance of adequate long-term intensive care. The AWBZ stimulated the development of nursing homes where specialized nursing home care could be provided, and existing homes for the elderly could now organize themselves to become nursing homes. In addition, special facilities were designed to operate as nursing homes right from the beginning. Now that the financial aspects were taken care of, nursing homes had the resources with which they could finance their own nurses, nursing aids, physicians, social workers, psychologists, chaplains, occupational therapists, physiotherapists and speech therapists.

In the beginning, however, nursing homes perceived themselves as *hospitals* for the chronically ill and the dying. The design was often more or less a copy of what existing hospitals looked like. In fact the buildings resembled small hospitals possibly because there was no experience of what facilities for the chronically ill and the dying should look like. Little was known about their specific needs. Consequently the rooms on the ward would cater for five to ten patients; the toilets and the bathrooms were situated across the hallway, opposite the rooms, just like in the hospitals of that time. The number of wheelchairs was limited to a few on each ward. Since these patients had been discharged from hospital because further treatment was futile, all that they required was a bed and a chamber pot. In the course of time these views have changed. As caregivers struggled to understand better their specific responsibilities towards the chronically ill and the dying, care for these patients was reassessed. A major change in attitude by the caregivers became evident. They became aware that care in the nursing home should not focus on that which patients were no longer able to do for themselves, and that the role of the caregiver should be to stimulate patients to do whatever they were still capable of doing. Attending to the wishes and needs of each individual patient while at the same time helping them to realize their desires whenever possible, therefore, became a turning point in the approach.

Gradually nursing homes discovered that, as health care institutions with a specific mandate, they had to reconceptualize the care they provided. The development of a nursing home philosophy and the care they provide is rather unusual in the world and is characteristic of the developments in health care in The Netherlands. One should remember that during the same period the first hospices for terminally ill patients were established in the UK. The policy behind their development was quite different from the outset. The one big difference between the two systems is that while the hospices in the UK are dependent upon money coming from grants and charity, in The Netherlands care of the chronically ill and the dying in nursing homes is paid for through social premiums.

Today nursing homes have become well established organizations rendering all sorts of health care services to many. Although they are primarily occupied with providing care for elderly people, the number of young patients is also on the increase. Of the 326 Dutch nursing homes, 67 are for somatic patients only and 64 serve only psychogeriatric patients. The other 195 nursing homes are so-called 'combined homes', and have a mix of both categories of patients. Today the nursing homes in The Netherlands can accommodate a total of almost 56,000 patients and about 5,000 patients are admitted to day care.

Many patients who are not officially admitted to a nursing home take advantage of its programme by simply spending their time there several days a week. In addition, an increasing number of patients with complex chronic diseases, who stay at home or in homes for the elderly, receive help from the nursing home in their neighbourhood. This can range from simple treatment to specialized nursing home care equivalent to that received by residential patients.

Only recently have nursing homes set up a range of consultation programmes to help neighbouring hospitals with the care of post-stroke patients, psychogeriatric patients and terminally ill patients. In some hospitals we find nursing home physicians cooperating with the hospital staff to provide for the care of patients who have been admitted to the hospital, but who are waiting to be admitted to the nursing home.

Nursing home care

Today the basic task of the Dutch nursing home includes reactivation and rehabilitation, care for patients with chronic or protracted illnesses (somatic and/or psychogeriatric illnesses), special forms of care (for example, care of young patients with non-congenital brain damage, comatose patients, post-stroke care, care of patients on respirators or of patients with motor neurone disease). Not every nursing home provides every sort of care. Over the past ten years a growing number of nursing homes have developed specialisms in certain fields, and one of these is palliative care for terminally ill patients.

In line with these initiatives, not only have they set up specialized wards in combination with specific services, they have also initiated educational programmes to share their experiences with organizations that have taken similar initiatives. Nursing home care has developed and greatly expanded from what it was in the early days and is now best characterized by its composite nature, catering for patients with complex needs. These needs are not only the direct result of their vulnerable medical conditions, but also arise from other problems related to that situation, such as the loss of physical functions or other disabilities caused by the ageing process or psychological disorders. Often it is not the patient but the family, relatives and friends that run out of sufficient resources to provide proper care. The care that has been developed in nursing homes today takes these different aspects into account, resulting in an integral package of care geared to meet the specific needs of the patient and the relatives concerned. It is clear that this requires a multi- and interdisciplinary approach. At present, inter-disciplinary teams in nursing homes provide patients with all the aspects of care included in the definition of palliative care by the World Health Organization (WHO 1990).

Dutch nursing homes have specialized nursing home doctors, nurses, social workers, psychologists, pastors, paramedics and occupational therapists at their disposal. However, these professions no longer work individually, but render their services on the basis of joint deliberations in interdisciplinary teams. In this context the role of volunteers should also be mentioned, since they help to facilitate much of the care giving in Dutch nursing homes.

Some facts and figures about terminal care in The Netherlands

The total population of The Netherlands numbers 15,460,000 people; that is, 452 inhabitants per square kilometre. There are 100 acute hospitals with 50,000 beds, 326 nursing homes totalling 56,000 beds and 1,200 homes for the elderly, offering another 120,000 places. These homes for the elderly are institutions for supported living when people can no longer cope independently in their own home environment. As people get older, there are a growing number of residents who, during their stay in a home for the elderly, need some sort of nursing home care. Accordingly, many nursing homes and homes for the elderly have integrated their services, thus providing residents with an adequate continuum of care.

The number of people expected to die in nursing homes will increase in the coming years. Out of a total number of 124,000 deaths in 1988, 41 per cent occurred in hospital, 15 per cent in nursing homes, 14 per cent in homes for the elderly and 30 per cent at home. In 1996, from 135,000 deaths, 36 per cent took place in hospital, 17 per cent in nursing homes, 16 per cent in homes for the elderly and 30 per cent at home. In 2030 the expected total number of deaths will be 214,000, rising to 250,000 by 2050. Compared to other Western countries the number of people dying in hospital in The Netherlands is low; for example, in the USA 65 per cent of the population dies in hospital, and in the UK the figure is roughly 55 per cent.

With these statistics in mind, a growing number of nursing homes and homes for the elderly in The Netherlands are interested in expanding their services to patients who cannot or do not wish to die either at home or in hospital. By the end of 2001, 30 nursing homes had opened special units (141 beds) for palliative terminal care. A similar development was taking place in homes for the elderly. The number of hospices was also increasing, to 32 hospices with 135 beds by the close of 2001. Nursing homes play an important role in helping to set up these facilities. They are also actively preparing for mobile palliative care teams for home care consultation.

Specialized palliative terminal care is provided in and outside the nursing home

We can see that nursing homes and nursing home care in The Netherlands have come a long way since the 1960s. Developments in Antonius IJsselmonde serve as a good illustration of what has happened during this period. On the basis of the outcomes of a small project in 1977, Antonius IJsselmonde (230 beds) was the first nursing home in The Netherlands to start a major research project aimed at improving care for the dying. The project was subsidized by the government and was executed over a period of five years (1980–5). After a thorough evaluation of the outcomes of the project and on the basis of a great variety of experiences, major adjustments were made to provide for a specialized unit (eight beds) for the palliative care of the dying. The unit was opened in 1993. Two years after the unit opened, the Ministry of Health had the project and the experiences of the participants in the project thoroughly evaluated again.

Over the next seven years nearly 700 patients died in these eight beds, and the average stay was nearly three weeks. A large majority (95 per cent) of the patients had a malignant disease. Some 50 per cent were admitted directly from their own homes (normally this figure is about 20 per cent), 50 per cent of the patients came from neighbouring hospitals (normally 80 per cent). But the numbers alone do not reflect the success of the unit.

The success lies in the way families, patients, physicians and staff manage to cope with this new phenomenon. The unit demanded a new approach to the care of those in the last phase of life. Adequate control of pain and symptoms forms the basis of good palliative care. But this alone is not enough. In our experience, palliative care also implies communication and the exchange of relevant information. It aims to provide the patient with rest and comfort, appreciation, knowledge, real support and, last but not least, loving care to meet the needs of the patient and his or her relatives (Baar 1998). Today the workers on the team are specially trained to provide palliative care to terminally ill people, collaborating closely with patients and their families, and with volunteers.

It is remarkable that many patients, together with their relatives, acknowledge that if they had known about the kind of care beforehand they would have applied to be admitted to the unit at an earlier stage of their illness. The reason for this may well be that in the minds of many there persists the old perception of what the nursing home used to be. This perception is not very appealing.

Special units for terminally ill patients are reserved, in the main, for patients suffering from cancer. An important bonus of the care provided in these specialized units is the insight 'we' have gained. The question arises as to whether we should also offer the benefits of palliative care to patients who stay in the nursing home only temporarily for ailments other than terminal care and to chronically ill patients with non-malignant diseases. As their disease progresses, they require the same degree of care as terminally ill patients and their relatives. We have discovered from our own experience that palliative care for the chronically ill and their relatives is often more difficult than care for the dying. The former undergo a protracted process in their disease, they often suffer from multiple pathology and they may be on the verge of death several times before they are finally allowed to die.

The outcomes of the endeavours in Antonius IJsselmonde have not only been well documented and evaluated (Baar 1998), but also found their way into official policy concerning the role of the nursing home in palliative terminal care within the Dutch Association for Nursing Home Care (Arcares). This policy states that nursing homes are not only capable of rendering adequate terminal care to their own residents, but also well equipped to render their services to patients who for some reason do not want to die at home or who can no longer stay in hospital. Today more than 25 nursing homes have built special provision in the form of separate units with single bedrooms where patients can stay comfortably over a short period of time. In a physical sense it is important that this environment is well adapted to the needs of the patient and family in the last phase of life. These palliative services to the terminally ill may be offered in close cooperation with 'high' and 'medium' care hospices in the area. This form of cooperation is now considered one of the main tasks of the nursing home. It has led to a broadening of the task of the nursing home. Together with other organizations in the area, the nursing home is also responsible for organizing an adequate continuum of care (*ketenzorg*), mentioned above. Consequently the following tasks are allotted to the nursing home:

- Consulting with home care organizations and homes for the elderly, together with pain teams and representatives of other, similar, kinds of transmural initiatives.
- Consulting with and supporting physicians, nurses and other disciplines occupied in home care. These services may also be extended to those working in the local hospital.
- Organizing regional mobile palliative teams together with local hospitals, other palliative units and hospices.
- Providing nursing home professionals for the terminal care of patients in the hospital.
- Serving as a back-up system for homes for the elderly and home care organizations.

With regard to initiating improvements and coordinating developments in the field of palliative care in The Netherlands, nursing homes hold a key position on the basis of their knowledge of and experience with the care of terminally ill patients. For example, together with other parties, nursing homes can help to develop policy for the region they serve, or they may offer other parties an exchange of expertise. In so doing, nursing homes contribute to advances in the education of caregivers in the area.

Remodelling nursing home care

In remodelling the concept of nursing home care 'we' learnt from experience the importance of close cooperation with caregivers who refer their terminally ill patients to our institution. Equally important is the ability of the family and others to have the opportunity to visit the nursing home and see the ward where the family member will come to die. Upon arrival the attending nursing home physician together with the nurse in charge extends a warm welcome to the patient and family. This personal approach works miracles. It is our experience that the question 'How are you doing today?' elicits answers which are too much attached to the medical and nursing model. We now rephrase the question as 'Can you tell me a little bit about yourself?' and find that a question of this sort provides more possibilities for the initiation of good communication between the parties. This sort of question enables patients to tell their own stories. It provides caregivers with information about the experiences patients have before being admitted to the nursing home, and also helps patients to reflect on and perhaps evaluate why it is they are here.

In nursing homes there is a strong drive among attending health care professionals to work in ways that are multidimensional, multi- and interdisciplinary and methodical. Today this 3M model is recognized as characteristic of Dutch nursing home care. The 3M model, which replaced the former CLSM model (chronic, long-term, systematic and methodical), has been developed over the years on the basis of experience with the care of chronically ill and dying patients. In Antonius IJsselmonde we have broken the model down to form a checklist for the caregivers, helping to identify the specific needs and the possible problems that may arise in the care of a particular patient. In its abbreviated form, we call this checklist SCAMMSPSLL. Each letter reminds the caregiver to check or attend to a specific aspect of care: Somatic, Communication, Activities belonging to every day routines, Mobility, Means and specific measures to be taken, Status and social context, Psyche, Spiritual and religious needs, past Life-events and biography and everyday Life. Most nursing home physicians would use this checklist to help them to assess the needs of the patient.

On the basis of this checklist and what it reveals, the care team sits down to draft a plan of care for the particular patient. The care plan contains information about the main diagnosis and underlying secondary diagnoses. It will list the measures to be taken with regard to the well-being of the patient, ensuring the stay is as comfortable as possible. If the situation demands an alteration to the care plan, the team will come together to discuss whatever action is required and the care plan will be changed accordingly.

Soon after the patient has been admitted to the nursing home, details will be circulated as to what is expected of the staff and the personnel in the event that the condition of the patient (suddenly) deteriorates. The issue of whether or not to prolong the patient's life is discussed openly at a very early stage. We have found that this is always much appreciated by the patient and family. Patients have always shown that they can cope with the 'truth'; often they have already discussed this issue with the family before actually arriving at the nursing home. Most patients seek rest and relief from symptoms, and do not want to prolong life if this implies more suffering. The information is gathered and collated in the care plan in the clearest of terms in order to avoid any misunderstanding among those involved in the care of the patient. The attending physician only needs to check the care plan to know what is expected if the condition of the patient suddenly deteriorates. The care plan of the terminally ill patient is discussed and evaluated on a weekly basis.

In the units for (short-term) terminally ill patients specific measures must be available to relieve pain and suffering. The personnel will require additional training to make the parenteral relief of symptoms possible. The application of intravenous infusions, of subcutaneous lines for the administration of (a combination of) drugs, of catheters, the care of complex wounds or injuries or care for paralysed patients occur repeatedly within these kinds of units. Owing to extensive educational programmes, physicians and nurses on these wards are much more alert to these situations and can handle them accordingly. The situation is assessed on a day-to-day basis. Together with the attending nursing home physician the nurses will make the appropriate choices regarding the daily care of these patients. If the dosage of medicine is increased, or if breakthrough pain or dyspnoea require treatment, these needs are carefully reported in the care plan. Following this procedure promotes the relief and comfort of the patient, the family and other colleagues involved in the care.

Reassessing the process of decision-making in nursing home care

In the early years of nursing homes, respect for the autonomy of the patients was paramount. If it was possible, patients were expected to decide for themselves what it was that caregivers should do in the case of calamities. However, it has been our experience that the capacity of nursing home patients to assert their autonomy is overestimated. In addition, over-emphasizing the autonomy of the patient can create difficult situations for the patient and caregivers. These patients are often very vulnerable. Before they are admitted to the nursing home, they have often died multiple 'deaths' owing to too many medical interventions elsewhere. As a result these patients no longer have the strength to voice their desires and requirements. Often their will has to be reconstructed before a decision concerning their care can be made.

As a consequence we are more inclined to integrate the insights of what we call the *ethics of care*. The concept focuses on the way the patient and the caregiver interact and relate to each other. It focuses on process issues. The care plan can only be made on the basis of an open relationship and mutual understanding, on the basis of respect for the increasing dependency of the patient, their wishes and requirements, as well as those of family and others involved. Members of the interdisciplinary team talk to the patient, discussing and explaining the benefits of various treatment options. In the course of this conversation it must become clear which treatment fits the patient's requirements and desires most adequately. An important part of the deliberations is to incorporate significant moments in the biography of that patient into the plan of care. This helps caregivers to decide the most appropriate course of action to take while attending to the care of the patient during the last phase of life. Special attention to life events, emotions and the need for intimacy and spirituality is an essential element of the care rendered to each person. We find that the caregivers themselves and the nursing home as a whole benefit from this model (Widdershoven 2000), contributing to and changing the culture of care within the organization.

Towards a new culture of care in nursing homes

To achieve what has been described here, a specific culture of care needs to be developed. This is not only to the advantage of terminally ill people and their relatives, but is also important for the other patients residing in the nursing home. Such institutions form small communities where people may stay and live over a shorter or a longer period of time. Here they will receive treatment and special care and support from caregivers who also spend an important part of their professional lives within these communities. These professionals not only look after the residents as best they can, they are also engaged in research, in setting up educational programmes and in developing new forms of care.

The general atmosphere in the nursing home should be one where everyone feels welcome. The information about the services rendered should be transparent and easily accessible. All the personnel should be open and friendly. The building itself should be a pleasant and colourful facility to be in and to walk around, nicely decorated with art and attractive furniture. Plants and flower arrangements, music, even pets, should be part of the atmosphere too. It is good policy to allow people to bring some of their own furniture and whatever 'little things' are dear to them. The home should breathe an atmosphere of hospitality where relatives, friends and neighbours are welcome at any time of the day. The underlying reason motivating people to come to the nursing home is often that they themselves do not see any alternative. Consequently it is important that everything should be done to make their stay as pleasant and as meaningful as possible, creating a safe and caring environment. A gentle and loving environment creates opportunities for the individual and family to explore personal history and review life experience. The underlying philosophy is that each individual is a unique person and deserves our respect and undivided attention (van den Berg 2000).

In Antonius IJsselmonde we have become aware that caregivers should not only approach the patient on the basis of their professional knowledge, but also be prepared to speak to that patient from a different perspective. Part of the learning process for health care professionals is that they render a care that is multidimensional in character. This is related to the fact that the focus of their care is not on what they think or what they have to offer on the basis of their specific knowledge and experience alone, but on what the patient really asks of them. It is concerned not with 'our' offer, but with the needs of patients and families, and these should be the focus of our professional response. Consequently chaplains may be engaged in the medical needs of the patient, while the physician may relate in a spiritual way where the patient is engaged in a search for making sense out of suffering (van den Berg 2001). Of course, each discipline is called upon to make its own professional contribution, but caregivers should also acknowledge that they do not always hold the key to the problem. The main characteristic of this kind of care is that it is interdisciplinary and complementary in nature: complementary to the needs of patients and the family; complementary to what the other disciplines on the care team have to offer.

The role of the nursing home physician

Over time the role of the nursing home physician in The Netherlands has changed dramatically. In the late 1960s the doctor was a family physician with an interest in the care of the elderly, and was neither professionalized nor specialized in this area. Nevertheless, the position of the physician ranked highest among caregivers, and the physician took the key decisions about care and treatment. Among the staff there were not many disciplines with comparable academic qualifications to balance the influence of the physician. In the process, nursing home physicians developed their own specific knowledge and skills. They became experts in their field as they focused more and more on the functional consequences of the diseases with which they were confronted. Perhaps more than in other areas of medical expertise, they consulted other disciplines, seeking interdisciplinary co-operation. On the basis of these endeavours a so-called functional geriatrics (Hertogh 1999) developed as a new specialism. In addition, new moral quandaries were recognized as specific to the care of elderly people (Aghina 1994).

These developments have resulted in the provision of an academic educa-tion for nursing home physicians which is now available at several univer-sities in The Netherlands. In the curriculum all aspects of nursing home care are highlighted. Much attention, for example, is given to good symp-tom control, to how the suffering of the patient affects relations with kin, how suffering affects communication with caregivers and other patients, how suffering affects moral reflection and even the organization of the care as a whole. Although nursing home physicians carry final responsibility for the care plan as such, the specific nature of nursing home care today has affected the traditional medical model: nursing home physicians function less hierarchically. The nursing home physician relates to the patient and relatives on the basis of mutual understanding and respect, and cooperates closely and equally with other disciplines in establishing the care that is needed.

The nursing home physician coordinates the care and can best be com-pared with a master of ceremonies watching over a complex process of a wide range of different care-related activities. This involves supporting the patient and identifying the problems that may lay ahead, providing possible solutions as to how to cope with them. Nursing home physicians can draw on personal expertise but will also make use, from a medical perspective, of the insights and the talents of the patient and relatives, as well as the opinions and feelings of the other caregivers involved in the case. The medical knowledge of the physician in itself is not decisive in the process. At the end of the life of a patient the physician has the privilege to be a sojourner for a short while, listening carefully to whatever the patient wants to share and remaining sensitive to specific needs and wishes. The physician must help the patient to cope with suffering, giving support to the patient in efforts to come to terms with life and death. The physician must seek ways in which the patient and relatives can be best supported.

Palliative care helps physicians to discover their talents and their personal shortcomings. Specific knowledge is required to recognize symptoms and other related problems, and skill is required in communicating and organizing the care that is needed under these specific circumstances, where it is essential to understand how to support the patient and family when important decisions need to be made. In these circumstances, physicians need to pay attention to their own vulnerabilities.

Along with the coordinating nurse in charge, the nursing home physician forms the core team in the care of the patient. Together they determine which other disciplines are needed to optimize the patient's care. For this to occur, physicians must realize the need to be team players. By developing a number of protocols, Dutch nursing home physicians have, over time, made a considerable contribution to the improvement in the quality of palliative terminal care. For example, they have developed a protocol aimed at improving the treatment of pain and other related symptoms, as well as protocols to help decision-making in cases of emergency, such as cardiac arrest and non-resuscitation orders. In this context a particular protocol is worth mentioning: *complex situations of care – suggestions for management and for professionals, based on experience with coma cases* (Aghina 1994). The protocol is based on the experience of coping with problems that arise in the care of comatose patients and their relatives, and highlights the need for and the importance of paying attention to all aspects of palliative care, including good communication with patients, relatives and the care team. Attention is also given to the ethical aspects of coping with patients in difficult and complicated situations.

Research, education and training

The knowledge and skills required in palliative terminal care are disseminated in special courses for nursing home physicians. In close cooperation with the Integral Cancer Centre in Rotterdam (IKR), Antonius IJsselmonde has developed an introductory as well as an advanced course in palliative care. The programme is aimed at nursing home physicians and nurses specialized in palliative terminal care. Started in 1995, it continues to attract many health care professionals from all over the country.

With regard to the wider promotion of palliative care, the Dutch government decided in 1997 to establish six academic Centres for the Development of Palliative Care. These centres cooperate with other specialized palliative terminal care services. Extensive research programmes have now been set up. One of the main issues addressed concerns the question: why is it that some patients die at home whereas others are unable to do so? Another aspect under investigation is: what kind of organization is required to develop specialized palliative care units and what are the effects of such units on the culture of those organizations as a whole?

In 1995 a quality protocol for the care of acute terminally ill patients was developed. This was done in conjunction with other nursing homes and with the help of the National Institute for Hospitals and Nursing Homes. A protocol for terminal care in nursing homes has now been added to this. It contains directions not only for the palliative terminal care of the 'mainstream' residents, but also for the care of terminal patients admitted to specialized wards/units and for the care which can be given by mobile palliative care teams.

Task for management: care for the caregivers

Palliative care for terminally ill people involves the organization as a whole. In this respect those on the board, together with those in the office of the institution, carry a great responsibility. Little is known about the ways in which the culture of an organization should be managed and administered in order to realize the rather ambitious goals we have described here. Transparent and coherent institutional policies, well defined professional responsibilities and reporting lines and social cohesion among the personnel are, in themselves, not enough. We have mentioned the ethics of care. Research is being done on how health care institutions can sensitize ethical awareness and moral responsibilities. This requires the nursing home management to reassess its own role. Different behaviour from that of the traditional managerial patrons will be expected from the board and the directors of such health care institutions. The management group will need to be aware that they too serve as role models for the organization as a whole. Palliative care demands team players, and consequently the administrative officers and other members of the management will have to become less hierarchical; in fact they will have to become team players themselves. Palliative care implies that managers will need to be of an open mind; they will become coaches, also attending to the emotional side of whatever care is given. Creating sufficient funds and providing for additional training programmes and other forms of support for the personnel is a prime responsibility for the management too.

In Antonius IJsselmonde we have developed a programme called 'Care for the caregivers'. We have learnt from experience that only by taking good care of themselves can health care professionals provide good care for others. The training and continuous care of the caregivers is part of the responsibility and the skill of the nursing home management. The management must create 'time' for the teams to evaluate the way they operate and how members relate to each other in the care process, professionally as well as personally. The responsibility of the management is twofold: first, to see to it that the team has protocols at its disposal on the basis of which the care team can adequately evaluate the quality of the care it is providing; second, it is important for the management to ensure that there is sufficient time for members of the care team to reflect on each other's contribution to the care of a particular patient, in a more personal way. 'Time' has to be made available to consider and discuss questions like: what, at the end, has been the focus of our endeavours or have our minds and hearts been preoccupied with other matters? Are we still motivated by what we consider to be our primary task as caregivers? And do we continue to have in mind the common good of the other person?

In addition we must realize that individual team members are regularly confronted with their own grief and feelings of inadequacy. This challenges them with thoughts of their own vulnerability and, ultimately, the awareness of their own mortality. Sharing these feelings in the care team in a systematic manner is meaningful and can provide individual team members with the personal support necessary to continue their work.

The managers of the nursing home should be prepared to lead the way and act as role models. They should be prepared to question whether they understand the difficulties their employees face on a day-to-day basis and what it means for them to be properly motivated to do this work. We have learned from experience that close cooperation among the different nursing home disciplines enhances the whole of the care offered by these institutions. Cooperation results in efficient and effective care plans, in protocols, in educational programmes. It upgrades the skills of workers, the insights of the disciplines are raised to a higher level and it creates better medical provision. From a wider perspective it contributes ultimately to a better system of health care and to a better society (van der Kloot Meijburg 2000).

Conclusion

Compared with other Western countries the number of people dying in health care institutions in The Netherlands is rather low. Yet data on people dying in hospitals show that, given the opportunity, more would prefer to die at home, in specialized units for palliative care for the terminally ill in nursing homes or in specialized hospices (Francke and Willems 2000).

In The Netherlands units for palliative care in nursing homes and in homes for the elderly could be considered the Dutch counterpart of the hospices in Anglo-Saxon countries. On the basis of their experience with the palliative care of patients with chronic diseases, Dutch nursing homes offer all the skills needed for palliative care of terminal patients. In this respect much has changed since the first nursing homes were built. New insights into the care of the chronically ill and the care of those in the last phase of life have not only altered the way we now build these facilities, but have also initiated new kinds of educational programmes to support health care professionals and other caregivers. Nursing homes have become quite distinctive in their aproach. Having found its own identity, the management is responsible for developing a culture of care within these institutions that not only reflects the needs and wishes of the patients but also supports those who care for them – nurses, chaplains, physiotherapists, psychologists, bereavement counsellors, volunteers, physicians. Programmes like 'care for the caregivers' have now been introduced everywhere in the country. Over a period of 30 years, medical care in nursing homes has developed into a new specialism with characteristics of its own, reaching beyond pain treatment, and focusing on many other needs of the patient, including the spiritual.

Palliative care for the terminally ill is now high on the political agenda in The Netherlands and the Dutch government has launched a new programme to enhance the quality of palliative terminal care. Nursing homes, with all their experience in the palliative care of patients with non-malignant diseases, now fulfil an important complementary role to care given in hospitals as well as to the care which is provided by home-care organizations.

For patients who cannot die at home and who do not wish to die in hospital, nursing homes and homes for the elderly offer a serious alternative. More specialized units in nursing homes for the palliative care of terminally ill patients are being established across The Netherlands. Likewise, the exchange of insights and experiences from other countries elsewhere has had a great impact. The results of research and educational programmes, developed in conjunction with universities and several other institutions, are now leading to substantial improvement in the quality of palliative care in The Netherlands, and work in nursing homes has a substantial part to play with this (Baar 1999).

Implications for practice

- Experience in The Netherlands shows that nursing homes can develop their own high-quality culture of care.
- In order to do this a strong sense of team working must be developed, including all staff, whether involved clinically or not.
- Caring for caregivers should be an important aspect of the nursing home culture.
- The specialization of physicians in nursing home medicine is a particular feature of the Dutch system and merits close attention elsewhere.

References

Aghina, M. J. (1994) *Complex Situations of Care: Suggestions for Management and for Professionals, Based on Experience with Coma Cases* (in Dutch). Utrecht: Dutch Association of Nursing Home Care.

Baar, F. P. M. (1998) *Lessen van levenden. Twintig jaar palliatieve en terminale zorg in Antonius IJsselmonde*. Rotterdam: KVV.

Baar, F. P. M. (1999) Palliative care for the terminally ill in the Netherlands: the unique role of the nursing homes. *European Journal of Palliative Care*, 6(5): 169–72.

Francke, A. L. and Willems, D. L. (2000) *Palliative Care, Today and Tomorrow: Facts, Opinions and Scenarios* (in Dutch). Amsterdam: Elsevier.

Hertogh, C. M. P. M. (1999) *Functional Geriatrics: Problem-oriented Care for the Chronically Ill Elderly* (in Dutch). Maarssen: Elsevier/de Tijdstroom.

van den Berg, M. (2000) *Betrokken zorg. Verhalen over spiritualiteit en geloof in de zorg*. Intro: Baarn.

van den Berg, M. (2001) Rondetafelgwesprek over spiritualiteit. Sta er voor open, anders komt het er niet van. *Pallium*, 3(4): 15–19.

van der Kloot Meijburg, H. H. (2000) The lessons we learn: palliative care in the Netherlands. *Illness, Crisis and Loss*, 8(2): 109–19.

Widdershoven, G. (2000) *Ethics in the Clinic, Modern Approach in the Clinic* (in Dutch). Amsterdam: Boom.

World Health Organization (1990) *Cancer Pain Relief and Palliative Care*. Technical Report Series No. 804. Geneva: World Health Organization.

7 | Ethics and end-of-life decision-making

☐ JO VALLIS AND KENNETH BOYD

The ethics of end-of-life decision-making in nursing homes is a subject of intense social concern. This chapter clarifies some traditional and more recent ethical principles as they relate to nursing home settings. It also discusses the scope for respect for autonomy and the role of 'protective responsibility' with particular reference to advance directives. The need for 'candour' in relation to treatment and medico-legal issues is also explored, highlighting the importance of staff knowing residents' wishes and defending their best interests in relation to various treatment options. Finally, issues of justice, relating to the finite financial and human resources available for nursing home care, are examined. Throughout the chapter, the potential for extending traditional ethical frameworks, to encompass new, more applicable principles for this changing care sector, is explored and illustrated with reference to some recent empirical research in Scottish nursing homes (see Box 7.1 for an outline of the study).

Ethical principles

Ethics has always been part of health care, but the modern discipline of medical ethics or bioethics, originating in the 1960s (Holm 1997), provides some helpful new ways of analysing medico-moral issues. Among the best known is the deontological approach based on the four *prima facie* ethical principles of respect for autonomy, beneficence, non-maleficence and justice (Gillon 1994; Kuczewski 1999); see Table 7.1.

This approach is called *deontological* (from the Greek word for 'duty') because each principle encapsulates a duty which health professionals ought to fulfil, and thus patients have a right to expect from them. The four

Box 7.1   Summary of the Scottish study

Title	*End-of-life decision-making: the thinking and practices of doctors and nurses*
Project	A qualitative study using interviews to explore doctors' and nurses' views on end-of-life decision-making for frail, elderly patients.
Participants	Primary, secondary and independent sector staff.
Location	Three contrasting (urban, rural and mixed) Scottish health board areas.
Dates	February 1998 to July 2000.
Funding	The Chief Scientist Office.
Aims	There were four main aims:

- To explore doctors' and nurses' thinking and practices surrounding ethical decision-making for elderly patients in hospital geriatric units and nursing homes.
- To do this with special reference to ethical reasoning and perceived dilemmas surrounding withholding and withdrawing life-prolonging treatments.
- To identify practices which facilitate appropriate decision-making, including in nursing homes.
- To contribute to the generation of effective guidance, particularly for nursing home staff and general practitioners.

Design	Two hundred and twenty-one (20 pilot) semi-structure, tape-recorded interviews were conducted. Interviews covered the thinking and practice behind end-of-life decision-making. Analysis, using the framework designed for the research, entailed numerical coding in SPSS, supplemented by selective transcribing of emergent contextual themes.
Outcomes	Outcomes were in four main areas:

- Quality of life and 'a good death' were the basis of participants' implicit ethical reasoning/decision-making.
- Families' wishes were seen as important but not decisive. Fear of litigation and complaints, especially from families with unrealistic expectations may influence decision-making.
- Most participants distinguished between palliative use of opiates and euthanasia. They favoured palliative approaches, including improved education and resources, to changes in the law on euthanasia. However, they were sceptical about prescriptive terminal care guidelines.
- Although personal experience was seen as contributing to professional insight and empathy, professional education was seen as inadequate preparation for end-of-life decision-making.

Table 7.1 The four principles of health care ethics

Name of principle	Duty
Respect for autonomy	To respect the patient's considered wishes
Beneficence	To act in the patient's best interests
Non-maleficence	To do no harm
Justice	To treat all patients (and others) fairly

principles are called *prima facie* (literally 'at first sight') because each refers to a duty which ought always to be obeyed, except when it is in conflict with another equally binding duty. When there is conflict between the principles, according to this approach, there is no pre-arranged way of deciding between them. Instead, those confronting the conflict must take all the circumstances into account, and come to a considered view of which duty is the most important in the particular case under review.

Although, in principle, no one of these duties has priority over the others, in health care practice priority has traditionally been given to non-maleficence and beneficence. Non-maleficence, *primum non nocere*, is one of the oldest medical duties, dating back to Hippocrates, while beneficence, acting in the patient's best interests, is the basis of medical paternalism. Today, by contrast, respect for autonomy and justice are often uppermost. In the current 'user-driven' health care climate, 'respect for patients' autonomy has become, perhaps the premier principle in medical ethics' (Kuczewski 1999: 17). But, since this involves respecting the autonomy as well as promoting the interests of *all* patients, questions of justice have also become pressing.

In long-term care settings today, the relevance of all four principles is clearly evident. With respect for autonomy: how can and should elderly nursing home residents and/or their families be involved in end-of-life decision-making (Teno *et al.* 1997; Tsevat *et al.* 1998)? In keeping with beneficence and non-maleficence: what are the most appropriate ways of promoting the best interests of vulnerable residents, especially those who are incompetent or otherwise unable to decide for themselves? And in what ways can and should vulnerable residents be protected from harm? In arguing for justice: what social arrangements are needed to ensure the fair distribution of health care resources in relation to nursing home residents (Hamel *et al.* 1996; Massie 1999; Sutherland 1999)?

While it is clearly relevant to health care and often useful for analysing ethical issues, the four principles approach has been criticized, particularly for being overly simplistic, too medically orientated and culturally and gender specific (Gilligan 1982; Holm 1997). The principles are nevertheless often found helpful by doctors in acute health care settings (Holm 1997), where discussion tends to focus on curative interventions and dilemmas. Nursing homes, by contrast, may lend themselves more to an 'ethic of care' approach (Gilligan 1982). Staffed largely by women, these homes emphasize nursing 'care' rather than medical 'cure' (Nolan *et al.* 2001), and this can have implications for applying the four principles. For example, with rising dependency levels in nursing homes (Shemmings 1996), patient involvement in end-of-life decision-making may be limited, with implications for autonomy. At the same time there may be greater emphasis on beneficence, especially where residents are unable to make their own decisions (Gray 1994). However well intentioned, beneficence can become unduly paternalistic if, as a result of assessing older people with dementia, or simply frail and old people as 'incompetent', others override their wishes and fail to balance residents' needs for protection with respect for their autonomy (Gray 1994).

A further criticism of the four principles approach is that, having originated in North America, where the social drive for individuality and autonomy is more established, it may be less applicable in Europe (Holm 1997), particularly concerning current nursing home populations. The four principles remain very general and have been described as 'not going far enough' to address the subtleties of contemporary nursing home care (Norberg 1994; Kuczewski 1999). In contemporary health care, moreover, new emphases, such as that on 'person-centred care', are unfolding (Nolan *et al.* 2001). These are likely to raise new ethical issues, and frameworks such as that of the four principles may need to be extended to encompass them (Kuczewski 1999).

One way of doing this, relevant to nursing home settings, is by employing three additional ethical principles. The first, identified by Holm (1997), is the concept of protective responsibility. The other two have been identified by Kuczewski (1999): the principle of candour and the principle of narrative integrity (see Table 7.2).

These three principles clearly have affinities with respect for autonomy, beneficence and non-maleficence, and more generally with justice. But they also have the advantage of being more specific than the four traditional principles. Together, these additional concepts may help to extend the bioethical framework, rendering it more applicable to nursing and care home contexts.

Table 7.2 Additional ethical principles

Name of principle	Meaning of principle
Protective responsibility	Professional responsibility to protect vulnerable patients from harm
Responsibility for narrative integrity	Knowing residents well and defending their best interests
Candour	Being completely open and truthful with residents

Before we explore these additional ethical principles in the light of end-of-life decision-making in nursing homes, a final general point should be made about the language of ethics. The traditional biomedical and philosophical language of ethical difficulties and dilemmas may itself be problematic (Higgs and Jones 1995). There is little consensus about the meaning of these terms, and perceptions of dilemmas vary according to levels of expertise (Benner 1984). For example, whereas experts may recognize dilemmas and know how to handle them, novices may simply be unaware of them (Benner 1984). These factors raise methodological issues for research. Questions asked, including the precise language used, determine the responses obtained (Milburn *et al.* 1994; Lofland and Lofland 1995). When participants in a Scottish study (see Box 7.1) were asked about the ethical difficulties, dilemmas and decisions they faced, this initially produced little response. However, approaching the question in terms of 'challenges' faced with the issue of end-of-life decision-making produced a flood of responses. Although this could partly reflect the limited decision-making status of nursing home staff, it may also suggest limits to the meaning of traditional bioethical language for these participants.

Additional ethical principles in relation to nursing homes and end-of-life decision-making

Autonomy and protective responsibility

In an age when autonomy is highly valued, many people also have unprecedented expectations of health care. Such people, who are often well informed, want involvement in medical decision-making and can resent professional dominance. This growing consumer sentiment appears to be spreading from the private health care fields of North America. In Britain, it is encapsulated in the *Patient's Charter* and recent government endorsement suggests that it is here to stay (Scottish Executive 2001). The public demand for greater autonomy also extends to matters of death and dying. Increasingly, people perceive a right to 'a good death'. For Emanuel and Emanuel (1998) this means 'making the last weeks . . . of life valuable and meaningful'. Failure to meet expectations can have profound implications, not only for the dying person but for the family's adjustment to bereavement. If professionals, in private nursing/care homes as elsewhere, get things wrong, there is potential for litigation. This trend too seems to have originated in North America, where patient involvement in end-of-life decision-making is formalized in the Patient Self Determination Act (PSDA) (Teno *et al.* 1997; O'Rourke 2001). Introduced in 1991, this legislation makes documentation of patients' end-of-life wishes mandatory. Its main provisions are that, by law, health care facilities must:

- give incoming patients a statement of rights regarding health care decisions;
- discuss and document the existence of advance directives with patients;
- explain their own policies regarding advance directives, including their acceptable limits;
- fulfil their legal obligations to staff education and training (O'Rourke 2001: 1).

Advance directives are statements (usually written) of clients' wishes about their treatment and care, particularly towards the end of their lives. Although better known in the USA, they are becoming more common in Britain. Most of the health professionals participating in the Scottish study mentioned above had at least heard of them. Most were in favour, particularly for themselves personally. However, they had mixed views and perceived potential drawbacks to their use with nursing home residents. Among the drawbacks perceived were:

- legal and practical difficulties in drawing up advance directives related to residents' mental capacity;
- the possibility of residents subsequently changing their minds or of their condition improving;
- the potential for advance directives being ignored on the one hand or abused on the other.

These perceptions of advance directives echo wider views (e.g. Teno *et al.* 1997; Bogle 1999; Craig 1999a; Doherty 1999; O'Rourke 2001). Participants in the Scottish study were generally sceptical about the ultimate efficacy of living wills for frail elderly people. This may be a generational divide. The concept of exercising autonomy over end-of-life care and treatment is probably more familiar to and favoured by the younger, post-Second World War generation and is associated with a rising demand for control over death. For many very elderly people in nursing and care homes, by contrast, such notions may remain relatively alien.

Given the rising numbers of very elderly people in long-term care, the question of living wills raises pressing ethical questions. How are carers to know their wishes if residents cannot tell them? Should residents even be expected to contribute in this way? Meisel *et al.* (2000) suggest not, and question the ultimate value of eliciting their wishes. Yet that leaves this very elderly population potentially vulnerable to wrong decisions. Traditionally isolated from the outside world, care home residents lack autonomy. Or at least, as Callopy suggests, their autonomy is of *negative* quality (Callopy 1988; see also Chapter 3). Certainly, some forward-looking care homes have residents' forums; but these are quite rare and in most cases residents (competent or otherwise) lack the ability to make themselves heard and/or effect any real change. Some, moreover, prefer to leave treatment decisions to the 'experts'. Typically, the older generation has more direct faith in doctors (Jepson *et al.* 1991).

In practice, responsibility for protecting nursing home residents' end-of-life wishes more often than not falls to the family. In Scotland, carers' (including families') protective roles have received official recognition through the Adults with Incapacity Act (Scottish Executive 1999). This legislation aims to empower carers by making them formal 'public guardians' of vulnerable older people. In nursing/care homes, family involvement is seen as integral to holistic terminal care delivery (Shemmings 1996; Bradley *et al.* 1998; Scottish Executive 1999; Brown *et al.* 2001; General Medical Council 2001; Nolan *et al.* 2001). Staff and families often develop close working relationships and there is scope for genuine partnership. However, many families are scattered and some residents have no family at all visiting. For those that do, relationships between families and staff can be uneasy. Within the charged atmosphere of terminal care, families are understandably distressed. It is often their first experience of death. They can be frightened, angry, frustrated and grief-stricken. This can be particularly challenging for staff and is a potential recipe for blame. In the Scottish study, families' unrealistic expectations were a recurrent theme. Thus a typical comment was: 'Some family members think miracles can happen. Some are not realistic at all' (Enrolled nurse, NHS continuing care).

But is it appropriate that families are always seen as those entitled to speak on behalf of their elderly relatives? Their stronger voices can, potentially, drown residents' true wishes. And how can professionals be sure of family motives? What is to stop them from advocating courses of action, such as withdrawal of treatment, largely for personal (financial) gain? Health professionals and government are well aware of the potential for such abuses. The *Adults with Incapacity Act* has built-in safeguards, such as good record keeping being a prerequisite to guardianship, with care standards being closely monitored. Legal sanctions will be imposed as necessary.

Clearly, then, there are major ethical issues at stake. O'Rourke (2001: 2) sums these up in the American context: 'Potentially the most serious ethical issue resulting from the PSDA is the implied assumption that physicians are simply to carry out the wishes of the proxy or attorney-in-fact.' Problems may arise here as a consequence of mismatches between proxies' and residents' views and wishes. Tsevat *et al.* (1998) suggest that proxies tend to underestimate the zeal which older people have for life. They wrongly assume that elderly residents are willing to trade remaining life years for better health and to forgo curative interventions such as CPR. The authors conclude that 'because proxies . . . cannot gauge health values of elderly hospitalized patients accurately, health values of the very old should be elicited directly from the patient' (Tsevat *et al.* 1998: 371).

What if residents simply cannot contribute in this way? Health professionals clearly have a duty to protect them (GMC 2001). This often entails balancing their interests against those of the family. Participants in the Scottish study echoed recent British Medical Association (BMA) and General Medical Council (GMC) guidance when they said that, although families play a central role, the ultimate responsibility for treatment decisions rests with the 'treating team' (BMA 1999a; GMC 2001). That is, doctors have the ultimate *executional autonomy* to act on the decisions made (Callopy 1988). Is this protecting the wishes of elderly people or simply patronizing them? Holm's (1997) concept of 'protective responsibility', defined as a specific responsibility to protect, was derived from interviews with 40 doctors and nine nurses and is particularly pertinent to nursing home settings.

Holm (1997) shows that health professionals take their protective responsibilities very seriously, often assuming considerable responsibility for protecting their patients from harm. Spanning several ethical approaches, 'protective responsibility' sits most comfortably with 'virtue ethics', in which it is the player's (or agent's) disposition towards a particular action that matters (such as withdrawing curative interventions). A virtuous disposition spells ethical action. Protective responsibility is also grounded in the concepts of 'relationship' and 'paternalism'. Essentially, it is getting the right balance of closeness and distance within the therapeutic relationship. Too much can interfere with professional objectivity and judgement, whereas too little appears cold.

Protective responsibility is appropriate in relation to treatment decisions, including patient and family involvement in such decisions. Whereas professionals generally want to include patients in decision-making, they may, on occasions, feel compelled to override their wishes in order to protect them from inadvertent harm. For example, given British law, no wise nurse or doctor would comply with a nursing home resident's request for euthanasia. Similarly, whereas nursing home staff may value family involvement, they will not always comply with demands for curative interventions. Although doctors are ultimately responsible for treatment decisions, they are often only sporadic visitors in nursing homes. As a result, nursing home staff have growing 'gatekeeping' roles in this respect. This is a big responsibility involving considerable power and is echoed in Webb's discussion of advocacy, which she defines as 'the professional having a role in acting or speaking on behalf of an individual patient or group because of their knowledge, power or influence' (Webb 2000: 71). As residents' advocates, care home staff must deploy such power wisely. Without adequate attention, advocacy can appear like paternalism, or, as in the case of nursing home staff, suffocating maternalism. There is again the danger of underestimating residents' ability to contribute to end-of-life decision-making. Some clearly do welcome involvement in this, even if just to request non-intervention. Participants in the Scottish study said that many of their elderly residents asked to be allowed to die peacefully: 'A lot of them don't want to live. "I've had my time" . . . you hear that often' (Staff nurse, nursing home).

However, such a viewpoint cannot simply be assumed. Other residents may want more proactive intervention. How can professionals discover what they want? One way is through getting to know the residents intimately. This includes learning about their unique life stories and defending their best interests on that basis. This is Kuczewski's concept of 'responsibility for narrative integrity'. It is more personal than advocacy. Such a concept enables nursing home staff to empower their residents without detracting from their autonomy. This is best achieved through communicating openly and honestly with residents and their families.

Candour

Candour with elderly people in nursing homes is a central issue. Few would disagree that the resident's views and wishes come first. The Scottish study participants were unanimous on this. However, as Shemmings (1996) explains, discussing matters of death and dying is easier said than done:

> On entering residential care there is a covert understanding that an elderly person will end their days there, and yet it is often not considered 'decent' to broach the subject of how they wish to be cared for when dying, and what services the Home offers.
>
> (Shemmings 1996: 32)

In the Scottish study, too, there was a contradiction. Despite prioritizing residents' needs and wishes, participants found broaching end-of-life issues particularly hard. At least a quarter of all interviewees said this explicitly. This was mainly because of the sensitivity surrounding the subject. A typical comment was: 'It's a horrible, horrible subject to tackle at any time . . . a very difficult subject to broach' (Sister, nursing home).

The timing of such discussion is crucial. There seems to be no ideal or easy time. However, most are agreed that it should not be at admission 'because of the tension, pain and depression experienced by many people when they are admitted to a nursing home, this is a poor time to make decisions concerning future health care' (O'Rourke 2001: 1). This is put starkly in the following quote from the Scottish study:

> You're meant to ask that [about funeral arrangements] on admission. But I dinnae. 'Welcome to this nursing home. What happens when you die? Do you want buried or cremated?' It's not a very nice question to ask somebody.
>
> (Enrolled nurse, nursing home)

Study participants felt that discussion of end-of-life issues was best tackled as it arose. Even then it was difficult and they preferred to avoid it if at all possible. Yet at the same time they claimed to accept death in elderly (as opposed to younger) people as natural and normal. Even in the USA, there is little evidence to suggest that the PSDA has resulted in any more direct staff–resident discussion about these matters (Bradley *et al.* 1998; Levin *et al.* 1999). In their study of 600 nursing home residents, Bradley *et al.* (1998) found that although documentation of discussion about future treatment wishes had increased since the PSDA, most residents (71.5 per cent) still had none. Does this imply that end-of-life decisions are being taken without full account of competent patients' wishes? This is particularly problematic, since the literature suggests that many competent elderly people welcome greater openness and honesty about these matters (Bradley *et al.* 1998; Tsevat *et al.* 1998).

What does the lack of candour really signify? Social 'taboos' about death and dying? Although health professionals may have more experience of death than the general public, they are part of society. As such, they are not necessarily uninfluenced by such taboos. Indeed, faced with death and dying on a daily basis, nursing home staff may be more prone to this. Yet is death really a taboo subject? We are surrounded with media images of it everywhere. Cancer deaths are common and many of the Scottish staff reported personal experience of bereavement and loss. Perhaps residents' mortality is just an uncomfortable reminder to the staff of their own mortality? Walter (1993) suggests that, whereas society is embracing the concept of death, individuals may not be. In this sense death continues to be a taboo subject.

In reality, it may be that many nursing/care home residents are simply too old and/or have advanced dementia to discuss death and dying. Such discussions are often impractical. Even so, there is a danger of assuming that people with dementia cannot communicate. Communicating with them is a specialist art. With expert guidance, it can be learned (see Chapter 5). However, it can be time consuming and, rightly or wrongly, it is often with families that discussions about residents' end-of-life wishes actually take place.

As with autonomy, then, questions of candour may often be more relevant to families than to the residents. But given families' distress, together with their heightened consumer expectations, there is ample room for misunderstanding. Even where nursing home residents are very elderly, families can deny their impending death. Whereas health professionals may favour palliative approaches, involving symptomatic rather than curative interventions, families can go on having high expectations of treatment. '*Enough's enough*' was the recurrent refrain among the staff participating in the Scottish study. But failure to treat a frail, elderly nursing home resident can result in public suspicion of professional motives. Withholding or even withdrawing curative treatments can be construed as ageism and/or hastening death by omission. In this context, knowing residents well and defending their best interests, including treatment decisions, is vital. Kuczewski's (1999) concept of 'responsibility for narrative integrity' is now discussed in relation to various treatment options; for example, the giving of antibiotic therapy, artificial nutrition and hydration, 'flu vaccinations and transfer to hospital for curative investigations and interventions.

Narrative integrity

Responsibility for narrative integrity is more personal than advocacy. It involves staff knowing their residents intimately, including their unique life stories. Such a concept enables nursing/care home staff to empower their residents without detracting from their autonomy. Narrative integrity is relevant to Singer *et al.*'s (1999) qualitative study of end-of-life care of frail elderly residents in nursing/care homes. It reiterates five themes that appear to be important to elderly residents, namely: good pain and symptom control; the strengthening of relationships; not being a burden; having control; and not prolonging life. This last issue is particularly important in nursing homes, where prescribing antibiotics near the end of life is commonplace. Weak and dying residents are prone to infection. Few GPs would quibble about prescribing antibiotics for them, despite questions of cost, efficacy and resistance (Bradley 1999). Antibiotics are minimally invasive, and they can, at the very least, help to relieve pain and discomfort. However, they may also alleviate the carers' (nurses' and families') sense of helplessness. 'Something is being done' when an antibiotic is prescribed. But is it right to treat dying people largely for the sake of the carer or family? Is this really in the best interests of an elderly, frail person? Much probably depends on specific residents and their individual circumstances.

These questions are particularly acute in relation to more invasive procedures, such as artificial fluids and feeding. Artificial (intravenous and/or subcutaneous) fluids are relatively uncommon in nursing homes. This is changing, however, especially with the expansion in registration categories to include more acute care sectors. Subcutaneous fluids are easy for nurses to administer and supervise. They did so routinely in at least one of the nursing homes involved in the Scottish study. Opinions about the pros and cons of artificial fluids vary. They may actually compound discomfort, and keeping the mouth moist – for example, by means of artificial saliva – may be more beneficial (NCHSPCS 1999). It is difficult to be certain about this in all cases, however; and whereas staff and families may come to accept withdrawal of feeding, they often feel uncomfortable in stopping artificial fluids (Craig 1999b).

Decisions to insert percutaneous endoscopic gastrostomy (PEG) feeding tubes are rare in nursing homes, though much more common in the care of elderly people in acute hospitals. When they are used, they tend to stand out as dramatic and can be the source of considerable staff and family tension. For example, staff in one Scottish nursing home described the case of a youngish woman with motor neurone disease:

We had terrible, terrible dilemmas working through that lady's family on that topic [PEG tube insertion]. The lady herself was very bitter but had lost her ability to voice what she wanted to say – that was a very big dilemma. It took a long time.

(General manager, nursing home)

This is less likely to affect 'the oldest old' and the dying (Nolan *et al.* 2001). More commonly, residents arrive with PEG tubes already *in situ*. In this case, dilemmas can arise where families feel they have been rushed into making the wrong decision and now want the tube removed. It can be hard for them to witness prolongation of an otherwise moribund life. For care staff too, withdrawal of a PEG tube is a weighty ethical decision. While it may be uncommon, is there scope to prevent such heartache arising in the first place?

Ensuring adequate pain relief is probably the main treatment challenge faced by nursing home staff. But as we see throughout this book, palliative care knowledge and practices are unevenly distributed. Some homes get it right more often than others. Much depends on local circumstances, including team relationships. Inadequate prescription of analgesia can be a main source of tension between nurses and GPs. For example, one of the Scottish nurses said:

You find some doctors are very reluctant to prescribe analgesia for some residents. I would like to sit down with a couple and ask them 'Do you have a problem with this?' Because it's very distressing especially when you're doing your basic care – turning them – and they're screaming. To put someone who's constantly screaming on Paracetamol is a piece of nonsense – I think you maybe get some GPs who don't like elderly people.

(Night nurse, nursing home)

Families' expectations of treatment can result in demands for transfer to hospital for investigations and invasive procedures. This can result in the sad spectacle of nursing/care home residents dying alone in unfamiliar hospital beds with unfamiliar staff. Nursing home staff deplore this, seeing it as contrary to a 'good death'. They usually prefer to avoid hospitalization if at all possible. In many cases, the GP will not know the resident. She or he may be able to weigh up the situation and, with the aid of the nursing staff, arrive at a measured decision. If in doubt however, the GP may simply bow to family demands, to the detriment of the dying resident.

Flu vaccine is yet another challenging area. Vaccination programmes are expensive and, at least in the case of residents with advanced dementia, they can be of dubious efficacy. In this case, flu-related death can be seen as a relative blessing. Yet some nursing homes implement blanket vaccination programmes.

Staff who know residents well and defend their best interests can help to ensure appropriate treatment decisions. However, one thing constantly uppermost in the minds of professionals, residents and families alike is the need for adequate resources, so that appropriate end-of-life decisions can be arrived at with respect to the resident, the family and the health care professionals involved in the caring. For this to happen issues of justice need to be grasped.

Justice

As the full impact of population ageing unfolds, the relevance of justice to the current nursing/care home sector is self-evident. It may even be over-taking autonomy as the 'premier' principle involved. Questions of resource constraint and rationing are key, with implications for the fair distribution of scarce health care resources. For example, how can society decide between life-saving treatments like cardiac surgery and kidney dialysis on the one hand, and the long-term care needs of elderly people in nursing homes on the other?

Increasingly, very elderly people die in private nursing homes. They are now more dependent than ever on entry to these facilities (Shemmings 1996). With multiple health problems (co-morbidities) they can present major care challenges. Providing 'good deaths' demands resources, including adequate staffing, facilities, equipment and access to specialist back-up. All this is costly and the ongoing publicity reflects the intense social concern over the ultimate quality of the care.

Business considerations, moreover, cannot be ignored. As one Scottish study participant said: 'It all comes down to money and the hard fact is you have to break even' (General manager, nursing home). Nursing homes are businesses, like shops and hotels, although some owners would argue about their ultimate profitability. Like other businesses, it is the smaller, independent units that struggle. The market is competitive and smaller nursing homes are having to close. The situation is not helped by lack of government support. In the UK, for example, the NHS pays a fee for every patient referred to a private nursing home, but the inadequacy of this is a constant source of irritation to many home owners. The result is nursing home closures at a time of unprecedented demand. This exerts back-pressure on the NHS, causing severe congestion or 'bed blocking' in acute hospitals. It is far more expensive to keep an elderly person in hospital than in a nursing home (Scottish Executive 2001). Proprietors know they are saving money for the government, and feel that this justifies remuneration. Meanwhile, the vicious circle of supply and demand has ethical implications for elderly people and their families.

A lack of nursing home beds means elderly people die inappropriately in acute hospital beds or, worse, are transferred to or from hospital while actually dying. On the other hand, nursing/care home residents may be denied necessary hospitalization because of a lack of available hospital beds. Fears of rationing and ageism abound (e.g. Bowling 1999), and there is growing suspicion that nursing homes represent 'backdoor' rationing. Costs now falling largely to the consumer (in this case, the family) can represent an immense financial burden which many cannot afford. Yet how else is the alleged 'demographic time bomb' to be funded? Even if it has been exaggerated, this trend will not evaporate overnight. On the other hand, is it fair and just to expect families to pick up the considerable nursing/care home bills? Is this the basis of their increasingly militant responses to end-of-life decision-making? Is there a cross-over here between autonomy and justice? If families are paying for the service, they understandably expect a real say in how it is delivered.

Much depends on particular circumstances, such as geographic location and population characteristics: nursing/care homes may be urban or rural and serve varying populations. Local relationships with other sectors, such as hospital and community health authorities, are also important. In some areas there is a feeling that staff in acute hospitals hold nursing homes in some contempt. For example, a study participant remarked: 'They [hospital staff] think we're all idiots. They see someone coming in with a fractured femur . . . and they just think "a nursing home"' (Enrolled nurse, nursing home).

To some extent, hospitals could even be said to be washing their hands of nursing homes: 'Hospitals don't appreciate the fact that because somebody's in a nursing home, they're just as entitled to as much care as someone off the street who has fallen. They just say, "Oh God, another nursing home"' (Night sister, nursing home).

Interdisciplinary communication can be poor and disputes can arise; for example, over whether hospitals or nursing homes should themselves provide important equipment such as air mattresses and syringe drivers. Nevertheless, where the private nursing/care home sector is more well established, some of these problems are less acute and there are examples of good, local collaboration. In the Scottish study, moreover, an increasing number of staff skilled in the care of the elderly had moved from the hospital to the private sector, where they said that they experienced better conditions and felt better supported. By drawing valuable palliative care skills into the private sector, this trend could contribute to better interdisciplinary and hospital–nursing/care home relationships.

Resources within individual nursing homes are still very variable, however, and staffing is clearly a major aspect of this. 'Staffing is the key expense in the whole game. But it's also the key issue in providing good care. I think staffing is at a bare minimum in most nursing homes' (Doctor, general practitioner).

In contrast to NHS units, which have trained doctors and nurses, nursing homes in the UK are traditionally unidisciplinary and staffed largely by unqualified care assistants. Nursing homes have minimum staffing ratios (usually five residents to one member of staff) that form part of the inspection requirements. But there is also a national nursing crisis in many countries of the Western world. Pay is traditionally low in the private nursing/ care home sector and in the UK and is not comparable with that for staff working in acute hospitals or in the community. Scottish study participants described this situation as 'scandalous'. It is mainly unqualified staff who deliver the care, many of whom work part-time, and there is often a high staff turnover: 'When people leave you've got to replace them and it's nearly impossible' (Staff nurse, nursing home).

All this interferes with continuity of care. How can staff ever know their residents intimately under these circumstances? What are the implications for 'responsibility for narrative integrity'? Staff shortages may also result in less rigorous recruitment processes, leading to variable calibre of recruits. Basic health professional training does not appear to prepare practitioners adequately for terminal care and end-of-life decision-making. At least 60 per cent of those in the Scottish study said this explicitly. With the advent of palliative care, specialist in-service training is more widely available in nursing homes (see Chapters 9 and 10), but access to palliative care specialists remains patchy. For example, in the Scottish study, nursing home staff had good access to Macmillan nurses in one large rural area with a robust palliative care infrastructure, but in an urban area studied, provision was more limited. All participants in the study strongly desired more palliative care education and support and this was their main perceived area for development. Yet the cost of educational courses is an issue in nursing/care homes and staff shortages hinder the possibilities of releasing nursing/care home staff to such courses. The result is that staff may be less skilled than they might be, with profound implications for residents' equitable access to 'a good death'.

Conclusion

The end-of-life care of elderly people in nursing homes is fraught with potential dilemmas. Existing ethical frameworks are strained in trying to keep abreast of these developments, and standard ethical principles, while still relevant, may need some re-emphasis and/or extension. Nurses, not doctors, are the main 'gatekeepers' of nursing/care home interventions. Much depends on their knowing their residents' intimate wishes and, on that basis, advocating for them ('responsibility for narrative integrity'). This also involves being gently candid with residents and their families about the ultimate value of curative interventions. This is not always easy. Many residents are unable to participate in such discussions. At the same time, effective long-term and terminal care is expensive. It involves juggling costs and benefits. There is a need for realistic discussion at governmental and societal levels to establish what really is most important for residents who are dying in nursing homes.

Implications for practice

- Although respect for autonomy remains a key ethical principle, it may be as relevant to families as to nursing home residents themselves.
- Focusing on 'protective responsibility', moreover, can help to extend the principles of beneficence and non-maleficence through its greater emphasis on the importance of relationship. This is particularly appropriate in nursing homes where staff–resident–family relationships are the main focus.
- Given questions of ageism and resource distribution, the principle of justice certainly deserves greater emphasis.

Acknowledgements

The authors wish to record their thanks to the study grant-holders, Dr J. Bishop-Miller, Dr B. Chapman and Dr N. Hewitt, and for the willing participation of respondents from Scottish nursing homes, hospitals and general practice.

References

Benner, P. (1984) *From Novice to Expert: Excellence and Power in Clinical Nursing*. Reading, MA: Addison-Wesley.

Bogle, J. (1999) Advance directives: proposed legislation. In *Advance Directives: Gagging the Patients? Tying the Doctor's Hands?* London: Centre for Bioethics and Public Policy.

Bowling, A. (1999) Ageism in cardiology. *British Medical Journal*, 319: 1353–5.

Bradley, E., Peiris, V. and Wetle, T. (1998) Discussions about end-of-life care in nursing homes. *Journal of the American Geriatric Society*, 46: 1235–41.

British Medical Association (1999a) *Withholding and Withdrawing Life-prolonging Medical Treatment: Q and A Briefing*. London: BMA.

British Medical Association (1999b) *Physician-assisted Suicide*. Conference project-debating pack. London: BMA.

Brown, J., Nolan, M. and Davies, S. (2001) Who's the expert? Redefining lay and professional relationships. In M. Nolan, S. Davies and G. Grant (2001) *Working with Older People and Their Families: Key Issues in Policy and Practice*. Buckingham: Open University Press.

Callopy, B. J. (1988) Autonomy in long-term care: some crucial distinctions. *The Gerontologist*, 28 (suppl., June): 10–17.

Craig, G. (1999a) No man is an island: some thoughts on advance directives. In *Advance Directives: Gagging the Patients? Tying the Doctor's Hands?* proceedings of conference at the Royal Society of Medicine, 7 November 1998. London: Centre for Bioethics and Public Policy.

Craig, G. (1999b) Palliative care from the perspective of a consultant geriatrician: the dangers of withholding hydration. In *Palliative Care: the Way Forward*, proceedings of conference at Hospital of St John and St Elizabeth, 14 November 1997. London: Centre for Bioethics and Public Policy.

Doherty, P. (1999) 'Advance directives: would they constrain the doctor? In *Advance Directives: Gagging the Patients? Tying the Doctor's Hands?* proceedings of conference at the Royal Society of Medicine, 7 November 1998. London: Centre for Bioethics and Public Policy.

Emanuel, J. and Emanuel, L. (1998) The promise of a good death. *The Lancet*, 315: 21–9.

General Medical Council (2001) *Withholding and Withdrawing Life-prolonging Treatments: Good Practice in Decision-making* (http://www.gmc-uk.org/standards/endoflife/home.htm).

Gilligan, C. (1982) *In a Different Voice*. Cambridge, MA: Harvard University Press.

Gillon, R. (ed.) (1994) *Principles of Health Care Ethics*. Chichester: John Wiley and Sons.

Gray, J. A. M. (1994) The health care of the elderly. In R. Gillon (ed.) *Principles of Health Care Ethics*. Chichester: John Wiley and Sons.

Hamel, M. B., Phillips, R. S., Teno, J. M. *et al.* (1996) Seriously ill hospitalized adults: do we spend less on older patients? *Journal of the American Geriatric Society*, 44: 1043–8.

Higgs, J. and Jones, M. (1995) *Clinical Reasoning in the Health Professions*. Oxford: Butterworth-Heinemann.

Holm, S. (1997) *Ethical Problems in Clinical Practice: The Ethical Reasoning of Health Care Professionals*. Manchester: Manchester University Press.

Jepson, M., Jesson, J., Kendall, H. and Pockock, R. (1991) *Consumer Expectations of Community Pharmaceutical Services: A Report for the Department of Health*. Birmingham: Aston University.

Kuczewski, M. G. (1999) Ethics in long term care. *Theoretical Medicine*, 20: 15–29.

Levin, J. R., Wenger, N. S., Ouslander, J. G. *et al.* (1999) Life-sustaining treatment decisions for nursing home residents: who discusses, who decides and what is decided? *Journal of the American Geriatric Society*, 47: 82–7.

Lofland, J. and Lofland, L. H. (1995) *Analyzing Social Settings: A Guide to Qualitative Observation and Analysis*. London: Wadsworth.

Massie, A. (1999) Death by hospital 'limitation'. *The Scotsman*, 7 December: 17.

Meisel, J. D., Snyder, L. and Quill, T. (2000) Seven legal barriers to end-of-life care. *Journal of the American Medical Association*, 284(19): 2495.

Milburn-Backett, K., Fraser, E. and Secker, P. S. (1995) Combining methods and health promotion research: some considerations about appropriate use. *Health Education Journal*, 54 (September): 347–56.

NCHSPCS (1999) *Ethical Decision-making in Palliative Care: Artificial Hydration for People Who Are Terminally Ill*. London: National Council for Hospice and Specialist Palliative Care Services.

Nolan, M., Davies, S. and Grant, G. (2001) *Working with Older People and Their Families: Key Issues in Policy and Practice*. Buckingham: Open University Press.

Norberg, A. (1994) Ethics in care of the elderly with dementia. In R. Gillon (ed.) *Principles of Health Care Ethics*. Chichester: Wiley.

O'Rourke, K. (2001) *Coming Soon to Your Neighbourhood Health Care Facility: The Patient Self-determination Act*. Saint Louis, MO: Centre for Health Care Ethics, Saint Louis University Medical Centre.

Scottish Executive (1999) *Making the Right Moves: Rights and Protection for Adults with Incapacity*. London: HMSO.

Scottish Executive (2001) *The National Health Plan*. London: HMSO.

Shemmings, Y. (1996) *Death, Dying and Residential Care*. Aldershot: Avebury.

Singer, P. A., Martin, D. A. and Kelner, M. (1999) Quality end-of-life care. *Journal of the American Medical Association*, 281(2): 163–8.

Sutherland, S. (1999) *With Respect to Old Age: Long Term Care Rights and Responsibilities*. The Royal Commission on Long Term Care. London: HMSO.

Teno, J. M., Branco, K. J. and Mor, V. (1997) Changes in advance planning in nursing homes before and after the patient self-determination act: report of a 10-state survey. *Journal of the American Geriatric Society*, 45: 939–44.

Tsevat, J., Dawson, N., Wu, V. *et al.* (1998) Health values of hospitalized patients over 80 years or older. *Journal of the American Medical Association*, 279(5): 371–5.

Walter, T. (1993) Modern death: taboo or not taboo. In D. Dickenson and M. Johnson (eds) *Death, Dying and Bereavement*. London: Sage in association with the Open University.

Webb, P. (2000) Advocacy. In P. Webb (ed.) *Ethical Issues in Palliative Care*. Manchester: Hochland and Hochland.

8 The performance of the hour of death

CAROL KOMAROMY

When it occurs at the end of a long life, death is often constructed as a natural and timely event. In care homes for older people the lack of medical intervention at the time of death serves to emphasize the seeming appropriateness of death as natural and 'homely'. This chapter considers how death and bereavement are managed in these settings, where death is a controlled and timely product of homes in which older people accept the natural ending of their lives (Komaromy and Hockey 2001). Goffman's (1959, 1961) work on institutions and the presentation of self helps to explain how 'performance' at the time of death enables professionals to produce 'good' deaths in this context.

The construction of death in this way can be partly explained by the way that death is culturally shaped by care home practices. Yet there is an inherent tension in homes that are both private ('domestic') and public ('institutional') settings, and care homes as public places vary considerably in the extent to which they are open to the wider community. Indeed, many care homes occupy a private space in the community, in which older people are ghettoized (Komaromy and Chant 1999) and in which people live in a state of what Sudnow would call 'social' death (Sudnow 1967). My observations here are based on data from an ethnographic study of the management of death and dying in care homes for older people (Sidell *et al.* 1997); see Box 8.1 for details of this project.

The quality of death in the midst of life

In 1990 the NHS and Community Care Act resulted in a shift from institutional to community-based care, one of the consequences of which was

---

Box 8.1   A national study of nursing and residential homes

Stage 1   A postal survey of 1,000 homes in three geographical areas in England.

Stage 2   Tape-recorded interviews with 100 heads of homes sample from stage 1.

Stage 3   Case studies of a purposive sample of 12 homes from stage 2.

---

delayed admissions into residential care homes for older people. Together with the closure of long-term hospital wards, this resulted in a changed profile of people in care homes (for older people) to one of older and frailer residents. Furthermore, as Sidell (1995) highlights, this cohort of older people tends to suffer from more symptomatic chronic illness and disability, including arthritis, cardiac and pulmonary conditions, blindness and deafness.

Despite the changing needs of their residents, much of the emphasis in care homes remains on the quality of life and the main ethos of care is on rehabilitative 'living'. What was once a worthy aim – to counter the induced dependency of institutional life – seems to be increasingly inappropriate given the condition of many of the residents of care homes. The boundary between living and dying thus becomes increasingly blurred, but despite this emphasis, the day-to-day reality for care staff is one of constant 'management' of the slowly disintegrating bodies of residents who are washed, cleaned, fed and presented as 'living'.

At the same time, care home staff clearly recognize that a substantial proportion of their residents die each year and acknowledge this through an expressed aim to keep residents in the home until they die. As one head of home in our study observed, 'This is their home and they should have the right to die here.' Care home staff also want to enable dying residents to achieve a 'good' death, summarized in the words of one head of home thus: 'peaceful, pain free and in familiar surroundings' (ideally in what had become their home). Another head of home stated, 'It is our way of showing them that we care. It is also important to other residents that they see that they will be cared for when their turn comes.'

It is the *public* spaces within care homes, the hallways, lounges and dining rooms, which are constructed as the *living* spaces. The daily routine in most of the care homes we studied was for residents to be washed and dressed and 'taken' into the lounge by care staff and presented as the finished product of their work. As part of avoiding the dangers associated with dependency of institutionalized care, one of the main aspects of the role of care staff in these homes involved the need to 'keep residents going'.

By contrast, dying takes place in *private* bedrooms, even though it is the product of home life. It is not always possible to achieve a 'good death', however, and study findings revealed that some residents were transferred out of homes and subsequently died. Even for those residents who were able to stay in the 'home' until they died, some experienced pain and suffering, while others died lonely and afraid.

Dying trajectories

Providing good quality terminal care to dying residents was considered to be dependent upon being able to predict death. Retrospective accounts, by heads of homes, of recent deaths therefore highlighted the ways in which dying trajectories were constructed. In all, heads described 140 deaths and it was possible to categorize them into four main types. First, nearly 40 per cent of deaths were described as part of a process of 'general deterioration', which was sometimes imperceptible and which had no specific event to mark the beginning of a decline. Those residents who were described as 'fading away' were still afforded a dying status and given terminal care, although this was often only a few weeks or days prior to death, when death became more clearly imminent. The second most common category accounted for 35 per cent of all deaths and was that where an acute episode, such as pneumonia or a serious fall, marked the beginning of the dying period. Such an event clearly served to delineate living from dying. The third category, which accounted for only 15 per cent of deaths, differed significantly from the two previous ones in that the 'terminal illness' status was applied to conditions such as cancer or Parkinson's disease, which were not age-specific. In other words, those conditions which might also affect younger people were privileged above less clearly defined dying trajectories, even though the culmination of multiple chronic conditions also led to death. For example, it was more likely that support services could be legitimately utilized for residents with clearly identified and unambiguous terminal conditions and, for example, care staff called upon the services of Macmillan nurses for residents with severe cancer pain but were unlikely to do so for residents with equally painful arthritis. Likewise, residents with Parkinson's disease were more likely to receive medication to control their symptoms than those with illnesses categorized as age-related. The fourth and final category of 'sudden deaths' accounted for less than 10 per cent of all deaths, but created enormous distress to both home staff and relatives. These sudden deaths served to emphasize the need for the control and separation of death and dying even in settings in which death was such a regular event.

The control and separation of dying is dependent upon the ability of staff to predict death. But separating dying residents from those who are living is problematic in settings where death is viewed as the natural and timely outcome of a long life. Observations revealed the extent to which these boundaries between life and death were maintained and the strategies that staff deployed in order to do so. In a spiral of gradual decline, which is the case for many older and frail residents, the boundary between living and dying is not easily demarcated and therefore predictions are difficult to make. Together with this and the emphasis on quality of life, it is not surprising that the dying trajectory is interpreted very narrowly as a few weeks or days before death.

Making predictions of death

Glaser and Strauss (1966) highlight the importance for those people who work in the area of death and dying to be able to make temporal predictions of death. Part of their explanation for this is the need to reduce the uncertainty associated with death, and thus 'temporal predictions of dying trajectories' enable staff to prepare for death. In care homes, this includes the expressed aim of affording residents the benefit of terminal care. Senior home staff with experience of death and dying were more likely to be able to assess whether or not a resident was dying and if so how imminent the death might be.

However, while staff often speculated about the significance of particular signs of dying, the status of dying had to be confirmed by, or conferred on to specific residents by, a doctor, most often their GP, although some residents received a diagnosis from other doctors. Thus doctors as imprimaturs would formalize the period of dying and also decide on whether or not to launch a rescue for those residents whose lives were considered to be worthy or capable of being 'saved'. They might also decide to transfer residents if it was agreed that it was beyond the capacity of the home to care for them in this 'terminal' phase.

Therefore, despite the fact that it was usually the resident's general practitioner who made any formal diagnosis of dying, the senior staff members were the people who orchestrated the management of death and dying. For example, a senior staff member or head of home would summon a doctor and request his or her opinion; and once confirmed would draw up a plan for terminal care and notify any close family members. These were also the people who managed the disclosure of information about a resident's condition to relatives and made decisions about how much information should be given to other home residents. Accordingly, when a resident called Jim was dying, the senior care assistant in charge of the unit told me, 'The others don't notice because he was so confused and even aggressive, and they didn't bother with him. In fact he spent a lot of time alone, he preferred to really and so what's the point?' This contrasts with the time when Alice was thought to be dying and the senior staff nurse and matron kept informed the residents who had shared the same lounge with her. 'She is *so* poorly', the matron told residents the day before Alice died. At no time were the residents told that Alice was 'dying', however. It was not until Maisie, a close friend of Alice and fellow resident, went to visit her that she saw Alice was close to death. Maisie told me later that she had prayed to God that Alice would be spared.

As described in the retrospective accounts of death, there were some specific events which marked more clearly the process of dying. But signals that the dying process had begun derived more from a change than from the marker itself as an inherent sign of dying. For example, care home routines were largely geared around those residents who were designated the status of 'living'. This is illustrated by one of the most firmly established routines of mealtimes, which were highly significant events in all homes and which set the parameters for many of the activities in the home. It was a time at which most residents would be gathered into a communal dining area and served food and drink. In most of the homes many of the residents were unable to feed themselves (a task that most frequently befell me as the participant observer) and in some of these homes residents who could not feed themselves were separated from those who could. Staff explained that it was distressing to those residents who were able to feed themselves to witness others being fed. In these homes the perform-ance of eating in the public space of the dining room contrasted with the private feeding which took place in the margins of space. Despite the reality that some of the residents would spit out their food, the act of feeding was slavishly followed. But food and the activity of eating are not only life-sustaining, they also serve as powerful symbols of life, and it seemed that food was serving a non-nutritional purpose of symbolizing life and living.

It is not surprising, therefore, that one of the most common predictions of death which staff made was when residents stopped eating. In itself, this was not a sign of dying since many residents had no interest in food; instead it marked a significant event for particular residents. In this way and despite commonalities, the signs of death were individualized rather than universal and intrinsic. Furthermore, without any medically sanctioned reason for not eating, such as a specific illness, staff sometimes interpreted the refusal of food as something which a particular resident had willed and, in their words, residents were 'wanting to die' or 'giving up'.

Another common marker which signalled the start of the process of 'dying' was a significant decrease in mobility. The matron of a nursing home told me about a resident who had died recently and explained the point at which she was considered to be dying. 'Then she had a fall and although there were no fractures it seemed to severely affect her confidence and she became less and less mobile; less able to walk about and I think this time she decided that she had had enough and I think that people can decide that they have had enough.' This head of home went on to interpret the resident's reduced mobility as a choice which the resident had taken, not only to stop walking, but to do so in order to die. 'I loved her independence – all right it could be trying, but right to the end she was an independent lady. She knew what she wanted and even although the decision was that *I now want to die* one had to respect that.'

These two illustrations of markers of the beginning of dying trajectories are more easily related to a distinction between living and dying, and can be distinguished from those that herald the *proximity* of death. This is because, even when residents were ascribed the status of dying and were in receipt of terminal care, staff still wanted to be able to predict the time of death. Unlike the individualized markers of the beginning of trajectories, this senior nurse in one home elaborated on how she predicted the proximity of residents' death by using a universal marker. 'I think sometimes they tend to lose a spark. You do know that there is a change, whether we would link it with them knowing, or us knowing that they might be near to death, I'm not sure, but they lose a certain spark about them, don't they?' Ann, a night nurse in a large care home, explained what she considered to be a significant change indicating that a resident (called Betty) was nearing death. 'Betty is talking about her husband today and he died some years ago. She has never mentioned him before.'

Care assistants, whose formal role did not include making predictions about death, were also interested in when it would occur and detailed specific signs for which they looked. For example, when Eve was thought to be dying, one of the care assistants, Carole, described the signs she used in this way: 'First of all she was not eating and had lost her appetite; later, the shape of her face had changed, particularly around the nose.' Carole further explained how, in her experience, this was an important (universal) sign: 'The face sags and becomes indented on the inside of the cheeks.' The next day when the same resident Eve had deteriorated further Carole told me, 'Her nose is changing and her face is sinking. She is seeing people and talking to them, in fact someone has come for her.' Staff quite often explained that when dying residents saw someone it was because the apparition had come to collect them and, as in the earlier example, the messenger was often someone who had pre-deceased the dying resident.

While staff wanted relatives to be aware that a resident's death was imminent and would often want them to share in the deathbed vigil, they did not always share openly their predictions. The experience of Laura (the wife of a deceased resident) highlights a lack of clarity about what information was being disclosed. She explained, 'The matron came up and she – this was Christmas day – and she came up and she said she was sorry about it being, as the day was – didn't make any difference to me whether it was one day or the other day, you know. I think I knew then, well prior to that, you know. But they didn't discuss – she didn't say – she didn't say "he is dying". But I think it was implied that, you know.'

As Laura has indicated, she already thought that Derek was dying. In November the matron had called Laura to the home because Derek 'wasn't well'. She explained, 'They said he had a chest infection. But when I looked at him I thought it was pneumonia. And I thought, *Oh, golly, I bet he's, you know, this is the end – or the beginning of the end.* Because, you know, I mean people that are ill, or been ill for a long time, they don't always die of the – of what they're ill with. They die of pneumonia, don't they? . . . And I sort of guessed that he hadn't long to live, you know.'

It is not surprising that relatives, left to draw their own conclusions about the imminence of death also made predictions based on different and less medical criteria as this account by Mavis (whose father had died) illustrates. 'My dad had a happy life and he didn't want to die . . . I think he knew that he had to give up his wonderful life. He was never depressed. He was never depressed – he was full of life, he used to sing all the time . . . His singing was good and when he lost his voice he couldn't sing any more and I thought I would never be able to hear him sing any more.' By contrast, Jean recounted how difficult it was to predict when her mother would die during her gradual deterioration into death. 'It was my birthday, 17 March, and I wondered whether she'd be here for Mother's Day. And she was. And then I wondered whether she'd be here for Easter. And she was. And then, by the time Whit was coming, which was when she died, I thought, *God, how long can this go on?* And so, that's when I started to think *this is the end.* But she went on for an incredible time.'

The status of dying and terminal care

The privileged status of dying afforded a routine that was distinct from other forms of care. By setting up a routine of terminal care, usually through a care plan, staff differentiated 'dying' care from that given to 'living' residents. This involved residents being nursed in the private space of their own bedroom and no longer sharing the communal spaces of the home. Therefore, the absence of dying residents from public spaces not only separated dying from living residents but also signalled to those residents who were 'living' what was taking place.

But if the status of dying was one of privilege, what were the material benefits which that status bestowed? The rhetoric of a 'good' death was not always the reality. Interviews with care home staff and observations revealed that in most of the homes the main focus of end-of-life care was on the physical needs of residents. In particular, keeping residents clean and free from pressure sores was the main aspect of this care.

Staff expressed the aim of avoiding a 'lonely' death by sitting with dying residents, but this seemed to be compromised by staff shortages and different priorities. If relatives were not available to keep a bedside vigil then staff would drop into the room of a dying resident at regular intervals. For example, Alice was dying over a period of two days and the matron set up a care plan which included the need to change Alice's position every two hours to avoid pressure sores and to offer her liquids. The staff visited every hour and when the two-hourly care was due they spent longer with her, sometimes up to ten minutes performing the tasks of physical caregiving. Likewise, Jim was a resident who had been very confused for many months. Despite all attempts to transfer him out of the home, the staff had to resign themselves to giving terminal care that they felt ill equipped to provide. As with Alice, they also gave two-hourly care and came in at half-hourly or hourly intervals. Despite this regular surveillance, Jim was alone when he died.

It was not only staff and relatives who needed to be prepared for death; another closely associated feature of good death was that the dying residents should also be ready and resigned to death. Some staff members I talked to considered this to be dependent upon the resident's faith. As one head of home put it, 'I find that people who have more of a simple faith, no matter what their beliefs are, tend to have an easier time.' This resignation to death in old age is part of the wider construction of death as natural and timely. Staff recounted stories of distressing periods of dying which were peacefully resolved. The following account of Herbert's death highlights the resolution which they achieved. 'He was really agitated all day – the previous day, that is – and we were worried that he was in pain, but he calmed down at night and died peacefully a few hours later.' Although being resigned to death was seen as important, many staff members did not see it as their role to introduce the subject of death to residents who were dying. But it was an important aspect of being able to orchestrate a peaceful death, since residents who fought death threatened the ideal, peaceful death. Exceptions to this were religious homes in which the spiritual preparation for death was an integral part of home care and something that was ongoing for all residents. However, in these homes it was exclusively the ministers of religion who managed this aspect of spiritual care.

Separating living from dying residents forms part of the routine of terminal care, but the practice of moving residents to a sick bay has largely ceased and dying residents were nursed in their own rooms. Most commonly they occupied a single room, although in some of the homes in the study residents shared with a roommate. In this way residents were sequestrated *within* homes which were themselves often concealed within the local community. When dying residents spent an unusual amount of time in their room, other residents who previously had shared the same public space noted their absence. Some explanation therefore had to be provided by the staff, and the person in charge of the home usually decided what this should be. My observations revealed that it was rare for staff to tell other residents that someone was dying. Instead they would use a range of euphemisms, most commonly 'not very well', 'poorly' and 'failing'.

A care assistant explained to me that when someone was ill and stayed in their room the head of home was the person who needed to provide an explanation to the other residents. In any case, as she explained, 'It's their job and what they are paid for.' As well as the use of euphemisms, there were other signs that residents were dying which could be interpreted. From observations and talking to care home staff and residents it seemed that staying in one's room served as a metaphor for dying. For example, Molly, a care home resident, told me that she knew that Bert was very ill, because he had stayed in his room and that this was very unusual. 'I didn't see him for a few days and I was worried – well in case – you know – in case he was dying.' When Alice was dying, the residents who were her friends sat in their regular chairs, which were en route to the corridor to the bedrooms. This afforded them a view of the traffic to Alice's room and they speculated about the events and what was happening to Alice. In this way they were also keeping their own vigil. In a minority of homes the dying space in the form of the resident's bedroom was open to anyone who wanted to visit, as this nun explained, 'We leave the door open so that they can visit. It is a special time. Having said that, not many of them do.'

The management of death as a special event

The burden on care staff was increased because they had to manage the difficult task of producing death and dying not only as a 'normal' and 'good' event, but also as one which carried individual significance. There was also a tension between the view of death in general as a natural and timely event and the impact of individual deaths on the care staff. In many ways the transformation of a resident's death into a special event was one way of conferring significance upon a life which had become meaningless.

The work of Goffman offers a helpful insight into what is taking place in two main ways. First, despite the home-from-home rhetoric, homes are institutions. Goffman (1961) claimed that, in institutions, the separation of inmates from their social world erodes the sense of self in a way that leads to what he called the 'mortified self'. The extent to which this erosion takes place in care homes is the subject of continuing debate, particularly since it was partly Goffman's work that led to a backlash against institutionalization. Whatever the degree of loss, Goffman described the self as an entirely social product and claimed that although people are able to manipulate the impression of what others make of them, they are not able to choose freely the image of themselves. Second, Goffman's description of the regulation of people in 'total institutions', in which there are restrictions and deprivations, also contributes to an understanding of how deaths in the institutional territories of care homes can be produced as significant, timely and natural events. The loss of self which older people suffer contributes to the need to give more meaning to life through death-bed rituals. There are remarkable similarities between death-bed scenes and the theatrical performance which Goffman (1959) calls 'dramaturgy'. Observations of deaths in homes suggest that the event of death is one that needs to be carefully managed. My earlier points suggest that the pendulum might have swung too far – in that the focus on living seems to have overshadowed death and dying. Thus experienced staff need to manage the end stage of dying so that it does not appear to be discrepant with and thus threaten the boundary between life and death. Furthermore, Goffman would argue that home staff do not need to realize the moral standards, in this case of being both the surrogate family member and the professional; instead, they need to give a convincing impression of this realization.

For Goffman the performance is all and his interest lies in how it is produced. Accordingly we can identify the many institutional devices which help staff to manage this dualistic role of treating death as a significant event and also behaving in a professional manner. It was clear from observations and talking to staff that the head of home was the person who directed these 'scenes of death'. In particular, removing dead bodies from care homes required careful stage management. There was a distinct hierarchy and division of labour in all homes and junior staff were not expected to have to orchestrate death or dying. Instead, as with the orchestration of dying care, the duty fell to the more senior staff members who had professional experience of death and dying, as the following extracts from field notes illustrate.

Alice died at 4 p.m. and Matron was called. She felt for a carotid pulse and delegated two care assistants to straighten Alice's body. At 5.30 p.m. the GP arrived to certify the death. Matron individually informed those residents whom she believed would be affected by the death that Alice had died, 'I'm very sorry to have to tell you that on this day of the Lord at four o'clock Alice passed peacefully away.' She then instructed the care staff to serve tea while she laid out the body. The undertakers arrived shortly after being called. They took Alice's body out of the bedroom via the French doors and were unseen by the other residents who were eating their tea.

In another home Jim died at 8 p.m. and a GP came immediately and certified the death.

The two care assistants on duty were delegated to quickly wash him and put him into clean pyjamas and they called the undertakers who removed the body just before 9 p.m. The routine of the home was not disrupted and it was decided that it was too late to tell the other residents in the home since they might be upset at bedtime. However, one of the residents told a care assistant, who was helping her to bed, that she had seen the hearse arrive to collect Jim. After a brief discussion the care assistants agreed that it was better to tell those other residents who might also have seen the hearse arrive.

Residents were being protected from the sight of death in the form of the dead body as both a dangerous container of death and a physical reminder to residents of their own impending death. The senior staff who managed these two deaths maintained the 'living' routines for the other residents and in doing so kept the boundary between life and death secure.

Staff bereavement

The role of care staff involves managing difficult boundaries between living and dying and life and death. In many care homes in the study staff described the home as comprising one 'big family', which suggests that they had to manage being both the professional carer and the surrogate family member. During the study care staff were very keen to discuss with me their own needs in relation to bereavement and to recount feelings of loss or to rehearse how they managed to cope with loss. Some of the heads of homes talked about their need for both themselves and their staff to manage the balance between being 'caring' and being 'too caring'. There was a tension between having to maintain what heads of homes saw as an appropriate demeanour, the 'stiff upper lip', and feeling enabled to express their feelings by getting upset in front of relatives and other residents. One head of home summarized the need to manage the right level of emotional display following a death thus: 'We had to pick ourselves up very quickly for the rest of the residents because otherwise the place would have gone down with a very unhappy feeling.'

What is clear from the study data is that there were many devices which staff deployed to achieve this balance: to make death 'normal' and emotionally manageable. One such device was ritual and routine. For example, homes had written and non-written policies with clearly established routines, which formed a script for staff to follow without them having to confront the reality of the authenticity of death. Furthermore they drew upon repertoires of compensation which included 'death as a natural event at the end of a long life', 'death as a relief from suffering after a difficult period of dying' and 'death as a sudden event and *good* for the person who had died.'

Residents' bereavement

In general, staff did not expect residents to grieve in any prolonged way for other residents, but it seemed to be important that residents should be affected by a death. Therefore, residents also had a balancing act to perform, which involved being 'appropriately' affected by the death of their fellow residents. Some care staff provided accounts of the callousness of residents who were 'uncaring' and gave accounts of how residents were 'better off' when a particular person died. One example of this was when a resident who appeared to show no emotion asked if she could have the bedside lamp of the deceased resident. Conversely, residents like Bob, who became very depressed following the death of his room-mate and close friend, were thought to be overreacting. This expectation of a minimal and consistent grief reaction stands in contradiction to care staff's performance of the concealment of deaths and the need to spare the feelings of the other residents because of their temporal proximity to death.

Conclusion

Death and dying in care homes is likely to be constructed as a natural and timely event in settings where older people occupy a space between natural and medicalized death. Increasingly, old and frailer living residents separated from society experience what Sudnow (1967) would call a social death. But residents are encouraged to look upon the home as their own and expected to take part in and focus on the activities of 'living'. The home is both a public and a private place, but within the home dying residents are further sequestrated into dying spaces (Hockey 1990). Senior home care staff manage the production of natural and timely deaths; however, the final say on what has occurred is left to medical people who have the power to define both dying and death. When dying takes place it is orchestrated as a significant event but one which occurs over a short period of time, lasting only weeks or days. Some of the residents were described as slowly fading away and because the moment of death could be almost imperceptible the performance might be serving the function of conferring significance upon a life when that significance has been lost. It also provides staff with the means by which to manage the tensions in and boundaries between life and death. Foregrounding death-bed scenes as performances must inevitably draw upon the work of Goffman, in that the dramaturgy in which people present themselves in everyday life is dependent upon convincing the audience that their actions are authentic. Senior care staff direct the drama and 'caring' relatives who keep a bedside vigil are significant actors within it. The successful outcome of a 'good death' requires that everyone should be convinced of the performance.

Implications for practice

- Residents of care homes who are afforded the dying status usually receive the best care that staff can deliver.
- Nevertheless, when dying trajectories are narrowly defined there is a failure to recognize the need to control the symptoms of *all* residents with chronic illness to a degree that is acceptable to them and achievable within current palliative care practice.
- The requirement for home staff to focus on living has resulted to varying degrees in the sequestration of death and dying and a consequent failure to recognize the need for bereavement care and support for both residents *and* formal and informal carers.
- In order to provide good quality care for dying residents, home care staff need specialist education and training that is relevant to older people in the care home setting.

References

Glaser, B. G. and Strauss, A. (1965) *Time for Dying*. Chicago: Aldine.

Goffman, E. (1959) *The Presentation of Self in Everyday Life*. London: Penguin.

Goffman, E. (1961) *Asylums*. London: Penguin.

Hockey, J. (1990) *Experiences of Death*. Edinburgh: Edinburgh University Press.

Komaromy, C. and Chant, L. (1999) *Better Health for Older People*. London: HEA commissioned report.

Komaromy, C. and Hockey, J. (2001) Naturalising death among older adults in residential care. In J. Hockey, J. Katz and N. Small (eds) *Grief Mourning and Death Ritual*. Buckingham: Open University Press.

Sidell, M. (1995) *Health in Old Age: Myth, Mystery and Management*. Buckingham: Open University Press.

Sidell, M., Katz, J. and Komaromy, C. (1997) *Death and Dying in Residential and Nursing Homes for Older People: Examining the Case for Palliative Care*. London: Department of Health commissioned report.

Sudnow, D. (1967) *Passing On: The Social Organisation of Dying*. Englewood Cliffs, NJ: Prentice Hall.

9

Changing care practices: beyond education and training to 'practice development'

KATHERINE FROGGATT

The policy, demographic and cultural contexts outlined in the previous chapters raise a number of issues about how the delivery of appropriate end-of-life care in nursing and residential care homes can best be facilitated. This chapter focuses on the way in which the process of staff development can be used to shape care home practices at the end of life. Staff development in end-of-life care is mainly offered by and sought from the specialist palliative care sector, leading to a methodology of staff development that can be characterized as 'outside-in'. This has the consequence of emphasizing a particular approach to care that is directly beneficial for only some of the residents living within care homes. It is a particular way of framing end-of-life care which may not always be the most appropriate for the care of residents whose passage from life to death follows a different trajectory. The effectiveness of education and training as a means to ensure that organizational care practices are achieved can also be questioned. An alternative approach to changing care practices is explored that places staff development within the wider context of collaborative practice development.

Staff development

Within health services, staff development normally takes place through educational routes in order to enhance the quality of care delivered to patients. It is accepted at a policy and regulatory level that there is a need for staff to be appropriately qualified and professionally developed (UKCC 1999;

Department of Health 2000b). Within such a framework of organizational support, learning is regarded as an individual responsibility (Department of Health 2000b). There is an underlying belief that through staff development activities the people who learn will change and consequently be better 'practitioners', which in turn will improve the quality of care offered (TOPSS England 2000; Dalley and Denniss 2001). There is pressure within the health service to ensure that minimum levels of qualification are adhered to for all groups of staff (Department of Health 2000a). The way in which this is worked out for the different groups of staff working in care homes reflects the varying regulatory requirements to which each group is subject.

Nurses working within the care homes sector are subject to the professional development regulations laid out by the nursing regulatory body. In order to stay on the professional register and to be able to practice, nurses are required to undertake a specified amount of professional development every three years: five days or 35 hours of learning activity (UKCC 2001). In contrast, the professional development needs of health care and social care assistants have been less well addressed to date, reflecting primarily the lack of regulation of this particular group within the workforce. There is wide variation between care homes with respect to the level of training offered to care assistants (Dalley and Denniss 2001). National Vocational Qualifications (NVQs) in health and social care are available and some care homes support care assistants to undertake training in these. There are no NVQs that are specific to work in nursing or residential care homes. Training also exists in mandatory areas such as handling and lifting, and food hygiene, where statutory requirements enforce the provision of training in these areas. It has also been recognized that not all managers of residential care homes have the relevant qualifications recommended to be in this position (TOPSS England 2000). This problem is compounded by a lack of funding and the availability of a large number of different accredited courses with inconsistent aims and qualifications. Even less is known about the developmental needs of ancillary staff, such as domestic staff, kitchen staff, hairdressers, administrative personnel and recreational coordinators. Some areas of work may be supported by NVQ qualifications, such as catering, whereas other roles require no formal qualification (for example, domestic work) and there is therefore little opportunity for professional development.

This situation is changing, however, with increased central control becoming more apparent (Chapter 1). National training strategies, in the form of Occupational Standards, are being developed in the different countries of the United Kingdom. These will set out best practice in specific areas of work, identifying the knowledge and values required for competent practice. Mandatory standards of education for health care assistants, managers and the Inspectorate are also to be implemented.

Changing practice through *staff* development

Two broad approaches for staff development can be identified (Froggatt 2001). One focuses on the provision of formal education and training for staff; a second uses designated specialists (usually nurses) with an implicit role to develop staff through clinical encounters. The delivery of palliative care education has been primarily focused upon education for qualified staff (NCHSPCS 1996). More recently, however, there have been calls for the education of staff in general settings to focus upon the 'palliative care approach' (NCHSPCS 1997). There have also been repeated recommendations for palliative care education in the care home sectors of the USA (Ersek *et al.* 1999), Australia (Maddocks 1996) and the United Kingdom (Gibbs 1995; Bosanquet 1997; Sidell *et al.* 1997).

In the absence of educational resources specific to the care homes there has been an increasing number of projects in the UK since the mid-1990s that have been undertaken to meet identified local needs (Avis *et al.* 1997, 1999; Welton 1999; Froggatt 2000; Fergus 2001). Details of these projects are outlined in Table 9.1 and are explored in detail here.

The care home educational initiatives originated from a number of sources, including: a specialist community palliative care nursing team (Case 2); a specialist palliative care provider and education centre (Case 4); the nursing home sector (Case 3); and as part of a health authority initiative (Case 2). The projects all had the aim of improving care for residents in nursing homes, although the emphasis was different in each case. One initiative focused upon residents with cancer (Case 2), while other initiatives specified residents with identified terminal care needs (Case 1) or palliative care needs (Cases 3 and 4), regardless of diagnosis.

The projects were run by designated staff appointed to take responsibility for each project. These included clinical nurse specialists in palliative care (Cases 2 and 4), an educator (Case 3) and a nurse adviser supported by six district nurses (Case 1). The projects worked within a defined geographical area, aside from Case 3, which was a stand-alone educational initiative catering for participants from a larger geographical area, across a number of health authorities. Needs assessment was undertaken in these initiatives prior to any intervention within the nursing homes. This varied from informal visits to nursing homes and interviews with managers (Case 3) to a more formal assessment of client needs (Case 1) or a training needs assessment of staff educational needs (Case 4).

Common to all the projects was the provision of education and training. Education varied from individual study days on a range of topics to accredited courses. In Case 1 study days were run on grief awareness, syringe drivers, the concept of palliative care, pain and symptom control and aromatherapy, and varying numbers of staff attended each day. In Case 3, a 12-day course was developed for qualified nurses, which was accredited

Table 9.1 Four examples of developmental projects with care homes, UK

	Case 1	Case 2	Case 3	Case 4
Project	Community Palliative Care Project (Avis *et al.* 1997, 1999)	Improving Palliative Care within Registered Nursing Homes (Welton 1999)	The Palliative Care Education Project in Nursing Homes (Froggatt 2000)	Hospice as a Resource Centre (Fergus 2001)
Location	Nottingham	Sheffield	North West England	Glasgow
Dates	1994–1997	1995–1999	1996–1998	1998–2000
Funding	NHS Trust	DSS using funding that had previously been allocated to hospices	Macmillan Cancer Relief and The Wolfson Foundation	Scottish Executive
Aim	To extend hospice standards of palliative care to people with a terminal illness being cared for in a nursing home with registered palliative care beds.	To improve the quality of care for terminally ill patients being cared for in nursing homes.	To improve the care of the growing number of patients in nursing homes who require palliative care or terminal care for a wide variety of diseases.	To develop services which would extend and improve local awareness of the principles of palliative care in nursing homes.
Design	• Project nurse advisor and six peer support District Nurses to work with the homes. • Assessment of client needs in nursing homes in order to identify training packages for staff. • Provision of training, support and advice for	• The project was run out of the local hospice and had the backing of the Nursing Home Inspectorate. • A designated Macmillan Nurse plus clerical support who offered: • Education to all staff working in nursing homes. • Nominated link nurses in each nursing home.	• Developed in partnership with the Registered Nursing Home Association. • Designated Lecturer and Administrator. • Three types of course – day release one day a week: Registered Nurses – 12 days, accredited to level 2.	• Dedicated clinical nurse specialist. • Work with staff to develop protocols. • Training provided in use of equipment, drugs and training. • Training needs assessment undertaken. • Education for two link nurses (qualified staff) from each home at hospice site.

staff through an open referral system. • Access to specialist palliative care advice and better communication with other professionals. • Provision of support and advice for patients and relatives.	• Specialist equipment was made available to support the care of dying residents; for example beds, syringe drivers. • Payments to increase staffing levels to care for terminally ill patients in the home.	Health care assistants – 7 days. Ancillary staff – 1 day. • Registered nurses acted as mentors to health care assistants in their own nursing home.	• Unqualified care staff received training in the homes. • Resource file for each home. • CNS acts as link to primary care team and specialist palliative care team.
Outcomes			
1 Training undertaken by staff in 39/43 homes registered for palliative care. 2 240 patient visits by project nurse adviser. 3 1,103 Staff attended training on courses: • Grief awareness ($n = 890$) • Syringe driver training ($n = 63$) • Concept of palliative care ($n = 40$) • Pain and symptom control ($n = 80$) • Aromatherapy ($n = 30$) 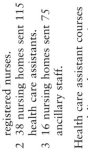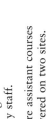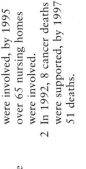	1 In 1993, 25 nursing homes were involved, by 1995 over 65 nursing homes were involved. 2 In 1992, 8 cancer deaths were supported, by 1997 51 deaths.	1 54 nursing homes sent 151 registered nurses. 2 38 nursing homes sent 115 health care assistants. 3 16 nursing homes sent 75 ancillary staff. Health care assistant courses were delivered on two sites. Ancillary days were run in 5 nursing homes in different localities to try and facilitate attendance. Areas which worked: • naming care; • communication skills; • accessing resources in community; • pain control. Individual learning rather than organizational change was apparent.	1 35/48 nursing homes in area involved. 2 44 patients referred to project CNS. 3 101 hours of education offered to qualified nurses, 60 hours to unqualified staff (numbers of participants not known).

at Level 3 by a local higher education provider; a seven-day course was also developed for the health care assistants in this project.

These four projects also addressed the development needs of the different types of staff working in nursing homes. In all projects training was provided for nurses and health care assistants. In Case 3 ancillary staff were also involved.

The initiatives featured a range of other 'interventions' alongside the educational input. Clinical nurse specialists, or the project worker, were available to give advice when residents were dying (Cases 1, 2 and 4). In two instances (Cases 2 and 4) 'link nurses' were identified in participating nursing homes. 'Link nurses' would be offered training and then supported to become a local resource within the nursing home and to liaise with the local clinical nurse specialists. In one project (Case 2) it was decided to provide specialist equipment as required for dying residents, such as special beds or syringe drivers. In this project, finance was available to resource increased staffing levels when a resident was dying. Also created within these projects was a resource file for staff (Cases 2 and 4), which contained information related to any educational training that had been offered. Less visible strategies employed within the projects included improving communication between the homes and other specialist palliative care providers and developing relationships between the homes and local resources (Cases 1 and 4).

The projects were all time limited, ranging from two to four years in duration. Evaluations were undertaken of all the initiatives and several different outcomes were identified, including the number of people attending courses and the numbers of residents referred to specialist palliative care services. What these outcomes do not indicate is to what extent the care received by residents and their relatives was different as a consequence of the projects being undertaken. Only one project (Case 4) attempted to interview patients or relatives about their experiences of care in the nursing homes, but problems of attrition meant that it was difficult to draw conclusions from the responses. There is also a lack of information about the lasting impact of all these projects.

The underlying approach integral to each of these initiatives is the 'outside-in' perspective. This exemplifies the way staff development has been characterized when it comes to developing palliative care practices in nursing and residential care homes. Specialist palliative care, external to this care sector, has taken the lead, which can create particular limitations. The straight transfer of palliative care knowledge from the specialist palliative care sector to another care sector, such as nursing homes, can be difficult (Froggatt 2001). The appropriateness and acceptability of palliative care as an approach to care for residents in care homes has not been fully explored. As we shall see in Chapter 10, the dying profile for many residents within care homes is different from that of patients usually looked after within a specialist palliative care context. How knowledge derived with one patient group can be applied to another group needs to be explored.

An 'outside-in' approach can also ignore wider knowledge about the care of older people, held by staff working within care homes. For example, gerontological expertise integrated with palliative care could create a powerful resource to promote appropriate care for all residents in care homes. The model of social care used within residential care homes also needs to be incorporated into the working practice of nursing homes. In turn, differences between nursing and residential care homes in terms of staffing profile affect the type of staff development that can be undertaken. Most initiatives, because of their origins within the specialist palliative care domain, have a health focus and address the needs of nurses and sometimes health care assistants, but rarely ancillary staff or managers. The needs of these staff also need to be clarified and addressed in a way that is appropriate to them (Chapter 6).

The long-term impact of such initiatives has not yet been clearly demonstrated. Although in each project described here it was possible to identify examples where a difference had been made to the care of individual residents, the extent to which the practices of care staff were changed in any lasting sense is not known. The efficacy of education to bring about changes in practice is debated generally (Dyson 1997; Hutchinson 1999), and also with respect to education in palliative care (Kenny 2001; Sneddon 2001). Placing the educational activities of *staff* development within a context of *practice* development offers a way to move beyond regarding the provision of education as an activity sufficient in itself. Education can then be regarded as a tool that may help in the process of developing practice. Quality initiatives also offer another way to facilitate changes in practice and are discussed in Chapter 10.

Changing practice through *practice* development

The development of care practices in any setting is a complex process that is influenced by a multitude of variables. Practice development has been defined as:

> a continuous process of improvement towards increased effectiveness in person-centred care, through the enabling of nurses and health care teams to transform the culture and context of care. It is enabled and supported by facilitators committed to a systematic, rigorous and continuous process of emancipatory change.
>
> (McCormack *et al.* 1999: 256)

It is clear from this definition that changing care practices is more than the provision of education and sending a person back into the setting to use this knowledge. There is a need to engage with the wider context within which care is being delivered. Some initiatives (Kenny 2001) with a clear educational focus do address this in choosing educational strategies that are explicitly collaborative with the participants and integrating practice experience with theoretical input, but these are the exception.

Kitson and colleagues (1998) have proposed a model for practice development that identifies the interaction of three factors – evidence, context and facilitation. Each of these factors needs to be addressed if effective change and the successful implementation of a new initiative are to occur. In this model, not only is knowledge required about the initiative (evidence), but there is also a recognition that the environment within which the initiative is to be implemented (context) and the way in which the change is brought about (facilitation) are equally important. This model offers a useful framework to explore how the development of end-of-life care practices could be taken forward in a more comprehensive and effective way within care homes.

Evidence, context and facilitation

The evidence that underpins the development of end-of-life care within nursing and residential homes has its origins in specialist palliative care. This body of knowledge is derived primarily from the care of people with cancer, across the age ranges (Froggatt 2001). This evidence is well established and relevant for people with cancer, but, as already indicated, we need to be cautious in assessing its application to people with other conditions being cared for in more general settings. The promotion of the 'palliative care approach' as a way to deliver appropriate palliative care in general settings still requires translation into care homes.

There is a need to evaluate the evidence being offered within educational courses. Education and training that are focused only on the end-of-life needs of people with cancer is not sufficient for the range of care homes in existence. There are currently two initiatives within the United Kingdom that will offer resources in palliative care tailored for staff working in these settings. Following empirical research with a large number of nursing and residential care homes (Sidell *et al.* 1997; Chapter 8), the Open University, funded by the Department of Health, is developing a distance learning package to be used in local settings aimed at all staff groups working in care homes, using written material, audio tapes and videos. Key to the package is the need for a designated facilitator to ensure workshops are run and motivation is maintained. The Royal College of Nursing is also developing distance learning material for staff working in a range of general settings, including care homes. Modules are being written for a number of issues, such as pain, breathlessness, fatigue, anxiety and depression. Core textbooks are also being published that will support work with people with conditions other than cancer (Addington-Hall and Higginson 2001).

There are issues about how specific the evidence needs to be. Often the approach of higher education providers is focused on NHS issues, and the particular needs of the independent sector may be ignored. Generic courses with a broad remit may therefore be less suitable for staff from care homes. Discrete areas of education – for example, concerning communication skills with residents who are disruptive (as a consequence of their underlying conditions) – have been undertaken and demonstrated according to specific outcome criteria to be effective in this care sector (Procter *et al.* 1999).

Evidence, 'context' and facilitation

The contextual factors which shape the extent to which end-of-life care can be developed concern cultural issues of resources, as well as relationships with other external care and educational agencies. The environment within which a proposed change is to be implemented also shapes the extent to which change can be brought about. Thus the regulations and standards set by central and devolved government shape the nature of changes within this setting by determining standards within institutions and professional standards for the different care groups working within these. In addition, there are also a number of factors at an organizational level that shape care practices in residential care homes and these have already been identified (Sidell *et al.* 1997). Resource issues become inevitable constraints and are reflected in tight staffing levels with little leeway for illness or absences for training. They also impose funding limits on staff development, and limited budgets for new equipment.

The manager of a home, whether a qualified nurse or not, is instrumental in shaping the care practices within that setting. The extent to which an individual manager can determine the culture of development within a home will sometimes reflect the type of home ownership. There are differences between homes that are owned and run by a single person, or partnership, as opposed to homes that are part of a larger corporate structure. Some institutions have a culture where the development of staff and practice is valued and encouraged. For example, homes that have achieved the *Investors in People* standard will already have structures in place to identify the learning needs of their staff and ways to meet them. Such institutions will be more easily able to address ways to improve end-of-life care within their environs. There have been calls for the development of the concept of a 'teaching nursing home' (RCP *et al.* 2000) that would address some of the needs for an academic, well supported environment to facilitate the education of both nurses and doctors in the care of older people, as seen in the Dutch context in Chapter 6. The creation of a care home that is focused upon education would be innovative in the UK and has the potential to create a new dynamic within the care sector.

Care homes are dependent on medical practitioners working within the community for their medical cover, and there is a reliance on community nursing services for nursing care. Even where staff working within a care home are motivated and willing to develop care practices, if the external health professionals are not able to engage with this, there may be conflict and subsequently no changes in practices.

The provision of education within the nursing and residential care home sector is also problematic for various reasons related to issues of funding, the structure and delivery of accredited courses and the focus of courses offered (Davies *et al.* 1999). The funding of education and training is complicated in this sector of care. The education of registered nurses working in nursing homes in the UK is not covered by purchaser contracts (RCP *et al.* 2000) and attendance on courses has to be paid for by the nursing or residential care homes or the individuals themselves. The level of training budgets varies between these homes, and funders' continuing squeeze on fees, which are rising at a lower rate than staff costs, means that training budgets are likely to be reduced where there is a shortfall.

The mode of delivery for many courses can affect the ease with which staff can attend them. Staff often attend in their own time, and attendance for a complete week can be more difficult than a day release each week, due to difficulties in covering staff absence in the home. Where training is offered to care assistants and ancillary staff, their low level of pay and dependence on public transport can limit attendance on courses some distance away. This issue was seen particularly in the project outlined in Case 3. Managers of nursing homes involved in this project, who chose only to send registered nurses, identified logistical difficulties in which the distance to the education centre created travel and financial problems for health care assistants and ancillary staff. The distance learning mode of educational delivery may solve some of these difficulties, although this approach to learning requires a high level of personal motivation and good organizational and educational support.

Evidence, context and 'facilitation'

Where staff development is used as a means to change end-of-life care practices there is an assumption that the individuals who are educated are able to bring about changes back in their work environment on the basis of the new knowledge they have attained. There is a change process that is integral to the development of care practices, and the implementation of new knowledge draws upon the principles of change. Unless practitioners are equipped with an understanding of how to bring about change, it is not surprising if care practices at an organizational rather than an individual level remain the same, despite the provision of education, as was seen in Case 3.

The need for a strong facilitator to support change within the clinical environment is advocated within the practice development framework outlined (Kitson *et al.* 1998). Three of the initiatives previously described (see Table 9.1: Cases 1, 2 and 4) used a designated clinical nurse specialist to lead the work. In conjunction with this person either link nurses from the homes were identified (Cases 2 and 4) or district nurses in the community were employed (Case 1) to enhance the process of using new knowledge.

The use of designated palliative care clinical nurse specialists (CNSs) or educators to lead the projects cited reflects the important role that CNSs can play in the provision of end-of-life care within care homes. A survey (Froggatt *et al.* 2001) of 610 Macmillan-funded community CNSs in palliative care and 120 comparable posts funded from other sources indicated that the majority of CNSs had undertaken some work with nursing homes (92 per cent of respondents) and residential care homes (80 per cent of respondents). Much of this work was not frequently undertaken and was reactive, responding to the immediate clinical needs of residents. Proactive development work occurred less frequently and the main activities undertaken by CNSs were the provision of education and training for home staff and the establishment of link nurse schemes. Some CNSs developed training courses specifically for nursing and residential care home staff, whereas in other situations care home staff were invited to join established courses for a range of personnel from community and acute settings. There are a few examples of designated CNSs in palliative care being appointed to work in a developmental capacity within the United Kingdom, and evaluation of their work may indicate whether or not direct focused facilitation from this role is helpful for the continued development of care practices within this sector.

Another source of facilitation might come from the development of the gerontological nurse specialist role (RCP *et al.* 2000). It is proposed that this person could take the lead on clinical matters and help to integrate health care support within care homes. One area of responsibility would be palliative and terminal care. Such a role would be ideally placed to work with specialist palliative care practitioners to take this work forward.

Conclusion

The promotion of staff development through education and training as a means to ensure the provision of appropriate, high-quality end-of-life care is problematic within the care home sector for a number of reasons. Care homes are located within a particular regulatory context with respect to the standards of care offered and the requirements to develop staff. These are changing and will put even greater financial and temporal pressures upon owners and managers of these homes to ensure staff are properly developed and supported.

The more fundamental issue of the sufficiency of education as a means to bring about changes in care practices also needs to be addressed by the specialist palliative care providers and educators who are offering education and training as a means to develop care. The knowledge provided for practitioners needs to encompass the breadth of conditions, and dying experiences, that the residents in care homes encounter. This knowledge would be best delivered in the broader context of a 'practice development' approach. Such a context seeks to address not only the evidence required for best practice, but also the wider issues within which it is to be used, as well as the process by which its introduction into practice will be facilitated. Without attention to these wider issues, attendance on educational courses may continue, but the benefits for residents at the end of their lives will be limited. Staff development through education is but one tool to help develop practice. Such a model is not external to the care setting but recognizes and works alongside the end-of-life expertise already held within the home. In this way, the diversity of the dying experience present within nursing and residential care homes is met and the organizational context addressed alongside individual learning.

Implications for practice

- Moving away from an 'outside-in' approach to partnership with care homes may be a more productive way to develop appropriate end-of-life care for residents within care homes.
- Educational initiatives for care home staff are an important way to influence the delivery of palliative care within care homes, but are not sufficient in themselves to ensure changes in practice.
- The knowledge about end-of-life care that is promoted within care homes needs to be drawn from specialist cancer care, gerontology and other specialities.
- It is important to address wider contextual issues specific to care homes, within which changes in practice are to be implemented, alongside the delivery of new knowledge.
- Different models for the facilitation of changes in practice are available and their effectiveness could be usefully evaluated.

Acknowledgement

Thanks are due to Heather Mercer for her comments and advice on the chapter.

References

Addington-Hall, J. and Higginson, I. (eds) (2001) *Palliative Care for Non-cancer Patients*. Oxford: Oxford University Press.

Avis, M., Greening-Jackson, J., Cox, K. and Miskella, C. (1997) *Evaluating the Community Palliative Care Project: Final Report*. Nottingham: Nottingham Community Health NHS Trust and Department of Nursing Studies, University of Nottingham.

Avis, M., Jackson, J. G., Cox, C. and Miskella, C. (1999) Evaluation of a project providing community palliative care support to nursing homes. *Health and Social Care in the Community*, 7(1): 32–8.

Bosanquet, N. (1997) Palliative care. Why it must be extended to the elderly. *Geriatric Medicine*, 27(5): 9–10.

Dalley, G. and Denniss, M. (2001) *Trained to Care? Investigating the Skills and Competencies of Care Assistants in Homes for Older People*. London: Centre for Policy on Aging.

Davies, S., Slack, R., Laker, S. and Philp, I. (1999) The educational preparation of staff in nursing homes: relationship with resident autonomy. *Journal of Advanced Nursing*, 29(1): 208–17.

Department of Health (2000a) *Care Homes for Older People. National Minimum Standards. Care Standards Act*. London: HMSO.

Department of Health (2000b) A *Health Service of All the Talents: Developing the NHS Workforce*. London: HMSO.

Dyson, J. (1997) Research: promoting positive attitudes through education. *Journal of Advanced Nursing*, 26(3): 608–12.

Ersek, M., Kraybill, B. M. and Hansberry, J. (1999) Investigating the educational needs of licensed nursing staff and certified nursing assistants in nursing homes regarding end-of-life care. *American Journal of Hospice and Palliative Care*, 16(4): 573–82.

Fergus, L. (2001) *Hospice as a Resource Centre Pilot Project: Final Report*. Glasgow: Marie Curie Centre.

Froggatt, K. (2000) *Palliative Care Education in Nursing Homes*. London: Macmillan Cancer Relief.

Froggatt, K. (2001) Palliative care and nursing homes: where next? *Palliative Medicine*, 15: 42–8.

Froggatt, K., Hoult, L. and Poole, K. (2001) *Community Work with Nursing Homes and Residential Care Homes: A Survey Study of Clinical Nurse Specialists in Palliative Care*. London: Macmillan Cancer Relief.

Gibbs, G. (1995) Nurses in private nursing homes: a study of their knowledge and attitudes to pain management in palliative care. *Palliative Medicine*, 9: 245–53.

Hutchinson, L. (1999) Evaluating and researching the effectiveness of educational interventions. *British Medical Journal*, 318: 1267–9.

Kenny, L. (2001) Education in palliative care: making a difference to practice. *International Journal of Palliative Nursing*, 7(8): 401–7.

Kitson, A., Harvey, G. and McCormack, B. (1998) Enabling the implementation of evidence based practice: a conceptual framework. *Quality in Health Care*, 7: 149–58.

McCormack, B., Manley, K., Kitson, A., Titchen, A. and Harvey, G. (1999) Towards practice development – a vision in reality or a reality without vision? *Journal of Nursing Management*, 7: 255–64.

Maddocks, I. (1996) Palliative care in the nursing home. *Progress in Palliative Care*, 4(3): 77–8.

NCHSPCS (1996) *Education in Palliative Care*. London: National Council for Hospice and Specialist Palliative Care Services.

NCHSPCS (1997) *Dilemmas and Directions: The Future of Specialist Palliative Care*, Occasional Paper II. London: National Council for Hospice and Specialist Palliative Care Services.

Procter, R., Burns, A., Stratton Powell, H. *et al.* (1999) Behavioural management in nursing and residential homes: a randomised controlled trial. *The Lancet*, 354: 26–9.

RCP, RCN and BGA (2000) *The Health and Care of Older People in Care Homes. A Comprehensive Interdisciplinary Approach*. Report of a Joint Working Party of the Royal College of Physicians, Royal College of Nursing and British Geriatric Association. London: Royal College of Physicians.

Sidell, M., Katz, J. and Komaromy, C. (1997) *Death and Dying in Residential and Nursing Homes for Older People: Examining the Case for Palliative Care*. Report for the Department of Health. Milton Keynes: Open University.

Sneddon, M. (2001) More, or more effective, education? *International Journal of Palliative Nursing*, 7(7): 316.

TOPSS England (2000) *Modernising the Social Care Workforce: The First National Training Strategy for England*. London: TOPSS England.

UKCC (1999) *Fitness for Practice*. London: United Kingdom Central Council for Nursing, Midwifery and Health Visiting.

UKCC (2001) *The PREP Handbook*. London: United Kingdom Central Council for Nursing, Midwifery and Health Visiting.

Welton, M. (1999) Nursing Initiatives. *Palliative Care Today*, 7(4): 35–6.

10

Organizational structures for enhancing standards of palliative care

JO HOCKLEY

End-of-life care in nursing and residential homes in the United Kingdom is being targeted, with the recommendation that knowledge and skills developed from within the hospice movement should be shared with other settings (Bosanquet 1997; Smith 2000). Care homes are not unused to caring for dying elderly people, but it may be that certain assumptions have been made as to how palliative care knowledge should be shared within them (Froggatt 2001). Rather than the simplistic transfer of a conceptual model developed in the context of diseases with a defined prognosis (such as cancer and motor neurone disease), a more collaborative sharing of palliative care skills between diverse areas of care might be more appropriate. When examining organizational structures to enhance the standards and quality of palliative care for older people dying in nursing homes, it is likewise important to consider an appropriate philosophy of care for this specific group of people. This chapter first addresses some of the differences between a philosophy of specialist palliative care and one for frail elderly people dying in care homes. It then complements the idea of changing care practice through staff development (Chapter 9) by examining organizational structures that might be used to develop such care through quality initiatives, including participatory action research.

A philosophy for end-of-life care

In a keynote address to the First International Conference on Palliative Care of the Elderly in 1989, Balfour Mount drew interesting analogies between geriatric practice and palliative care:

Both make the whole person and his or her family the focus of care, while seeking to enhance quality of life and maintain the dignity and autonomy of the individual. Judicious use of investigations are advocated and both eschew unwarranted treatment while providing symptom control and relief of suffering. Both are necessarily multi-disciplinary and both are areas which prompt phobic reactions from society at large. Finally, to carry the parallel still further, in medicine, both Geriatrics and Palliative Care are new medical technologies which challenge the restorative, often aggressive and increasingly technolog-ical practices in technological areas of medicine.

(Mount 1989: 7)

Despite such similarities there are also considerable differences between geriatrics and palliative care. The term 'palliative care' derives its meaning from the Latin verb *palliare*, meaning 'to cloak', and the term has been used extensively in the context of the hospice movement, where the inability to cure a person's cancer is recognized and accepted. In this context the care given concentrates on the control of distressing symptoms and promotion of quality of life. Throughout the growing gerontological literature on the care of the dying, however, it is interesting that the term 'palliative care' is far less common than 'end-of-life care'. From this, and from our own under-standing that humans are born, grow old and die, it may be that there are subtle but important differences between what are described as 'palliative care' and 'end-of-life care'. In 'end-of-life care' there is the same need for quality care and good symptom control and, indeed, good psychosocial care. There may also be an unwritten awareness that 'cure' may not be part of the equation of care in the elderly person who is already infirm from multiple medical pathologies, which might include dementia. For those over the age of 80 years, or even 90 years, it is recognized that one has to die sometime . . . from something. It could be argued that there is no *curative* treatment in old age and that because of this and other subtle differences, the transfer of a model specific to specialist palliative care becomes quite problematic when applied to end-of-life care.

Froggatt (2001) challenges the tendency to think that what has been developed with specialist palliative care for those with advanced cancer can automatically be transferred to the care of the elderly person dying in a nursing home. There are differences between these two areas of care; both in the care settings involved (care homes and specialist palliative care units) and in the care practices which occur within them. When looking more closely at these different areas of care, other variations can be identified (see Table 10.1).

The dying trajectory of frail older people in care homes can be so much a part of a slow, debilitating decline that the imminent dying phase may be easily missed if trained health care professionals are not anticipating it.

Table 10.1   Differences between cancer palliative care and end-of-life care in the elderly dying

Cancer palliative care	End-of-life care in the elderly dying
Focus on one disease process	Multiple disease processes
Emphasis on dying in mid-age or younger when life is generally seen as being 'cut short'	Natural ending of life often understood by both the resident and those caring within the context of care homes
Clearer concept of 'prognosis' so terminal care can be planned	Often quicker dying trajectory following a more dependent, lengthier disease process
Professional holistic relationship between patient and staff	Often a much closer/emotional relationship between resident and care home staff as resident 'part of the family' and may have lived in home over a year
More support from family/friends	Less support from family/friends – often care home staff and other residents seen as family
Both patient and family often want life extended	Elderly, frail people in nursing homes frequently speak about dying, and that it would be nice 'to go to bed one night and not wake up'
Morphine and other medication frequently used to control symptoms	Pain requiring strong opioids less common
Multidisciplinary model of care	Nurses and care workers having the greatest input of care
Patients more often cognitively intact	Greater percentage of elderly in nursing homes being cognitively impaired

As well as a differing dying trajectory, various studies show evidence of differing symptom control issues (Wilson *et al.* 1987; Blackburn 1989). The assessment of pain, for example, in someone with cancer versus someone with advancing dementia (Chapter 5) raises very different scenarios; the most striking being that in the first case it is possible to inform and describe the pain but in the second it is often not possible. A further difference can be seen concerning families. Many residents within the nursing/care home may come to rely on the staff as 'family', especially those with dementia, who find the regular face of care staff more familiar than family or relatives themselves. One of the more obvious differences is the greater acceptance of death of the very old in nursing/care homes where many frail older people may verbalize the fact that 'they are ready to go'.

With the increasing interest in care of the older person and palliative care, professional bodies are starting to consider what is meant by quality end-of-life care for elderly people. It has been defined as:

> an active, compassionate approach that treats, comforts and supports older individuals who are living with or dying from progressive or chronic life-threatening conditions. Such care is sensitive to personal, cultural and spiritual values, beliefs and practices and encompasses support for families and friends up to and including the period of bereavement.
>
> (Ross *et al.* 2000: 50)

The challenge here is to ensure that such a statement or philosophy of care underpins organizations entrusted with the care of dying elderly people in society. Before we discuss standards and organizational frameworks that might provide quality end-of-life care for elderly people in care homes, it is important to examine what components influence a 'good death' in this population.

A 'good death' and dying elderly people

Much has been written about the concept of a 'good death' (McNamara *et al.* 1994; Seymour 2001). Health professionals (Emmanuel and Emmanuel 1998; Fowler and Coppola 1999) have introduced frameworks for a good death, and qualitative studies involving elderly people themselves (Mui Hing Mak and Clinton 1999; Singer *et al.* 1999; Leichtentritt and Rettig 2000) have helped to clarify the 'user' perspective on this. Singer *et al.* (1999) interviewed 38 elderly patients in a long-term care facility in the USA about 'control at the end of life' and formulated five domains that address quality end-of-life care and can be seen as components for a good death:

- adequate pain and symptom management;
- avoiding inappropriate prolongation of dying;
- achieving a sense of control;
- relieving burden;
- strengthening relationships with loved ones.

Singer *et al.*'s research is similar to other studies (Fowler and Coppola 1999; Teno and Field 1999) where focus groups involving terminally ill cancer patients and health care professionals were used to gain information (Table 10.2).

Certain problems are raised, however, by the concepts of 'inappropriate prolongation of dying' and 'relieving burden'. These may well be more specific to elderly people dying naturally at the end of life than to those dying from cancer in mid-life. At an older age there is a greater expectancy

Table 10.2   Domains of quality end-of-life care

Fowler 1999[a]	Singer 1999[b]	Teno 1999[c]	Leichentritt 2000[d]
Control over pain and discomfort	Receiving adequate pain and symptom management	Importance of spirituality and transcendence	Dying a natural death (neither prolonging nor shortening)
Having as much control over other aspects of life as possible	Avoiding inappropriate prolongation of dying	Communication about condition and what to expect	Avoiding physical suffering
Having basic day-to-day needs met in a comfortable way	Achieving a sense of control	Not being a burden	Acceptance of my death by others
Having a chance to bring relationships to a comfortable point	Not being a burden	Autonomy	Having the choice whether family are with me or being on my own
Finding acceptance of one's own life and comfort with one's place in the universe	Strengthening relationships with loved ones	Being able to choose where one should die	Being able to say goodbye
		Symptom management	Finding spiritual consolation

[a] Results of ten focus groups including terminally ill patients, bereaved family members, nurses, social workers, oncologists, hospice workers and clergy
[b] 38 elderly residents in long-term care
[c] Patients and families involved in two large national focus group projects on dying
[d] 26 elderly people at home

of death and many elderly people will already have experienced the death and loss of old friends and siblings. Many are less frightened about death than about the process of dying (Field 2000). In Leichentritt and Rettig's study, death was mostly addressed as 'an inevitable completion of the life circle, a phenomenon that one has to accept since it cannot be avoided or overcome' (Leichentritt and Rettig 2000: 228). A sense of resignation and of waiting are important aspects of care at the end of life for the older person.

Box 10.1   Principles of a good death at the end of life

- To know when death is coming, and to understand what can be expected.
- To be able to retain control of what happens.
- To be afforded dignity and privacy.
- To have control over pain relief and other symptom control.
- To have choice and control over where death occurs (at home or elsewhere).
- To have access to information and expertise of whatever kind is necessary.
- To have access to any spiritual or emotional support required.
- To have access to hospice care in any location, not only in hospital.
- To have control over who is present and who shares the end.
- To be able to issue advance directives which ensure wishes are respected.
- To have time to say goodbye, and control over other aspects of timing.
- To be able to leave when it is time to go, and not to have life prolonged pointlessly.

Within the UK, the authors of *The Future of Health and Care of Older People* (CPA 1999) have identified 12 principles of a good death (Box 10.1). Smith (2000) advocates that such principles need to be incorporated into the plans of individuals, professional codes and the aims of institutions and whole health services.

It is clear that staff within care homes need to be aware of these principles. Indeed, several of them, such as dignity, privacy and autonomy, are already uppermost in the minds of those working with older people. However, other issues, such as the use of advanced directives, explanation about what is happening when someone is dying and access to a hospice for symptom control issues, may not be so easily grasped. Unfortunately, articles in medical and health care journals are often not read by those caring for elderly people dying in care homes. The 12 principles in Box 10.1 are therefore very appropriate, but unless they are translated through practice development initiatives (Chapter 9) or organizational frameworks they might as well not exist.

Organizational frameworks influencing and maintaining standards for good quality end-of-life care in nursing homes

The Centre for Policy on Ageing (CPA 1999) insists that it is essential for care homes to have clear policies and procedures in order to ensure that residents' last days are spent in comfort and dignity and that their wishes are observed. Policies, procedures and standards of care are important, but if staffing levels are not adequate, or there is a lack of continuity of staff, or an unbalanced mix of staff, then policies and procedures hold little value. Those finding their way into nursing homes are increasingly more frail, are admitted closer to the end of life and are thereby increasing not only dependency levels but also the frequency of death in nursing homes. Neither the number of staff employed nor the mix between untrained and trained staff has adapted sufficiently to secure good quality end-of-life care in these places (Shemmings 1996). It is recommended that nursing homes should have a ratio of one-third qualified nurses to two-thirds untrained staff (CPA 1999: 8).

The cost of good quality care for older people in nursing homes, alongside the setting of national core standards, is now being addressed in the UK (Chapter 1). Quality of care is defined as 'the degree to which health services for individuals and populations increase the likelihood of desired health outcomes and are consistent with current professional knowledge' (Lohr and Walkerm 1990). The increasing consumerism within health care means that users are looking to be satisfied. How might such care be monitored or evaluated?

Audit and setting of standards

The quality of long-term care can be improved by changing the strategies used to monitor it (Kane 1995). Historically, within the nursing home setting the 'regulation of care' has sought to eliminate bad care and to improve quality. Unfortunately, this regulation has often had a reputation for a 'policing' effect rather than encouraging new and dynamic practice. Interestingly, it has been shown that where nursing homes are involved in audit, improvements in standards of care have followed (Chambers *et al.* 1996).

The White Paper *Working for Patients* (Department of Health 1989) proved a major stimulus to standard setting and audit across health care in the UK. Quality of life and quality of care in time became an integral part of assessing, giving and evaluating care across different settings, and these are particularly important for frail elderly people who may feel they have no voice. Setting standards and audit have often been regarded as the responsibilities of individual professions, such as nursing or medicine (Higginson 1993), but in the context of care at the end of life, shared multiprofessional goals are likely to be more relevant. Trent Hospice Audit Group (THAG) (Hunt 1993) was one of the first to set core standards for palliative care and has worked to produce clinical standards for specialist palliative care specific to:

- collaboration with other agencies;
- symptom control;

- patient/carer information;
- emotional support;
- bereavement care and support;
- specialist education for staff.

It is important, however, that standards are set to achieve goals relevant to the philosophy of care for the specific setting. Engle (1998) suggests that nursing home quality indicators should include the resident remaining in the nursing home until death. This is clearly appropriate if staff and carers have been trained and have the necessary education and skills for a resident to receive high quality end-of-life care. Such care includes more than just a basic knowledge of pain management and often needs advanced care planning, with care staff taking a leading role to enable it to happen. Too often in the past the transfer of frail elderly people to hospital has meant that they end their lives in surroundings that are unfamiliar to them, away from the people they have come to know and trust.

It is widely reported that standards of care work best where there has been a local interest in looking critically at practice by examining standards and working together to improve aspects of care that are problematic. A project in north-west England has set standards that will help to monitor care, and share knowledge and expertise of end-of-life care in nursing homes. Three overarching standards are: a programme of education in general palliative care; implementation into practice of new knowledge and skills; and the systematic formation of 'link nurses' in care homes to be in regular contact with specialist palliative care resources. Each standard encompasses a standard statement, as well as structure, process and outcome criteria, with separate evaluative questionnaires (Shepherd 2002).

Setting clinical standards, however, is only one aspect of assuring the quality of care. Standard setting has to include the 'monitoring of practice' against the standard/goals that have been set. Results of the monitoring or auditing should then be fed back to carers, thus creating the audit cycle. Most audit groups have followed Donabedian's (1988) model of structure, process and outcome to help to frame the writing of core standards, but auditing them is most important. Audit results may also monitor patient/family satisfaction with clinical care given, or consider the effectiveness of certain documentation, or the results of an educational programme for staff.

Standards for 'specialist' palliative care, 'intermediate' palliative care and 'generic' palliative care are being devised by the Clinical Standards Board for Scotland (www.clinicalstandards.org). The standards for 'generic' palliative care could be seen as *guiding* the structure for good quality end-of-life care in nursing homes/care homes and in particular those care homes registered for 'palliative care' (i.e. taking patients who have advanced malignant disease). It is most important, however, that the actual standards set are devised by staff in care homes with particular attention to the needs of the frail elderly people who die there, and are not based on the simplistic notion of 'transfer' from specialist palliative care. Such generic palliative care standards would include: education and training; assessment and care planning; palliative care equipment; palliative care drugs; and palliative care symptom management.

In the USA, Denmark, Iceland, Italy and increasingly the UK, the Minimum Data Set (MDS) or Resident Assessment Instrument (RAI) is being used not only as a clinical assessment tool for elderly people admitted for care in a long-term facility/nursing home (Chapter 2) but as a tool to measure outcomes of care (Kane 1995; Phillips *et al.* 1997). The tool was developed in the USA to aid costing of care and offers a mechanism to generate data on many pertinent domains of care and outcomes. Kane (1995) advocates a dual approach to the use of the MDS, encouraging its use not only as an external monitoring tool, but also as an internal quality-assurance programme that directly addresses key process issues, including the appropriate use of guidelines. Assessments are done (albeit by the observation of the nurse rather than direct resident involvement) every three months, with some aspects of the tool being completed every month. By obtaining longitudinal data on both problem-specific and more global measures of quality (such as decline in the ability to perform the activities of daily living), information can be pooled (Philips *et al.* 1997).

No discussion of standards, quality and evaluation would be complete without consideration of the use of integrated care pathways (ICPs).

Integrated care pathways (ICPs)

Integrated care pathways (ICPs) are one approach to integrating standards and clinical guidelines, including a multiprofessional quality framework which not only records what is being done but at the same time can measure it within the clinical situation. New initiatives such as ICPs or multidisciplinary pathways of care (MPCs) are gaining increasing popularity in the evaluation of health care (Kitchiner *et al.* 1996; Wilson 1998). The care pathway acts as a guide to treatment and an aid to documenting the patient's progress. It also appears to provide a structure on which to assess not only the quality perspective but also the cost.

In the UK, Ellershaw *et al.* (1997, 2001) were the first to introduce the idea of an ICP to the field of specialist palliative care in a proactive move 'towards an outcome-based culture' (Ellershaw *et al.* 1997: 204). It was a tool to develop, monitor and improve palliative care in order to impact on the quality of dying patients' last few days in hospitals and in the local community. Members of the specialist team developing the ICP felt it was impossible for them to be involved with every dying patient in a hospital that had 2000 deaths a year. Using such a pathway might therefore help health

Box 10.2   Criteria to establish 'diagnosis of dying'

- Deteriorating without any reversible causes.
- Drowsy or reduced cognition.
- Essentially bed bound.
- Taking little food or fluid and having difficulty with oral medication.
- Not wishing further investigations or interventions.

care professionals to follow agreed guidelines of care, yet freely accommodate the individual needs of any given situation through the documentation of any variance on the pathway.

Ellershaw *et al.* (2001) collected data from 168 patients placed on an ICP for the last 48 hours of life and who died in a hospice over a 13-month period. For each of the symptoms documented (pain, agitation and respiratory tract secretions) 82 per cent of patients had complete control of symptoms after only one intervention. The ICP has provided a means 'to measure symptom control in the dying patient and set standards of care which is integrated into clinical practice' (p. 12). Ellershaw has also been using this ICP to monitor care in local nursing homes (personal communication).

Farrer (2001) has developed a similar tool for the last few days of life in the acute hospital situation. Like Ellershaw *et al.* (1997), Farrer determines that a 'diagnosis of dying' should be confirmed before the pathway can begin. Whereas Ellershaw *et al.* (1997) will start the ICP with at least two of the following being present (patient is bedridden; patient is comatosed; patient is able to take only sips of fluids; patient is no longer able to take tablets), Farrer's ICP insists on an affirmative answer to the criterion of 'diagnosis of dying', following British Medical Association (BMA) recommendations (see Box 10.2).

Both Ellershaw *et al.* (1997) and Farrer (2001) stress that once a decision has been made to start the pathway, the ICP documentation is the only documentation which should then be used. The pathway is split into four sections:

1 Nursing and medical goals and assessments.
2 Interdisciplinary communication.
3 Variance reporting.
4 Guidelines:

   (a) Management of pain.
   (b) Management of agitation or confusion and anxiety or fear.
   (c) Management of terminal breathlessness.
   (d) Management of other symptoms.
   (e) Giving bad news and communication in palliative care.
   (f) The final act of care.

Once a decision has been made to put a patient on an ICP, an *initial assessment* is carried out. Associated goals for the last few days of life will be carried out by the nurse and the doctor, such as comfort measures, psychological insight, patient problems, identifying family and communication with the primary health care team (Ellershaw *et al.* 1997: 204). *Ongoing assessments* are then carried out by the nurse. These further ongoing assessments include assessments of pain, agitation and confusion, anxiety and fear, breathlessness, nausea and vomiting, alongside four-hourly nursing interventions such as mouth care, pressure area care, urinary incontinence and catheter care, syringe driver use and patient safety. Daily assessments addressing patient awareness of dying, patient/family distress over unfinished business, preparation of the family/friends for the patient's demise, unmet spiritual needs and facilitation for the family while visiting are also noted. Each assessment along the pathway requires the health care professional to circle 'yes' or 'no' against achievement of the target. If 'no' is highlighted, then a 'variance' has to be recorded. Any variance from the established pathway is then recorded on a separate sheet within the pathway documentation. This is a most important aspect of the ICP, in that 'individualized patient care' means that variances are to be expected (Wilson 1998).

Farrer (2001) clearly points out that the ICP is a structure in the process of care and should not inhibit clinical decision-making and judgement, especially in complex cases. The variance sheet is there to clarify why a deviance from the pathway has been necessary. The ICP therefore provides a documented standard of routine care and also a measure of what has been done in more complex situations, in both instances providing outcome measures. The care pathway also documents care given, which in turn can be costed.

It appears that an ICP can result in improved outcomes of care in situations where specific areas known to cause distress are highlighted and actually guide the pathway. Applying such a structure of care for elderly dying residents in nursing homes has many advantages (Box 10.3), one of which is the provision of good documentation of care at the end of life. At present there is very little evidence of the standard of such care and how it differs from specialist palliative care. The ICP documentation would provide much more dynamic evidence from which to evaluate outcomes.

The ICP can also serve as a reminder of the essential aspects of palliative care for nurses in nursing homes. Because deaths are generally not as frequent in nursing homes as in hospices and hospitals, it is important to have a 'checklist' by which to trigger important communication and action. If there is a specific problem, such as pain or breathlessness, with an individual resident, then the relevant guideline within the ICP can provide the necessary up-to-date guidance to meet the individual needs for that specific situation.

Box 10.3   Advantages of Integrated Care Pathways in nursing homes

- Provide good documentation of the standard of care achieved from which to evaluate outcomes.
- Ability to give individualized care to older people dying in nursing homes.
- Act as a reminder for nurses working in nursing homes about the essential aspects of palliative care.
- Appropriate approach to palliative care can be adopted into nursing homes through recognized guidelines.
- Any deviation on the four-hourly assessments encourages the trained nurse to be proactive because of the need to document care.
- Bridge the gap between hospices and nursing homes, availing nursing homes with up-to-date guidelines.

Isolation in care and education has been an endemic problem associated with care homes in the UK. Through the determined use of ICPs adapted to the care of elderly people dying in such settings, however, local hospice units can help to support the care of the dying in these places and so help to bridge the gap. With the ICP *in situ* it may be that the nursing home will be prompted to seek direct advice from the hospice more often.

Nevertheless, there may be difficulties in translating such a framework into the care home situation. The underlying principle of ICPs is that they are multidisciplinary (Wilson 1998). It is as important for the dying person to be reviewed on a daily basis by the doctor as by the nurse. Within the nursing home setting where there is no daily medical presence this may be difficult, although not impossible (but see the Dutch context, Chapter 6). Families of dying residents value the fact that the doctor visits, even though everything may seem to be under control, and they may feel that such a visit adds quality to the care.

A joint report by the Royal College of Physicians, the Royal College of Nursing and the British Geriatric Society (RCP *et al.* 2000) stresses the importance of integrated care and the interdisciplinary approach to care for those in care homes. Such an approach needs to be present even within the last few days of life. This report also discusses the important role that gerontological nurse specialists can have in the care of older people in nursing homes. At present, with the *ad hoc* way UK residential/nursing care homes are supported by general practitioners, this could help to bridge care home facilities with both the general practitioner and more specialized gerontological care, as well as palliative care. Much in the same way that nurse specialists first highlighted the needs of those dying in acute hospitals (Dunlop and Hockley 1999), so gerontological nurse specialists may help to bridge the divide between care homes, general practice and gerontological services. Such specialist nurses could be responsible not only for new initiatives – for example, implementing ICPs – but also for helping the coordination of palliative care initiatives at the end of life.

A chapter examining organizational frameworks to improve and enhance practice for the care of the elderly at the end of life would not be complete without some attention being paid to the value of action research.

Action research

There is considerable similarity between action research and systematic practice development (McCormack *et al.* 1999; Chapter 9). Both advocate bringing about change to improve clinical practice through rigorous and systematic involvement in the setting. Both are also educative and often use reflective practice (Johns and Freshwater 2001) to underpin the learning experience in order to effect change.

Action research was first introduced by Lewin in the 1940s (Lewin 1946) but only since the mid-1980s has it had an impact on practice-based professions (Elliott 1991; Le May and Lathlean 2001; Winter and Munn-Giddings 2001). Action research is founded on a methodology that involves bringing about change. It is problem-specific (Hart and Bond 1995); the researcher alongside practitioners in the settings identifies problem issues. Difficult issues are thereby highlighted and action in response is planned collaboratively with those who understand the culture of the organization. In this way there is greater potential for change to take place and also for that change to be sustained (Titchen and Binnie 1994). The name 'action research' denies its complexity. Enormous skill is required by the researcher not to 'take over' but to empower co-researchers in the workplace, not only to evaluate critically the problem, but also to contribute suggestions for change. Democracy and participation are fundamental to action research (Meyer 2000).

An action research project is in progress to enhance the knowledge and practice of palliative care for older people dying in nursing homes in Edinburgh. This project includes a clinical practitioner/facilitator involvement in the nursing homes, alongside a specialist course specific to the palliative care needs of older people at the end of life. Material for the course has come from being involved in the care of those residents dying in the nursing homes where the researcher is facilitating change. The use of reflection to create a learning culture is a major thrust of both the research and the course.

Change is far easier to talk about than to see implemented in practice. Bringing about change in the care of older people is known to be difficult, not least because of high staff turnover, the under-establishment of staff, the frequent use of agencies and the presence of part-time staff (Smith 1986). Froggatt (2000) also found that many care homes might be resistant to change because of hierarchical structures. There are huge issues around the empowerment within the organizational structure of nursing/residential homes, where untrained carers do the majority of the physical work; for example, poor teamwork is an issue where division between the ranks of trained nurses and carers allows low morale and a feeling of repression to be fostered.

Critical reflection performed systematically in action research has the added advantage of being able to test theory already developed (Titchen and Binnie 1994). This in itself may help to identify differences between specialist palliative care and the growing interest in end-of-life care for older people.

Conclusion

In addressing organizational structures for enhancing standards of care at the end-of-life in care homes, this chapter has explored a philosophy for end-of-life care. It has looked at the similarities between the different specialities of geriatric care and palliative care, at the same time highlighting some of the differences between the two dying trajectories commonly found within each.

Some of the organizational frameworks mentioned within this chapter might help to revitalize the care of older people dying at the end of their lives, and thereby break away from some of the surrounding restraints. The importance of auditing care and setting standards specific to the end of life must be owned, however, by those local to the nursing home setting. Integrated care pathways (ICPs) are heralded as an important step in the right direction not only to guide quality end-of-life care but also to monitor and cost such care. ICPs that have been developed for the acute hospital setting may, however, need to be adapted to the less acute, unidisciplinary model of care homes. Participation in local projects involving action research, where the emphasis is on collaborative working and education, in order to bring about sustained change, is another useful change process that should be considered.

Greater integration between health care and social care of older people may well become a catalyst for some of these organizational frameworks to be put into practice. The collaboration between specialists within the field of caring for elderly people and in specialist palliative care, perhaps even the appointment of gerontological nurse specialists to help to coordinate good quality end-of-life care, is also likely to produce opportunities and support for change.

Implications for practice

- There may be a subtle but important difference between specialist palliative care and care at the end of life for the very old in nursing homes.

- Inappropriate prolongation of life for dying elderly people may undermine a 'good death'.
- The regulation of care homes has done little to enhance good quality end-of-life care for dying elderly people.
- The setting of standards and use of audit has been shown to improve care in nursing homes.
- The use of ICPs in guiding and evaluating the care of the dying, developed collaboratively between hospice units and nursing homes, is likely to develop appropriate knowledge for the end-of-life care of old people.
- Participatory action research, because it involves working collaboratively with staff from within a setting where there is an eagerness to change practice, may be a further way of enhancing good quality of care at the end of life for the dying old people in nursing homes.

References

Binnie, A. and Titchen, A. (1999) *Freedom to Practice: The Development of Patient-centred Nursing.* Oxford: Butterworth-Heinemann.

Blackburn, A. M. (1989) Problems of terminal care in elderly patients. *Palliative Medicine*, 3: 203–6.

Bosanquet, N. (1997) New challenge for palliative care. *British Medical Journal*, 314: 1294.

Chambers, R., Knight, F. and Campbell, I. (1996) A pilot study of the introduction of audit into nursing homes. *Age and Ageing*, 25: 465–9.

CPA (1999) *The Future of Health and Care of Older People: The Best Is Yet to Come.* London: Age Concern.

Department of Health (1989) *Working for Patients.* London: HMSO.

Donabedian, A. (1988) The quality of care: how can it be assessed? *Journal of the American Medical Association*, 260: 1743–8.

Dunlop, R. and Hockley, J. (1999) *Hospital Based Palliative Care Teams.* Oxford: Oxford University Press.

Ellershaw, J., Foster, A., Murphy, D., Shea, T. and Overill, S. (1997) Developing an integrated care pathway for the dying patient. *European Journal of Palliative Care*, 4(6): 203–7.

Ellershaw, J., Smith, C., Overill, S., Walker, S. E. and Aldridge, J. (2001) Care of the dying: setting standards for symptom control in the last 48 hours of life. *Journal of Pain and Symptom Management*, 21(1): 12–7.

Elliott, J. (1991) *Action Research for Educational Change.* Buckingham: Open University Press.

Emanuel, E. and Emanuel, L. L. (1998) The promise of a good death. *The Lancet*, 351, SII21–9.

Engle, V. F. (1998) Care of the living, care of the dying: reconceptualizing nursing home care. *Journal of the American Geriatric Society*, 46(9): 1172–4.

Farrer, K. (2001) Personal communication: unpublished Integrated Care Pathway for patients dying within the acute hospital. Lothian University Hospitals, Edinburgh, EX4 3XU.

Field, D. (2000) Older people's attitudes towards death in England. *Mortality*, 5(3): 277–96.

Fowler, F. J. and Coppola, K. M. (1999) Methodological challenges for measuring quality of care at the end of life. *Journal of Pain and Symptom Management*, 17(2): 114–19.

Froggatt, K. (2000) *Palliative Care Education in Nursing Homes*. London: Macmillan Cancer Relief.

Froggatt, K. (2001) Palliative care and nursing homes: where next? *Palliative Medicine*, 15(1): 42–8.

Froggatt, K., Hasnip, J. and Smith, P. (2000) The challenges of end-of-life care. *Elderly Care*, 12(2): 11–13.

Hanson, L., Davis, M. and Garrett, J. (1997) What is wrong with end-of-life care? Opinions of bereaved family members. *Journal of the American Geriatric Society*, 45: 1339–44.

Hart, E. and Bond, M. (1995) *Action Research for Health and Social Care*. Buckingham: Open University Press.

Higginson, I. (1993) *Clinical Audit in Palliative Care*. Oxford: Radcliffe Medical Press.

Hunt, J. (1993) Audit methods: palliative care core standards. In I. Higginson (ed.) *Clinical Audit in Palliative Care*. Oxford: Radcliffe Medical Press.

Johns, C. and Freshwater, D. (2001) *Transforming Nursing through Reflective Practice*. Oxford: Blackwell Science.

Kane, R. L. (1995) Improving the quality of long-term care. *Journal of the American Medical Association*, 273(17): 1376–80.

Karim, K. (2001) Assessing the strengths and weaknesses of action research. *Nursing Standard*, 15(26): 33–5.

Kitchiner, D., Davidson, C. and Bundred, P. (1996) Integrated care pathways: effective tools for continuous evaluation of clinical practice. *Journal of the Evaluation of Clinical Practice*, 2: 65–9.

Leichtentritt, R. D. and Rettig, K. D. (2000) The good death: reaching an inductive understanding. *Omega*, 41(3): 221–48.

Le May, A. and Lathlean, J. (2001) Action research: a design with potential. *Nursing Times Research*, 6(1): 502–10.

Lewin, K. (1946) Action research and minority problems. *Journal of Social Issues*, 2: 34–46.

Lohr, K. N. and Walkerm, A. J. (1990) The utilization and quality control peer review organization. In *Medicare: A Strategy for Quality Assurance*. Washington DC: Institute of Medicine/National Academy Press.

McCormack, B., Manley, K., Kitson, A., Titchen, A. and Harvey, G. (1999) 'Towards practice development – a vision in reality or a reality without vision?' *Journal of Nursing Management*, 7: 255–64.

McNamara, B., Waddell, C. and Colvin, M. (1994) The institutionalization of the good death. *Social Science and Medicine*, 39(11): 1501–8.

Meyer, J. (2000) Using qualitative methods in health related action research. *British Medical Journal*, 320: 178–81.

Mount, B. (1989) First International Conference on Palliative Care of the Elderly. Cited in R. Fisher, M. Ross and M. MacLean (eds) (2000) *A Guide to End-of-life Care for Seniors*. Canada: University of Toronto and University of Ottawa.

Mui Hing Mak, J. and Clinton, M. (1999) Promoting a good death: an agenda for outcomes research – a review of the literature. *Nursing Ethics*, 6(2): 97–106.

Phillips, C. N., Zimmerman, D., Bernabei, R. and Jonsson, P. V. (1997) Using the Resident Assessment Instrument for quality enhancement in nursing homes. *Age and Ageing*, 26–S2: 77–81.

RCP, RCN and BGS (2000) *The Health and Care of Older People in Care Homes*. London: Royal College of Physicians.

Reason, P. (1994) Three approaches to participative inquiry. In N. K. Denzin and Y. S. Lincoln (eds) *Qualitative Research*. Thousand Oaks, CA: Sage.

Ross, M. M., Fisher, R. and Maclean, M. J. (2000) End-of-life care for seniors: the development of a national guide. *Journal of Palliative Care*, 16(4): 47–53.

Saunders, C. (1987) What's in a name? *Palliative Medicine*, 1(1): 57–61.

Secretaries of State for Health (1989) *Working for Patients* (White Paper). London: HMSO.

Seymour, J. (2001) *Critical Moments – Death and Dying in Intensive Care*. Buckingham: Open University Press.

Shemmings, Y. (1996) *Death, Dying and Residential Care*. Aldershot: Avebury.

Shepherd, D. and Hunt, J. (2002) A standards framework for general palliative care. *The Foundation of Nursing Studies Newsletter* (Spring): 1–2. The Foundation of Nursing Studies, London SWIW 0RE.

Singer, P., Martin, D. K. and Kelner, M. (1999) Quality end-of-life care. *Journal of the American Medical Association*, 281(2): 163–8.

Smith, G. (1986) Resistance to change in geriatric care. *International Journal of Nursing Studies*, 23(1): 61–70.

Smith, R. (2000) A good death. *British Medical Journal*, 320: 129–30.

Stewart, A. L., Teno, J., Patrick, D. L. and Lynn, J. (1999) The concept of quality of life of dying persons in the context of health care. *Journal of Pain and Symptom Management*, 17(2): 93–108.

Teno, J. and Field, M. J. (1999) Research agenda for developing measures to examine quality of care and quality of life of patients diagnosed with life limiting illness. *Journal of Pain and Symptom Management*, 17(2): 75–82.

Tetley, J. and Hanson, E. (2001) Participatory research. *Nurse Researcher*, 8(1): 69–88.

Titchen, A. and Binnie, A. (1993) Research partnerships: collaborative action research in nursing. *Journal of Advanced Nursing*, 18: 858–65.

Titchen, A. and Binnie, A. (1994) Action research: a strategy for theory generation and testing. *International Journal of Nursing Studies*, 31(1): 1–12.

Wilson, J. (1998) Integrated care management. *British Journal of Nursing*, 7(4): 201–2.

Wilson, J. A., Lawson, P. M. and Smith, R. G. (1987) The treatment of terminally ill geriatric patients. *Palliative Medicine*, 1: 149–53.

Winter, R. and Munn-Giddings, C. (2001) *A Handbook for Action Research in Health and Social Care*. London: Routledge.

Conclusion

JO HOCKLEY AND DAVID CLARK

There is a growing acceptance that the benefits of palliative care should be extended beyond the work of hospices and specialist palliative care services, to encompass the broader population of those in need of high-quality end-of-life care. This means reaching out to other settings and services and also to those with diseases other than cancer. We fully support this viewpoint and in this book our contributors have made out a case for improving the care of older people in nursing and residential homes. We have seen that this is a multifaceted problem, encompassing questions of policy, practice, education and research. Until recently, there would have been little to report on this matter, such was the dearth of interest, but now there are encouraging signs of development and the chapters of this book point the way forward.

Cicely Saunders has been fond of saying that in any society the care of dying people is a measure of its civilization. By the standard of end-of-life care in many care homes, this might still produce an unfavourable judgement in most countries. Now, as political interest gets under way, as practitioners, planners and managers show an interest and as researchers and educators become involved, we can at last begin to feel optimistic about the possibilities of change. We present a summary here of some of the main conclusions that can be drawn.

1 *Older people at the end of life have become more central to health and social care policy*. In various countries – the UK, USA, The Netherlands and Australia – greater attention is being given in legislation and in policy-making to the needs of the care home sector. All these countries will continue to grapple with the question of how long-term care for frail elderly people is to be funded, but we see in each case evidence that

the quality of care for this group of people has become a matter of major political and public concern, and this is important for the specific issue of end-of-life care.

2 *The character of the care home population is changing.* Older people are being admitted into care homes in an increasingly frail condition. Multiple medical problems are common and a majority of residents die within 18 months of admission. We are therefore dealing with one of the most dependent groups within the health and social care system, yet it is clear that care home residents are not receiving palliative care proportional to their needs. The issue of pain relief for care home residents, particularly those with dementia, continues to give concern.

3 *Despite significant efforts at easing the transition, the move into a care home and subsequent life within it is for many residents an experience of multiple losses.* Entry into a care home seems only rarely to be a planned event that has been anticipated some time in advance. Relocation can therefore compound feelings of loss and guilt. There are losses concerning physical disability and incapacity, but also the sorrows associated with the deaths of friends and others elsewhere, as well as of residents within the home itself. Creating a sense of community within care homes and the nurturing of old and new relationships are important in this context. Care homes are complex, communal living environments where many aspects of human existence are to be found, and where opportunities can exist for quality of life and new experiences.

4 *A person-centred approach is pivotal to appropriate end-of-life care in care homes.* This approach is particularly relevant to the question of end-of-life decision-making. It creates an environment in which nurses and carers are encouraged to know the *personal* needs of residents rather than simply to meet physical requirements, however demanding they may be. Currently, the overarching philosophy in many care homes is one of 'normalization'; this is important and appropriate in many ways, but it should be enhanced by a wider view of end-of-life issues and the acceptance of death.

5 *We require a wider range of ethical concepts relevant to end-of-life issues in the care home setting.* We have seen presented here three important ethical principles relevant to nursing home settings: the principle of protective responsibility, the principle of narrative integrity and the principle of candour. These go beyond the more familiar bioethical concepts of autonomy, non-maleficence, beneficence and justice, and suggest new ways of preventing suffering through inappropriate care at the end of life. While the principle of autonomy continues to predominate, it should also be extended to the situation of family members, as well as residents themselves.

6 *Attention needs to be given to the level of training and the professional skill mix of the care home team.* There is an increasing need for

experienced nurses to be employed in care homes. Most of the staff working in care homes are untrained and are often caught by surprise at the number of deaths they encounter. At the same time there is huge scope for the work of physicians in nursing homes to be given more priority; indeed, for recognition of this work as a sub-speciality within medicine.

7 *The palliative care needs of care home residents must be identified more carefully and then acted upon.* Assessment of need and the use of specific assessment tools are important in determining the costs of care and in monitoring the outcome. The assessment tools in use do need, however, to be subject to more rigorous evaluation since some current assessment processes and instruments may fail to identify palliative care needs. Further work on extending the Resident Assessment Instrument (RAI) to develop specific assessment for palliative care needs should be carefully monitored as to its adequacy. Assessment should also be regarded as part of the continuing process of care and not as a single event.

8 *The spiritual care of residents in homes needs greater attention through education and research.* This is an aspect of holistic care that is lacking in many care homes, where competing physical needs of highly dependent patients challenge for attention. It may be compounded when residents have mental illness problems or dementia. Who is looking after the spiritual needs of people in care homes? Is the pattern as disjointed as for some medical input or can there be a more systematic way of allocating people within a local community to care for the spiritual needs of older people dying in local care homes? And what issues does spiritual care raise for staff of varying backgrounds, ages and belief systems?

9 *Staff working in care homes require far more support in their continued education and development than is currently available.* No number of tools alone will necessarily improve care. So much depends on the attitudes and skills of those giving the care as well as those helping to support, develop and educate staff within care homes. Traditional methods of education may not be wholly appropriate. The culture of nursing homes may be different from that of hospices and hospitals and may therefore need other methods on which to base educational initiatives. Encouraging learning through experience within a systematic framework of practice development has the potential to promote appropriate care specific to the palliative care needs of those dying in care homes. Attention must also be paid to the continuing support of care home staff in what is physically and emotionally demanding work.

10 *Partnerships with other service providers as well as with the family members and friends of residents can do much to improve end-of-life care in care homes.* The link with primary care services is particularly important in this respect. There is also great potential for collaboration

between clinical nurse specialists in palliative care and their emerging counterparts in the care of older people. There is evidence that the work of care homes can be viewed in a negative light, particularly by hospital staff, and this perception needs to change.

How much extra pressure can and should be put on nursing and residential homes in an effort to improve end-of-life care? Problems within the system of funding, difficulties in staff recruitment and low morale all combine to make change hard to achieve. We conclude by quoting an example, supplied to us by Deborah Parker and Alison McLeod (Chapter 2), which encapsulates what can happen when the circumstances are right. National standards of care and appropriate assessment tools in nursing homes are important, but from the experience of these Australian authors, such standards need to be matched by a commitment to palliative care in the staff employed to work in nursing and residential homes. The example they present encapsulates the importance of holistic, person-centred care, a multidisciplinary framework of operation and imagination about what can be done.

In Australia, Aged Care Standards and the accompanying Assessment Criteria go some way towards encouraging and prompting care home facilities to undertake adequate and appropriate assessment of those requiring palliative care. However, from our experience palliative care is more likely to be provided in facilities where the nursing directors and senior staff express a particular commitment to this issue. In such facilities staff will have received education that provides them with the confidence to deliver appropriate palliative care, and the management of the end of life will have become an integral part of the organizational culture.

In the southern region of Adelaide there is an aged care complex that provides accommodation for elderly people requiring independent living, high and low care. The Director of Nursing has a particular interest in providing appropriate palliative care. To this end, all staff have been funded to undertake a three-day palliative care course offered by the local specialist palliative care service. When interviewing for staff the Director of Nursing asks if prospective employees are interested in caring for the dying. Nurse and carers unwilling to undertake palliative care education are unlikely to be employed.

Palliative care updates are part of the in-service education programme over the year and all staff including the kitchen/domestic staff and the gardener are encouraged to attend. This facility has a specific assessment form which assists the staff in identifying the needs of patients with chronic disease who are facing the final stages of life. Working as a team committed to providing adequate symptom management, the nursing staff have confidence in their assessment and in identifying the needs of their residents. The general practitioners who provide services to this facility have consequently learned to trust and respect the nurses' assessments and willingly provide the medical support required to achieve good care.

The role model of the Director of Nursing and specialist nurses from the palliative care service has assisted the registered nurses to become competent in supporting relatives and residents through the last weeks and months of life. When a resident is dying a photograph is put on a table in the hallway with a candle burning beside it. Residents are informed that one of their colleagues is seriously ill. When death occurs the candle is extinguished and a rose is placed in a vase beside the photograph and remains for a few days. This ritual has become an accepted part of this facility's culture, alongside the six-monthly memorial service when family and friends of residents who have died are invited to an ecumenical service within the facility and all residents who have died are remembered individually.

While the staff in some facilities believe that providing palliative care is too hard, too expensive and too time consuming, others such as those in the one described here have been able to include expert and appropriate end-of-life care into the everyday running of a large and busy complex. The difference between the two viewpoints begins with the training of staff to recognize the needs of those who are dying. It continues with the documentation that identifies the needs of residents and families and which provides guidance to practice. And it is maintained by the commitment of the senior nursing personnel who continue to develop a culture of aged care that encompasses the terminal phase.

(Debbie Parker and Alison McLeod)

We can see from this example just how high-quality, appropriate end-of-life care can be incorporated into a busy care home for older people. This book has suggested that a model of caring for dying people developed within specialist palliative care might not be entirely appropriate when transferred with no adaptation specific to the culture of care homes, though clearly there is much to be learned from the expertise developed within palliative care facilities. Bringing about change in nursing and residential homes is not a simple task. It requires dedication and time. It also requires a 'vision' that is capable of enduring and adapting. Just like the wider development of hospice and palliative care, the improvement in the care of older people dying in care homes will have to be addressed systematically and with patience. We are confident that the outcome will be positive.

Index